Shattered Subjects

Trauma and Testimony in Women's Life-Writing

Suzette A. Henke

St. Martin's Press
New York

Contents

Acknowledgments

The inauguration of this project was made possible by a grant from the Camargo Foundation, which welcomed me to a scholarly community in Cassis, France during a sabbatical leave from SUNY-Binghamton in Spring 1985. Since 1991, my research has been generously supported by the Thruston B. Morton, Sr. Endowment and the Board of Trustees at the University of Louisville. A grant from the United States Information Agency in Summer 1990 funded a series of five lectures in India that bore fruitful exchange with scholars at the Indian Institute of Advanced Study, Himachal Pradesh University, Delhi University, Hyderabad University, and the American Studies Research Center in Hyderabad. A Fulbright Senior Fellowship took me to Australia in 1991-92 for research and teaching at the University of Western Australia and Adelaide University. I am grateful to Professor Debra Journet and the English Department at the University of Louisville for granting a 1997-98 sabbatical leave that enabled the completion of this project. Professor Sandra Morgen of the University of Oregon kindly invited me to the Center for the Study of Women in Society as a visiting scholar during the 1997-98 academic year. Jennifer Freyd organized an enlightening conference on "Trauma and Cognitive Science" at the University of Oregon in July 1998, just as I was finishing this book.

Sidonie Smith, Robert Spoo, and Suzanne Nalbantian generously read parts of the manuscript during its several incarnations and offered helpful advice. Bonnie Kime Scott read the entire text in near-final form and made invaluable suggestions for improvement. The influence of the late Frieda Flint, psychologist and feminist, survives throughout this study.

I wish to thank the Beinecke Library at Yale University for providing access to H. D. manuscripts and typescripts of *The Gift*. Parts of chapter 3 have appeared in print in earlier forms: "A Confessional Narrative: Maternal Anxiety and Daughter Loss in Anaïs Nin's *Incest*" in *ANAÏS: AN INTERNATIONAL JOURNAL* 14 (1996); "Life-Writing—Art as Diary, Fiction, Therapy," in *ANAÏS: AN INTERNATIONAL JOURNAL* 16 (1998); and "Anaïs Nin's *Journal of Love:* Father-Loss and Incestuous Desire" in *Anaïs Nin: Literary Perspectives*, edited by Suzanne Nalbantian, copyright © Suzanne Nalbantian, reprinted with permission of St. Martin's Press, Incorporated.

A seedling version of the first part of chapter 4 was published as "A Portrait of the Artist as a Young Woman: Janet Frame's Autobiography" in *SPAN, Journal of the South Pacific Association for Commonwealth Literature* 31 (1991).

I can only begin to express my appreciation to the many friends and scholars who have contributed intellectually to the development of this project. Humbly, I utter name upon name in acknowledging the following individuals. For discussions of trauma and its repercussions, I am grateful to Cathy Caruth, Margaret Higonnet, Claire Kahane, Dominick LaCapra, Marian MacCurdy, Jacqueline Rose, and Mary Wood. On the topic of autobiography: Meena Alexander, William Andrews, Louise DeSalvo, Laura di Abruna, Paul John Eakin, Rita Felski, Carolyn Heilbrun, Rebecca Hogan, James Olney, Hazel Rowley, Sidonie Smith, and Julia Watson. On feminist theory: Shari Benstock, Marilynn Desmond, Tamar Heller, Susan Koshy, Jane Marcus, Toril Moi, and Gayatri Spivak. On narrative theory: David Halliburton, Cheryl Herr, Brandon Kershner, Rosemary Lloyd, Robert Polhemus, Paul Ricoeur, and Robert Rawdon Wilson. On modernism: Beth Boehm, Thomas Byers, Alan Golding, Leslie Heywood, Marcelline Krafchick, Susan Suleiman, and Elizabeth Tenenbaum. On Colette: Dorchen Leidholdt and Jerry Aline Flieger. On H. D.: Jane Augustine, Rachel Blau DuPlessis, Susan Stanford Friedman, Angela Moorjani, Adalaide Morris, Perdita Schaffner, and Robert Spoo. On Anaïs Nin: Richard Centing, Noel Riley Fitch, Benjamin Franklin V, Evelyn Hinz, Joaquin Nin-Culmell, Rupert Pole, Diane Richard-Allerdyce, Anne Salvatore, Sharon Spencer, and Gunther Stuhlmann. On Janet Frame and New Zealand Literature: James Acheson, Chris Ackerly, Patrick Evans, Donald Hannah, Malcolm Page, Chris Prentice, Anna Rutherford, Susan Schwartz, and Mark Williams. On Audre Lorde: Carole Boyce-Davies, Ajuan Mance, and Alice Snyder.

For gracious hospitality in London, prolific thanks to the Bacrac family and to the Hunots. For friendship and assistance in Australia, Bruce Bennett, Marion Bennes, Penny Boumelha, Susan Davis, Patricia Giudice, Leonie Ford, Dennis Haskell, Jan Kavanagh, Kateryna Longley, Jenny Mutton, Kay Schaffer, and Robert White. For facilitating summer teaching at the University of Trento in 1996, Giovanna Covi. For hospitality in Oregon, the Bartletts and the Fischlers. For welcoming me to the academic community at the University of Oregon, Suzanne Clark, Linda Kintz, Michaela O'Connor, and Richard Stein.

Maura Burnett, my editor at St. Martin's Press, has provided rare support and encouragement at every stage of publication. She and Ruth Mannes, the production editor, have shown a patience and forbearance which I truly appreciate. Work on this project has been greatly facilitated by research assistants at the University of Louisville—Mary Barbosa-Jeréz,

Leah Graham, Kristin Kirsch, and Elizabeth Hawes Scheitzach, all of whom have cheerfully done much more than can be recognized in so short a space. Shirley Marc graciously expedited my research at the Center for the Study of Women at the University of Oregon.

Finally, I would like to thank the many friends and relatives who have enriched my life and the context of this work in countless intangible ways. My cousin Mary Ann Kish Drey offered hospitality in Bethlehem, Pennsylvania, during the H. D. Centennial Conference in 1986 and made a gift of *The Gift*. She, along with Mary Kish Strehlish, John Gish, Jeanne Hennemuth Kovacs, and Eileen Hennemuth Mullin showed warmth and familial concern during my mother's last illness in May 1995. My aunts and 29 cousins on the west coast have been the source of a gratifying sense of family, and I would like to acknowledge, in particular, Ada Fierst and Enna Bradley, Bettyann Clark, June Fessler, Bill, Frank, and James Fierst, Chuck Henke, Julia Rosborough, and Josie Walls. They have helped keep alive the legacy of my father, Allen James Henke.

This book is dedicated to three heroic women whose memory remains a precious part of my heritage. My maternal grandmother, Julia Alexa Kish, emigrated to the United States from Russia and Hungary in the early 1900s. After giving birth to four children, she succumbed to Spanish influenza in 1918. This dedication is, to my knowledge, her only memorial. My grandmother Alys Caffrey Henke displayed the courage of a twentieth-century pioneer and provided a model of strength and fortitude well into her seventies. The loss in 1995 of my own Sido figure, Elizabeth Kish Henke, was incalculable, and I continue to celebrate her extraordinary gifts of nurture, joy, and unqualified love.

For sustaining friendships, I am profoundly grateful to Hildy Miller, John Flint, and Elizabeth Tucker Gould and their families. For years of loving companionship, my debt of gratitude to James F. Rooney is beyond words.

Introduction

The twentieth century may well be remembered as a century of historical trauma. As citizens facing the third millenium, we daily confront the unthinkable in news and television reports, in bizarre public trials, and in relentless statistics exposing rape, murder, torture, battering, and child abuse in an increasingly violent society. Global disasters challenge our sensibilities with occasions for communal mourning too numerous to chronicle. How have we survived, both individually and collectively, in the face of unimaginable trauma?

Our medical and psychiatric understanding of trauma is a fairly recent phenomenon. The nineteenth century was well acquainted with symptoms of hysteria, a disease whose etiology had been allied mysteriously with the female gender through metaphorical associations with a wandering womb, as well as the presumed influence of uterus and ovaries on woman's mental stability.[1] Only with the manifestation of similar symptoms in males fighting on the front during World War I were physicians impelled to diagnose the devastating effects of "shell shock" on a ravaged military population. Even then, trauma appeared to be associated with active combat or the fear thereof. It was not until 1980 that the American Psychiatric Association acknowledged post-traumatic stress disorder in its official therapeutic manual as a real illness affecting countless men and women in all strata of society.

If one accepts the basic premise of Freud's talking cure—a psychoanalytic working-through of repressed memories brought to the surface and abreacted through the use of language and free association—then an intriguing question arises concerning the role of the analyst. Is he or she truly necessary? Might the therapeutic power of psychoanalysis reside more in the experience of "rememory" and reenactment than in the scene of transference posited by Freud? In other words, as James Pennebaker asks, "is talking necessary for the talking cure to cure?" (40). In *Opening Up*, Pennebaker presents fairly convincing evidence that the very process of articulating painful experiences, especially in written form, can itself prove therapeutic. "Writing about the thoughts and feelings associated with traumas . . . forces individuals to bring together the many facets of overwhelmingly complicated events. Once people can distill complex experiences into more understandable packages, they can begin to move beyond the trauma" (193). "By talking or writing about the traumatic memories," explains Jennifer Freyd, an individual "spontaneously creates an episodic interpretation and integration of previously disjointed sensory and affective memories" (170).[2]

A "life testimony," says Shoshana Felman, "is not simply a testimony to a private life, but a point of conflation between text and life, a textual testimony which can *penetrate us like an actual life*" ("Education" 14). Felman acknowledges Freud's discovery that "*it takes two to witness the unconscious*" (24), but argues that a surrogate transferential process can take place through the scene of writing that allows its author to envisage a sympathetic audience and to imagine a public validation of his or her life testimony. The very foundations of Freudian psychoanalysis valorize the "birth of knowledge through the testimonial process" by transforming the unconscious into a "conscious testimony that itself can only be grasped in the movement of its own production" (25).

My own interest in autobiographical testimony began more than a decade ago, when I embarked on a psychoanalytic study of women's life-writing during a 1985 sabbatical semester in Cassis, France. Supported by a grant from the Camargo Foundation, I set out to investigate the intriguing interface between autobiography and fictions of self-writing. My initial research engaged issues of gender and genre and the web of textual filaments that suggests an aesthetic continuum between fact and fiction, autobiography and self-inflected fabulation. The focus of this project dramatically shifted when a significant pattern of repressed trauma and psychological fragmentation began to emerge, often unexpectedly, in a large number of twentieth-century feminist autobiographies. The literary testimonies I was examining provided startling evidence that women often manifest symptoms of post-traumatic stress disorder after a crisis precipitated by rape, incest, childhood sexual abuse, unwanted pregnancy, pregnancy-loss, or a severe illness that threatens the integrity of the body and compromises the sense of mastery that aggregates around western notions of harmonious selfhood.

At the December 1985 Convention of the Modern Language Association in Chicago, I delivered a paper sketching a tentative paradigm for scriptotherapy—the process of writing out and writing through traumatic experience in the mode of therapeutic reenactment. I argued that the authorial effort to reconstruct a story of psychological debilitation could offer potential for mental healing and begin to alleviate persistent symptoms of numbing, dysphoria, and uncontrollable flashbacks. Autobiography could so effectively mimic the scene of psychoanalysis that life-writing might provide a therapeutic alternative for victims of severe anxiety and, more seriously, of post-traumatic stress disorder. These ideas may have struck a 1985 Modern Language Association audience as more psychoanalytic than literary, and even somewhat marginal to the field of critical theory.

Prevalent notions about literature and psychoanalysis began to change radically in the early 1990s, when Cathy Caruth brought out a provocative collection of articles on trauma in two issues of *The American Imago* (reprinted as *Trauma: Explorations in Memory*), and Judith Lewis Herman published her groundbreaking text *Trauma and Recovery*. As a practicing therapist, Herman was able to compare post-traumatic stress disorder precipitated by rape, sexual abuse, or battering with the symptoms of neurosis exhibited by war veterans and victims of terrorism. Reading her extensive array of case histories gave me a sense of reassurance, since a thesis I had so tentatively gleaned from the exploration of women's life-writing was reinforced by a study reflecting numerous individual testimonies and years of clinical practice. One could not have predicted, however, the virtual explosion of critical interest in survivor discourse and in narratives of recovery precipitated not only by Herman and Caruth, but by theorists like Dori Laub, Shoshana Felman, Dominick LaCapra, Jennifer Freyd, Anne Hunsaker Hawkins, and Thomas Couser, to name only a few. Over the last decade, scriptotherapy has infiltrated the imagination of therapists, literary critics, mental health workers, and narratologists alike. Charles Anderson and Marian MacCurdy have recently edited a richly suggestive collection of essays on *Writing and Healing: The Techne of Wholeness*, soon to be published by NCTE Press.[3]

At the outset of this project, I made a decision not to deal specifically with Holocaust narratives because these poignant testimonies constitute a field unto themselves and require a particular historical purview that should be investigated within a broader political, religious, and philosophical context.[4] My own study was intentionally more limited and geared to an examination of the unexpected eruption of repressed tales of traumatic experience in feminist life narratives—and to ways in which modern women authors have had recourse to sotto voce personal testimony in working through episodes of psychic fragmentation.

Emulating Virginia Woolf's own description of her autobiographical essays, feminist critics like Shari Benstock have proposed the term *life-writing* to challenge the traditional limits of autobiography through the use of a category that encompasses memoirs, diaries, letters, and journals, as well as the bildungsroman and other personally inflected fictional texts. This expanded genre embraces the flux and discontinuity that so frequently characterizes the orts, scraps, and fragments of self/life-writing found in confessional novels, romans à clef, biomythography, and tantalizing autofictions.[5] Both autobiography and autofiction offer a unique conflation of history and discourse, of verifiable fact and aesthetic fabulation. To a large extent, every autobiography imposes narrative form on an otherwise formless and fragmented personal history; and every novel incorporates shards of social, psychological, and cultural history into the texture of its ostensibly mimetic world. As Cathy Caruth observes in *Critical Encounters*, conflicts about issues of reference, materiality, and history "have long been at the heart of literary studies, where the status of the literary text—which is always by definition possibly a fiction—is in question" (2).[6]

Although one must acknowledge the perplexed and contested meanings currently ascribed to such beleaguered terms as *self* and *subject*, it is not within the scope of this discussion fully to delineate the ongoing controversy between humanist and deconstructive/poststructuralist epistemologies. Extensive analyses of the debate can be found in Paul John Eakin's *Fictions in Autobiography* and *Touching the World*, Paul Jay's *Being in the Text*, and Sidonie Smith's *Subjectivity, Identity, and the Body*. "*Self*," explains Smith, "signals an understanding of the human being as metaphysical, essential, and universal," whereas the term *subject* tends to denote "the culturally constructed nature of any notion of 'selfhood'" (*Subjectivity* 189n). Most contemporary critics would agree with Eakin's observation that "the self that is the center of all autobiographical narrative is necessarily a fictive structure" (*Fictions* 3) since, as Paul Jay insists, the "material recollected is less a 'pure' past than a narrative created in the present as the subject imaginatively reworks conscious and unconscious material" (25-26).

As Jacques Lacan would argue, the mirror stage of human development evinces a series of misrecognitions or "*méconnaissances* that constitute the ego" and situate "the agency of the ego . . . in a fictional direction" allied with the imaginary function (*Écrits* 6, 2). The human subject is always-already split and divided, a subjectivity "which is precarious, contradictory and in process, constantly being reconstituted in discourse each time we think or speak" (Weedon 32-33). Thus, when the reader of autobiography "is offered some kind of cohesion of the writing 'subject' which is guaranteed by the writing signature," she or he "is asked to submit to a fiction" (P. Smith *Discerning* 104). As Roland Barthes would argue, "*in the field of the subject, there is no referent*" (*Barthes* 56).[7]

Critics like Paul John Eakin, Sidonie Smith, Timothy Dow Adams, and Shirley Neuman, along with the majority of scholars working in the field of autobiography today, seem to have recourse to what Neuman calls a "both/and" strategy in dealing with the rhetorical jungle of theories that claim to be either constitutive or deconstructive of the "self" or "subject." Eakin believes that one must adopt a perspective recognizing "that the self and language are mutually implicated in a single, interdependent system of symbolic behavior" (*Fictions* 192).[8] Interrogating the meaning of the speaking subject in autobiography, Betty Bergland asks: "[D]o we read at the center of the autobiography a self, an essential individual, imagined to be coherent and unified, the originator of her own meaning, or do we read a postmodern subject—a dynamic subject that changes over time, is situated historically in the world and positioned in multiple discourses?" (134).

Despite the present poststructuralist moment in history, most contemporary autobiographers are engaged in fashioning coherent narratives of their own lives, even though they recognize that the concept of a stable identity allied with the myth of a universal subject has proven to be a fantasmatic cultural construct.[9] They respond to what Eakin identifies as an "existential imperative, a will to believe that is, finally, impervious to theory's deconstruction of reference as illusion" (*Touching* 30). Thanks to the "*pre-narrative quality of human experience*," Paul Ricoeur observes, "we have the right to speak of life as of an incipient story, and thus of life *as an activity and a desire in search of a narrative*" ("Life" 434).

The texts of both autobiography and bildungsroman exfoliate in the manner of mimetic histories but necessarily double back, like involuted Möbius strips, in haunting self-referentiality. At least three different subject-positions emerge in the text: first, the authorial consciousness, or subject of enunciation, narrating the autobiographical story in a series of recollected, sometimes discontinuous episodes; second, the early, fragmented (and often traumatized) version of the self; and, finally, the ostensibly coherent subject of utterance evinced through the process of narrative disclosure. Subjective reconstruction can take the form of aesthetic vocation, personal liberation from a cloying domestic or social environment, or successful integration into a larger discursive community. Whatever the framework, the author recasts his or her life narrative in the shape of a salutary paradigm that offers both a myth of origins and an implicitly teleological model for future development.[10]

What I would like to suggest in *Shattered Subjects* is that autobiography is, or at least has the potential to be, a powerful form of scriptotherapy—and that, as such, it lends itself particularly well to the evolution of twentieth-century women's life-writing. Autobiography has always offered the tantalizing possibility of reinventing the self and reconstructing the subject ideologically inflected by language, history, and social imbrication. As a genre, life-writing encourages the author/narrator to reassess the past and to reinterpret the intertextual codes inscribed on personal consciousness by society and culture. Because the author can instantiate the alienated or marginal self into the pliable body of a protean text, the newly revised subject, emerging as the semifictive protagonist of an enabling counternarrative, is free to rebel against the values and practices of a dominant culture and to assume an empowered position of political agency in the world.

In my own thinking about women's life-writing, I have defined the genre broadly, and sometimes metaphorically, to include confessional forms, autofictions, diaries, journals, and the bildungsroman, as well as autobiography and biomythography. What all these genres have in common is an author attempting to fashion an enabling discourse of testimony and self-revelation, to establish a sense of agency, and to unearth a panoply of mythemes that valorize a protean model of female subjectivity. Women daring to name themselves, to articulate their personal histories in diary, memoir, and fictional form, reinscribe the claims of feminine desire onto the texts of a traditionally patriarchal culture. In so doing, they begin to celebrate a semiotic discourse and a maternal subculture that has always generated experimental modes of feminine self-invention.[11]

As a psychoanalytic critic, I am particularly interested in the sexual/textual inscription of traumatic narrative as the focal point of a large body of autobiographical practice. Most psychoanalysts agree that traumatic experience generates inevitable psychic fragmentation—an etiology that a Lacanian critic might construe as a disruption and dismemberment of the imaginary subject, the version of an integrated self that emerges from *méconnaissance* or misrecognition of one's valorized mirror image. Whether attributable to fantasy or social construction, such misrecognition is vital to the individual's sense of agency and subjectivity. In order to function as an effective being in the world, one must necessarily cling to this Lacanian *mensonge vitale* as an enabling myth of coherent identity, despite its status as a fictional construct.[12]

In any autobiographical text, the narrator plays both analyst and analysand in a discursive drama of self-revelation, re-membering what Jacques Lacan would call the *corps morcelé* or "body in fragments" through the aegis of scriptotherapy. The subject of enunciation theoretically restores a sense of agency to the hitherto fragmented self, now recast as the protagonist of his or her life drama. Through the artistic replication of a coherent subject-position, the life-writing project generates a healing narrative that temporarily restores the fragmented self to an empowered position of psychological agency. The tenuous subject-in-process, the Lacanian *moi* contingent on the production of meaningful testimony, is valorized and reflected back in the implicit gaze of an auditor/reader who stands in for the (m)other of the early mirror stage.[13]

There seems to be little doubt that trauma precipitates a violent fragmentation of the (perhaps fantasized) image of the integrated subject. Traumatic events, Judith Herman tells us, "shatter the construction of the self that is formed and sustained in relation to others" and "cast the victim into a state of existential crisis" (*Trauma* 51). The fourth edition of the *Diagnostic and Statistical Manual of Mental Disorders* delineates the following symptoms associated with post-traumatic stress disorder: "recurrent and intrusive recollections of the [traumatic] event . . . or recurrent distressing dreams," "[d]iminished responsiveness to the external world, referred to as 'psychic numbing' or 'emotional anesthesia,'" and feelings of detachment and social estrangement characterized by a "markedly reduced ability to feel emotions (especially those associated with intimacy, tenderness, and sexuality)" (APA 424-25). A further constellation of symptoms tends to aggregate around interpersonal stress disorders that produce "impaired affect modulation; self-destructive and impulsive behavior; dissociative symptoms; somatic complaints; feelings of ineffectiveness, shame, despair, or hopelessness; . . . hostility; [and] social withdrawal" (APA 425).

Admitting that the definition of post-traumatic stress disorder must remain imprecise and contested, Cathy Caruth offers a summary of its symptoms: "there is a response, sometimes delayed, to an overwhelming event or events, which takes the form of repeated, intrusive hallucinations, dreams, thoughts or behaviors stemming from the event, along with numbing that may have begun during or after the experience, and possibly also increased arousal to (and avoidance of) stimuli recalling the event" (*Trauma* 4).[14] Returning to Freud's description of traumatic neurosis in *Beyond the Pleasure Principle*, Caruth goes on to suggest that the "experience of trauma repeats itself, exactly and unremittingly" in the form of a mental wound that is "not available to consciousness until it imposes itself again, repeatedly, in the nightmares and repetitive actions of the survivor" (*Unclaimed Experience* 4).

In *Trauma and Recovery*, Judith Herman classifies the symptoms of post-traumatic stress disorder in three main categories: "Hyperarousal reflects the persistent expectation of danger; intrusion . . . the indelible imprint of the traumatic moment; constriction . . . the numbing response of surrender" (35).[15] She further identifies the fundamental stages of recovery as a tripartite process that involves establishing safety, reconstructing the trauma story, and regaining a sense of community (3).

Traumatic memories, obtrusive and haunting, are nonetheless "wordless and static" (Herman *Trauma* 175). Stored in the brain during the adrenaline rush that accompanies the human biological response to danger, they "are not encoded like the ordinary memories of adults in a verbal, linear narrative" (37). Instead, they are imprinted on the brain like infantile recollections in "the form of vivid sensations and images" (38). In pathological configuration, traumatic memories constitute a kind of prenarrative that does not progress or develop in time, but remains stereotyped, repetitious, and devoid of emotional content. Iconic and visual in form, these images relentlessly intrude on consciousness as "a series of still snapshots or a silent movie; the role of therapy is to provide the music and words" (175). "What causes trauma," explains Cathy Caruth, "is a shock that appears to work very much like a bodily threat but is in fact a break in the mind's experience of time" (*Unclaimed Experience* 61). Popular cinematic representations of post-traumatic stress fail to convey the relentless nature of these flashbacks, which "are characterized by intense and absorbing visual imagery" and can sometimes assault consciousness hundreds, or even thousands of times per day (Schacter 216).

Bessel van der Kolk and Daniel Schacter have drawn on recent scientific brain research to show how traumatic memories are processed not in the cognitive cerebral cortex, but in the more primitive region of the amygdala.[16] Schacter hypothesizes that the "release of stress-related hormones, signaled by the brain's emotional computer, the amygdala, probably accounts for some of the extraordinary power and persistence that characterize many highly emotional or traumatic experiences" (217). Traumatic flashbacks make repeated intrusions into consciousness until their haunting reverberations take the form of an idée fixe. In order to break this torturous circuit of repetition, the victim must reenact the trauma in all its physical, sensory, psychological, and emotional detail.

The object of psychoanalysis—and of autobiography as scriptotherapy—is to "reassemble an organized, detailed, verbal account, oriented in time and historical context" out of "fragmented components of frozen imagery and sensation" (Herman *Trauma* 177). A great deal of evidence now suggests that the formulation of narrative cohesion can reconfigure the individual's obsessive mental processing of embedded traumatic scripts. "With this transformation of memory," Herman tells us, "comes relief of many of the major symptoms of post-traumatic stress disorder. The *physioneurosis* induced by terror can apparently be reversed through the use of words" (*Trauma* 183). In the very act of articulation, the trauma story becomes a testimony, a publicly accessible "ritual of healing" (181) that inscribes the victim into a sympathetic discourse-community and inaugurates the possibility of psychological reintegration. The trauma story, notes Janice Haaken, "anoints the survivor with a heroic status—as the bearer of unspeakable truths" (1083).

In her instructions for reclaiming a world, Herman has identified as crucial to the healing process the anatomization of both historical fact and emotional response. The primary goal of therapy is "to put the story, including its imagery, into words" (*Trauma* 177). If Herman's analysis is correct, then a major impetus behind autobiographical literature in general, and women's life-writing in particular, may be the articulation of a haunting and debilitating emotional crisis that, for the author, borders on the unspeakable. What cannot be uttered might at least be written—cloaked in the mask of fiction or sanctioned by the protective space of iteration that separates the author/narrator from the protagonist/character she or he creates and from the anonymous reader/auditor she or he envisages. Testimonial life-writing allows the author to share an unutterable tale of pain and suffering, of transgression or victimization, in a discursive medium that can be addressed to everyone or no-one—to a world that will judge personal testimony as accurate historical witnessing or as thinly disguised fiction. No matter. It is through the very process of rehearsing and reenacting a drama of mental survival that the trauma narrative effects psychological catharsis.[17]

There are possibly as many forms of women's (and men's) life-writing as there are authors committing their stories to paper, wordprocessing, and publication. It seems likely that marginalized individuals, both male and female, tend more frequently to invoke subversive and subvocal iterations to re-member the fragmented subject and regain an enabling sense of psychic coherence.[18] As members of the Personal Narratives Group affirm, life-writing "narratives of nondominant social groups (women in general, racially or ethnically oppressed people, lower-class people, lesbians) are often particularly effective sources of counterhegemonic insight" (7). The story of survival in the face of racial, cultural, and psychosexual adversity reconstructs a fragmented ego forced to the margins of hegemonic power structures. The act of life-writing serves as its own testimony and, in so doing, carries through the work of reinventing the shattered self as a coherent subject capable of meaningful resistance to received ideologies and of effective agency in the world. As Cathy Caruth reminds us, "trauma is not simply an effect of destruction but also, fundamentally, an enigma of survival" (*Unclaimed Experience* 58).

In *Shattered Subjects*, I examine a wide range of twentieth-century life-writing by women, from the Parisian *belle époque* to contemporary multicultural and postcolonial narratives. Beginning a book on narrative recovery with the case of Colette might, at first glance, seem anomalous, because the modernity and radicality of her literary production has largely been obscured to American audiences. Since Jerry Aline Flieger's publication of *Colette and the Fantom Subject of Autobiography*, however, it has been clear to psychoanalytic critics that Colette felt haunted by a powerful encrypted imago of the lost (m)other, a fantasmatic figure buried at the heart of her revisionist memoirs.

In Colette's biomythographies—*My Mother's House*, *Sido*, and *Break of Day*—the infantile sanctuary of Saint-Sauveur-en-Puisaye represents a green world of prelapsarian bliss presided over by the Mother/Goddess Sido and happily unencumbered by oedipal hostilities. When Colette is brutally abducted from the provinces by Henri Gauthier-Villars and introduced to the lascivious pleasures of a Parisian demimonde, the young girl feels literally and figuratively traumatized by her rude awakening to the perversion (*père-version*) of heterosexual desire. *My Apprenticeships* is the author's autobiographical attempt, at the age of sixty, to assert mastery over the master—to impose the rigorous control of symbolic language on the inscrutable specter that continues to haunt her. In recounting the story of her first marriage, she testifies to domestic battery, psychological manipulation, and conjugal imprisonment in a scenario that bears striking resemblance to paradigmatic captivity narratives.

Like Colette, Hilda Doolittle spent a lifetime reconfiguring a matrifocal and maternally inflected subjectivity. Whereas most critical discussions of H. D.'s literary production focus on traumas precipitated by World War I, chapter 2 of this work returns to an earlier defining moment that set the stage for the author's lifelong emotional vulnerability. The last chapter of *The Gift*, a narrative that H. D. described as "autobiographical fantasy" (*DA* 189), begins with the ten-year-old Hilda witnessing the effects of a mysterious accident that left her father wounded and bleeding. Unseen and unrecognized by Charles Doolittle, the distraught daughter sank into a state of mental dysphoria later rekindled by adult tragedy. Hence the powerful impact of severe losses suffered by H. D. during the Great War: an accidental pregnancy ending in stillbirth; the deaths of a brother killed in action and a father debilitated by stroke; and a second unexpected ("illegitimate") pregnancy followed by rejection and desertion by her husband Richard Aldington. H. D. would rehearse, reenact, and re-interpret these shocking events in a protracted series of autobiographical narratives that made use of scriptotherapy for purposes of self-analysis.

If Hilda Doolittle fantasized the emotional impact of paternal seduction in *The Gift*, Anaïs Nin literally enacted such fantasies in adult life. Using the psychoanalytic theories of Freud, Otto Rank, Jane Gallop, and Jessica Benjamin, chapter 3 traces Nin's disastrous internalization of the absent Father/God in the form of a stern, implacable superego who could be propitiated only by incestuous union. Capitulating to the imprecations of her long-lost Daddy, the thirty-year-old Nin consented to a love affair with the father who had been absent from her life for almost two decades. Her ingenious plan to ensorcell the man of her dreams, then to abandon him in a vengeful act of retribution, predictably backfired. The adult author was left doubly betrayed, reiterating the trauma of paternal seduction in voluminous diaries that functioned as self-analytic laboratories of the soul.

If Nin felt convinced that life-writing could serve as a powerful defense against the threat of psychosis and despair, the New Zealand author Janet Frame, the subject of chapter 4, would implicitly test this hypothesis in response to tragic experiences that shattered her childhood and adolescence. Frame's *Autobiography* testifies to the repercussions of grinding domestic poverty during the Depression; the traumatic loss of two beloved sisters, uncannily drowned a decade apart; and eight years of incarceration in a mental institution after a false diagnosis of schizophrenia. On a postcolonial odyssey to England, Frame recovered from a decade of "mind wastage" and managed to reconstruct her identity as an artist amidst the cacophony of London life. In an interview with Elizabeth Alley, she confesses that it was precisely the "point of loss" generated by trauma that motivated her autobiographical project (44). Poignant, indeed, is her unflinching record of emotional degradation in understaffed and primitive psychiatric facilities in New Zealand at mid-century.

Chapter 5 discusses the African-American poet Audre Lorde, for whom traumatic resonances produced by racial bigotry and ethnic polarities initiated a lifelong quest for matrifocal, woman-centered myths of creativity and heroism. In *Zami*, Lorde testifies to the intersection of multiple traumatic moments—from childhood rape by a boy who stole her glasses, through radiological assaults on her body in a dangerous and alienating work environment, to the nightmare of illegal abortion in the 1950s. The struggle against racism and homophobia became an ongoing challenge that informed her fight for survival. The writing of *Zami*, Lorde explains, was an experiment in scriptotherapy designed to work through traumatic experiences preceding the shock of breast cancer and surgical mastectomy. In contrast to the autopathography of Lorde's *Cancer Journals* and *A Burst of Light*, which function as intimate chronicles of the pain, humiliation, and rage evinced by life-threatening illness, *Zami* offers a retrospective bildungsroman shaped by the teleology of heroic self-invention.[19]

The final chapter of *Shattered Subjects* is devoted to Sylvia Fraser's Canadian memoir, *My Father's House*, and takes up the question of whether scriptotherapy might be considered an effective healing strategy for victims of childhood sexual abuse. Survivors of father-daughter incest often exhibit post-traumatic symptoms allied with multiple personality or "dissociative identity" disorder—a condition in which the victim literally enacts the metaphorical figure of a shattered subject, psychologically fragmented and emotionally in pieces (Schacter 238). Such was the case for Sylvia Fraser, whose powerful and tormented life narrative bears the weight of cathartic revelation. The construction of a coherent testimony—first as fiction, then as autobiography—eventually freed her to transfer filial affection from a seductive but treacherous patriarch back to the altruistic and long-suffering mother who had remained oblivious of her daughter's exploitation. By finally giving voice to repressed incest trauma, Sylvia was liberated to reinvent herself as woman and author, creative writer and historical witness to her own life story. As Sidonie Smith and Julia Watson declare in *Getting a Life*, by "citing new, formerly unspeakable stories, narrators become cultural witnesses insisting on memory as agency in its power to intervene in imposed systems of meaning" (14-15).

The term *narrative recovery*, now fairly current in the field of narratology, pivots on a double entendre meant to evoke both the recovery of past experience through narrative articulation and the psychological reintegration of a traumatically shattered subject. What the following study tries to illustrate is that much of the impetus behind women's life-writing in this century has been connected by emotional webs and filaments to a wide range of traumatic episodes; that many of these experiences have had a profound impact on the construction of female subjectivity; and that a number of women authors have instinctively turned to modes of autobiographical expression to implement the kind of healing made possible through the public inscription of personal testimony.

ONE

Colette's Autofictions: Genre and Engenderment

> It is the image in the mind that binds us to our lost treasures, but it is the loss that shapes the image. (*MA* 85)

I. THE EARTHLY PARADISE

"Is anyone imagining as he reads me, that I'm portraying myself?" Colette asks in *Break of Day*. "Have patience: this is merely my model" (*BD* 35). The model throughout Gabrielle Sidonie Colette's work is "Sido"—the mother portrayed as a "humbler artist" of physical creation, a woman completely in harmony with an idyllic world of infantile happiness. Much of Colette's autobiographical writing unfolds as a paean to a lost edenic landscape from which the adult author feels traumatically sundered. Consciously, Colette tries to emulate her mother's wonder at natural beauty and respect for everything that has life by reiterating Sido's perpetual litany of grace: "That child must have proper care. Can't we save that woman? Have those people got enough to eat? I can hardly kill the creature" (*MMH* 53). "I used to imitate her way of talking," Colette confesses, "and I still do" (*S* 167).

Throughout her nostalgic memoirs of childhood, Colette manages to introject what Nancy Chodorow calls a "preambivalent . . . preoedipal mother-image in relation to herself" (123). Her work celebrates the construction of a maternal imago that is large and omnipotent, but mythically benevolent, wise, and unfailingly generous.[1] Sido is at once a Delphic oracle, one of those "genuine Pythonesses" capable of "plunging to the bottom of another's being" (*S* 150), and a female python ready to (s)mother the children she loves too well. Colette sporadically perceives in her mother's countenance a "sort of wild gaiety" masking "an urge to escape from everyone and everything, to soar to some high place where only her own writ ran" (*S* 166).

In Colette's art, Sido emerges as a primary object of both narcissistic and libidinal pleasure, and Saint-Sauveur represents a green world of prelapsarian bliss unencumbered by oedipal hostilities. Colette tells us: "Sido and my childhood were both, and because of each other, happy at the centre of that imaginary star whose eight points bear the names of the cardinal and collateral points of the compass" (*S* 173). Bethimbled and nurturant, Sido's iconic figure sits at the symbolic apex of light, warmth, and maternal security. The lamp that illumines her needlework emanates from her figure and spreads out in concentric circles that portend the young Gabrielle's eventual loss of innocence. Within the protective circle of maternal love, serenity attends Sido's lamplit figure. "Beyond these all is danger, all is loneliness (*MMH* 25).[2]

When Gabrielle, at the age of nine, inherits the room of her ill-fated sister Juliette, a wild-eyed dreamer with Mongolian features and an inscrutable tent of hair, Sido becomes anxious about her younger daughter's potential fall from innocence. Regaling Gabrielle with stories of abduction and rape, she offers the cautionary tale of a Ghentish maiden forced to marry her seducer. "There was no other way out" (*MMH* 28), she explains ominously. Intrigued by these veiled allusions to a mystery she is too young to understand, Gabrielle becomes fascinated with a "small old-fashioned engraving, hanging in a dark passage" (*MMH* 28). The picture virtually seduces the prepubescent girl into perceiving rape and traumatic coercion as an acceptable, perhaps inevitable, paradigm of adult sexuality: "'*The Abduction!*' My innocent imagination was pleasantly stirred by the word and the picture" (*MMH* 28).

The iconography of this engraving casts the female in the mold of helplessness and vulnerability. Her mouth, framing an O, expresses the terror and astonishment of a victim whose screaming visage is shaped as an oral emptiness, a zero of negation suggestive of the vaginal hole about to be violated. Masochistic rapture accompanies the sexual anxiety that titillates its audience with a framed reality whose liminal border reassures the spectator of aesthetic sanction. Struggling with faint erotic apprehensions, Gabrielle cannot recognize the imminent threat of "a hypocritical and adventurous adolescence," whose burgeoning heterosexuality will transform her from a loving daughter into a "crafty accomplice of the stranger" (*MMH* 29). For the moment, however, the child is safely abducted by Sido herself, who carries her daughter back to an umbilical room attached to her own chamber.[3]

Sido functions, in large part, as the magic mirror of Lacanian fantasy, the (m)other whose gaze serves to construct a filial iconic image of wholeness and plenitude. The young Gabrielle, lost in the semiotic babble of infantile creativity, unsuccessfully attempts to uproot the fascinating word *presbytery* from its fixed linguistic community. She imagines fancifully that the word might refer to a horrible malediction, or it "might very possibly be the scientific term for a certain little yellow-and-black striped snail" (*MMH* 31). Enamored of the sound and texture of this elusive signifier, the child appropriates it for her own linguistic pleasure and tries to draw its vocative filaments into the malleable context of a fantasized mother tongue. A playful Gabrielle resists being inscribed into the symbolic register of the father/priest/lawgiver whom the presbytery shelters. At this point, however, she is reprimanded by her nonplussed mother, who connives with the patriarchy in demanding acquiescence to a harsh reality principle governing adult communication. "Call things by their proper names," Sido insists. And the future writer is left licking her wounds in a tacit battle for discursive innovation. The symbolic order triumphs temporarily: "I was craven and I compromised with my disappointment" (*MMH* 32).[4]

To other social conventions, the young Gabrielle will not so easily yield. She shrinks with horror, for instance, when confronted with the claustrophobic atmosphere of a matrimonial bower prepared for its sacrificial victims. At the center of the room stands a "high narrow bed" festooned with roses, "to stage the final scene of a day redolent of sweat, incense, the breath of kine and the aroma of sauces" (*MMH* 67-68). Having gorged herself on a sumptuous wedding breakfast, Gabrielle suddenly forges an alarming connection between food and mating, animal instinct and human sexuality. She envisions the married couple sinking helplessly "into that mound of feathers. The heavy shutters will be closed upon them, and the door and all the exits of this stifling little tomb" (*MMH* 68). Distraught by a Romeo and Juliet stage-setting of amorous asphyxiation, the young girl interprets conventional bourgeois marriage as psychosexual entrapment, a stultifying scenario that she finds inexplicably repugnant. Weeping and bewildered, she flees, in panic, to Sido's maternal embrace.

Throughout her portraits of childhood and adolescence, Colette seems to be engaged in a curious process of psychological splitting. She attributes to Sido those nurturant and loving qualities that imbue the mythic figure of her filial imagination, then introjects the more masculine aspects of this androgynous parent and sets out to woo the maternal object of desire through male-identified acts of autobiographical writing. This challenging engagement in literary production gives her the opportunity to construct an authorial subject-position as the renowned artist that her father, Captain Jules-Joseph

Colette, always aspired to be. Later adopting the single patronymic "Colette" as her literary persona, she usurps the name and authority of the father to fashion a unique signature: "So it came about that both legally and familiarly, as well as in my books, I now have only one name, which is my own. Did it take only thirty years of my life to reach that point, or rather to get back to it? I shall end by thinking that it wasn't too high a price to pay" (*BD* 19).

In the dreamworld of Colette's childhood, the figure of the Captain looms as an impotent, somewhat fatuous shade—so much so that the author expresses a sense of amazement at her own filial aloofness: "It seems strange to me, now, that I knew him so little. My attention, my fervent admiration, were all for Sido" (*S* 175). Colette acknowledges her progenitor in the role that Julia Kristeva would label the "father of personal prehistory," defined in terms of metaphorical identification rather than through metonymic displacements of desire and Eros. Because Colette's primary identification is with the object of her mother's desire, she evokes preoedipal narcissism as the ground for the mirror stage of infant development. In taking up a writing career, the adult author continues to attempt a psychological displacement of the father in her mother's passionate affections. She dares to assert the masculine side of her nature by practicing a craft that, throughout her childhood, had been reserved for the ineffectual patriarch of Saint-Sauveur.

The adult Colette recalls her father as "a wandering, floating figure, full of gaps, obscured by clouds and only visible in patches" (*S* 177). An opaque and mysterious progenitor, the Captain bequeaths to his daughter a passionate emotional temperament disposed to melancholia. "My father," Colette remarks, "fell before Melegnano, his left thigh shot away" at the age of twenty-nine (*S* 181). This symbolic castration was, to the members of his family, simply a fact of life—a disability so shocking that its obvious deformity was naturalized, then ignored. Colette confesses acute dismay at her youthful obliquity in the face of the Captain's misery. Only later in life could she penetrate his mask of insouciance and understand that despite an attitude of surface gaiety, he always "harboured the profound sadness of those who have lost a limb" (*S* 186-87). A mature Colette mourns the belatedness of her filial comprehension: "But while he was alive, ought I not to have seen through his humorous dignity and his feigned frivolity? Were we not worthy, he and I, of a mutual effort to know each other better?" (*S* 182).[5]

In the author's childhood memories, Jules-Joseph Colette is perceived by the young Gabrielle as virtually speechless. He is reduced to the status of helpless *infans*, in the original Latin connotation of a person "unable to speak." He cannot inscribe his masculine signature either in a literary text or in the domestic milieu he inhabits. A limb has been severed, a leg lost and forever grieved for. Psychologically castrated, Captain Colette depends on his wife for a maternal *langue* to give voice to his nostalgic iterations. Unable to enunciate an individual subject-position, he connives in being erased from the iterative skein of domestic *parole* and stands patiently watching as a vigilant observer. The Captain needs Sido to need him as husband and helpmate, but his all-consuming passion condemns him to a life of obsessive desire for the woman he can never fully possess.

Each afternoon, this taciturn soldier would retire to his library and ponder the huge notebooks, the *cahiers* in which he ostensibly was engaged in composing a history of his military campaigns. After his death, the family discovered the fruits of his labor—blank pages that revealed a mind incapable of translating dream into word, meditation into verbal inscription. Captain Colette had never gotten beyond the title of his magnum opus and its loving dedication:

> TO MY DEAR SOUL,
> HER FAITHFUL HUSBAND:
> JULES-JOSEPH COLETTE. (*S* 197)

It is perhaps understandable that Colette always identified the writer in herself as masculine and associated discipline and industry with male achievement. As Madame B., the voyant, insists when the spirit of Jules-Joseph Colette purportedly returns from the grave, the daughter who appropriates his surname has fulfilled her father's unrealized dreams. "You are exactly what he longed to be," she tells Colette. "But he himself was never able" (*S* 194). The ineffectual father offers his daughter a blank, virginal page on which to inscribe the elegy to Sido that he himself could never finish. He has bequeathed to her an "invisible cursive script," which she reproduces in her writing. This emotional legacy demands that Colette cunningly tease out an implicit tale of passionate devotion denied lyrical embodiment. "Your father is the modern Orpheus!" Sido had once exclaimed (*S* 192). Now the ghost of the father shines through the resurrected body of the phantom Sido/Eurydice, the mythic mother and lover summoned by the magical lyre of art from the inaccessible realm of the imaginary. With filial thumb bent in emulation of her father's withered phallic stump, Colette faithfully traces over the ghostly passions his shade implicitly calls forth. Her father's pen-name evinces his "spiritual legacy" (*S* 197), an all-consuming love that makes writing possible. The book we are reading constitutes the elegy the Captain might have written had he summoned the creative power to transform sexual obsession into textual embodiment.[6]

In later years, Colette would better understand that Sido herself had functioned as an artist of domestic creation who, in her epistolary communications, proved to be the writer that Jules-Joseph Colette had failed to become. "It was ironical that, equipped with every conceivable tool for writing, my father rarely committed himself to putting pen to paper, whereas Sido—sitting at any old table, pushing aside an invading cat, a basket of plums, a pile of linen, . . . Sido really did write. A hundred enchanting letters prove that she did" (*EP* 77). Colette so cherishes her mother's language that the words Sido speaks and (in)scripts take on iconic significance in *My Mother's House* and *Break of Day*. Sido becomes a repressed imago of the unspeakable mother, whose voice haunts the developing daughter as the Mother/Goddess/Demeter figure lost at the moment of "rape" by Dis/Hades/Willy. Throughout Colette's autobiographical writing, her unfortunate marriage to Henri Gauthier-Villars and subsequent separation from her mother is represented as a traumatic fall from grace succeeded by a lifelong struggle to recuperate maternal iterability. As Cathy Caruth would remind us, the paradigmatic nature of trauma is, in Freud's texts, "first of all a trauma of leaving, the trauma of *verlassen*. . . . [I]t is, finally, *the act of leaving* that constitutes its central and enigmatic core" (*Unclaimed Experience* 21-22).

In *My Apprenticeships*, Colette comments sardonically on the profound "difference between the condition of a maid and the condition of a wife" (*MA* 34), especially for ingenues initiated prematurely by "Lotharios half spoiled by time" (*MA* 56). Michèle Sarde suggests that, for the adolescent Gabrielle, the "dream of Prince Charming coexisted with the dream of some father-husband" (106). By virtue of Captain Jules-Joseph Colette's inscrutability, the young girl had apparently created a father/lover in fantasy to meet the more traditional needs of oedipal transference. Henri Gauthier-Villars eagerly fulfilled and played to the hilt the functional role of authoritarian Daddy/husband/master.

II. *MY APPRENTICESHIPS*: THE SPECTER OF WILLY

One suspects that a major impetus for Colette's own life-writing was the shock of her marriage, at the age of twenty, to Henri Gauthier-Villars, a Parisian playboy called "Monsieur Willy" by his friends and associates. Describing her conjugal initiation, Colette remarks acerbically: "Next day I felt separated from that evening by a thousand leagues, abysses, discoveries, irremediable metamorphoses" (*EP* 112). She portrays sexual defloration in terms of a grim metamorphosis—not from caterpillar to butterfly, but from innocent ingenue to scarred and knowledgeable woman. Colette's relationships with her father and then with her husband Henri Gauthier-Villars were characterized by a good bit of fantasy and idealization; and, in the latter case, by emotional terror, as well. It is probably not an exaggeration to speculate that Colette was both literally and figuratively traumatized by marriage to an exploitative lover who ruptured her dream of childhood innocence and introduced her to the ambiguous pleasures of a Parisian demimonde.

"I am recalling now an epoch when I lived in a singular state of . . . concealed wretchedness," Colette writes in *The Pure and the Impure*. "Two rooms had been set aside for me in the conjugal apartment, a bedroom and a studio . . . equipped with a trapeze" (*PI* 133-34). "I always knew," she realizes, "why my heart sank and why I trembled" in Willy's presence: "the shadow of that frightful shoulder, the expression of that vast back and the neck swollen with blood." Confessing to a fear of being alone, she asks rhetorically: "What name can I give to the so-called normal conditions that were foisted upon me?" (*PI* 149). Far from being normal, the marital environment she describes resembles a shocking scenario of domestic captivity.

Only the evocation of traumatic neurosis could explain Colette's obsessive need, at the age of sixty, to reenact the decade of conjugal bondage that she ironically labels her period of apprenticeship. Her inspiration is more urgent than a casual desire to recapture the past in vivid memoir. She feels compelled not only to record, but emotionally to exorcise the events of that ineffably painful period of her life. Three decades after her divorce from Willy, Colette still could not come to terms with the fact that she had spent her youth in the role of domestic prisoner to a man who forced her unwittingly to serve as his ghostwriter, concubine, plaything, and slave. Yet she feels the need to offer her audience an emotional disclaimer, telling us that she has directed both pity and laughter "at herself as much as at the chief character of her story" (*MA* 74).

If one is to believe Colette's impassioned testimony in *My Apprenticeships*, Willy literally held his wife hostage to her writing by incarcerating her in a sunless studio for several hours a day and, like a hard taskmaster, demanding a requisite number of "well-filled pages" before her release. One wonders if Colette parodically exaggerates in her claim that a "prison is indeed one of the best workshops. I know what I am talking about: a real prison, the sound of the key turning in the lock and four hours claustration before I was free again" (*MA* 71). In later life, she would express tongue-in-cheek gratitude for these exercises in enforced discipline. Scribbling under scrutiny, however, is hardly the fate one would wish for an aspiring writer. How could the fiercely independent Colette have submitted to the tyranny of such an egotistical and brutish mate? As Colette reveals in *My Apprenticeships*, she first had to surrender to the seductions of patriarchal power—to become enamored of the name and authority of the Father—before she could construct the kind of autonomous subjectivity traditionally reserved for males in western culture.

The bewildered young wife found herself apprenticed to a master who could generate ideas and choreograph their execution, but who was himself unable to produce art. Willy apparently "suffered from a sort of agoraphobia, . . . a nervous horror of the blank page" (*MA* 76). This popularly acclaimed journalist relied on a vast factory of ghostwriters to assemble piecemeal manuscripts that he would subsequently integrate and claim as his own. According to Colette, he lacked the kind of sexual/textual heroism demanded by the task of writing and "was frequently overcome by fits of weakness . . . before the virgin field, the naked page" (*MA* 77). Analogously, Colette had the misfortune to learn *ars amoris* from a jaded roué, who wallowed in voluptuous sensation but proved incapable of emotional reciprocity. Licentious rather than affectionate, critical rather than creative, Willy made imperious demands in the realms of love and literature but refused to gratify his wife's deepest needs for sympathy, intimacy, and male approval. Though an ungrateful editor and an unfaithful husband, he never relinquished control in the game of power that eventually destroyed their marriage.

Tragically for Colette, the two were playing entirely different games on the romantic battlefield of heterosexual conquest. An unscrupulous Lothario, Willy was determined to exploit the talented adolescent he had cunningly abducted from the provinces. His ingenuous bride took the game seriously and proceeded to enact traditional scripts of loyalty and devotion learned in childhood at Saint-Sauveur. "And what of the monogamous blood that ran in my veins, so inconveniently?" she asks (*MA* 119). Lost in a dream of amorous fantasy, Colette was genuinely fascinated by the man she had married. Adoring and mute, she voluntarily reduced her own personality to a tabula rasa. She became a zero, a pure and virginal page to be inscribed with the sexual discourse of her husband/father/lover. Colette unselfconsciously capitulated to Willy's manipulations and found herself losing every power struggle even before she had a chance to learn the rules of combat.

By sadomasochistic strategies of praise and blame, of lavish approval and devastating criticism, Willy kept his anxious pupil dangling in terror. Trembling under the weight of such authoritarian instruction, Colette had annealed on her psyche severe lessons in spousal docility. She quickly learned to be pliable in the face of her husband's outbursts and to eschew the soul-destroying effects of his harsh denigration. As avid disciple and intelligent student, this shell-shocked apprentice dared not risk the demeaning abjection provoked by her master's irascibility. As Judith Herman explains in *Trauma and Recovery*, in power struggles contingent on "the systematic, repetitive infliction of psychological trauma," the victim's fear is "increased by inconsistent and unpredictable outbursts of violence and by capricious enforcement of petty rules" (77).[7]

In her novel *The Vagabond*, Colette alludes more specifically to the experience of conjugal abuse: "What an expert master I had in him! How skillfully he alternated between indulgence and exigence! When I showed myself too intractable he even went so far as to beat me" (*V* 25). Was Colette, indeed, a battered wife? In a 1902 letter to Marguerite Moreno, she treats the subject with defensive levity in relation to her gymnastic exercises: "I venture the timid workouts of a lady who fears breaking something on the one hand and being beaten by her husband on the other" (*Letters* 3).

In Colette's remembrance of things past, Willy takes on mythic proportions. He was, she tells us, a mesmerizing lover who managed to dominate "several women's thoughts, at every hour of the day" (*MA* 123). His parsimoniousness, his mathematical preoccupation with figures and finances, and his anal-obsessive rage to "count, to amass, to hoard" gave him recognizably Dickensian features. In ridiculing Willy, Colette gains an empowering verbal mastery over this rotund and clownish boor: "M. Willy was not huge, he was bulbous," she observes. "It has been said that he bore a marked resemblance to Edward VII. . . . I would say that, in fact, the likeness was to Queen Victoria" (*MA* 54-55).

Such venomous caricature, however, in no way mitigates Colette's recollection of earlier intimidation. "It is indeed a very strange moment, in any life," she recalls, "when fear is born, seeds and takes root, spreads" (*MA* 55). The metaphor suggests a cancerous growth whose metastasis signifies emotional enslavement, either through amorous obsession or connubial obligation to a domineering partner. Colette confesses that she was bound to Willy not so much by law or religious belief as by the insidious power of sensual desire and physical "intoxication—a guilty rapture, an atrocious, impure, adolescent impulse" (*MA* 23). With the collusion of family and society, she became "the licentious masterpiece of some middle-aged man. It is an ugly dream . . . akin to the neuroses of puberty, the habit of eating chalk and coal" (*MA* 23). Colette's use of sadomasochistic imagery elicits morbid fantasies generated by a haunting conjugal nightmare and exacerbated by Willy's repeated infidelities.[8]

A proverbial Don Juan, Willy tormented his wife with a succession of love affairs that often reduced her to a state of emotional despair. Anecdotal evidence suggests that he shamelessly entertained his female guests in the small connubial apartment shared with Colette, who patiently waited on the landing or watched, in horror, the spectacle of exhibitionism proffered by her husband's mistresses. Colette reports a scandalous incident of implicit betrayal early in their marriage when, in response to an anonymous letter, she interrupted her husband and Mlle. Charlotte Kinceler in an intimate and compromising situation: "not in bed but sitting in front of . . . an open account book. . . . A dark little woman . . . was watching me, a pair of scissors grasped tightly in her hand" (*MA* 24)—evidently poised for a homicidal attack.[9] Another bizarre scene occurred when Willy brought home "a lively young model of Léandre's, the notorious Fanny Z—." Colette felt livid at the young woman's brash effrontery and recalls that when the model began casually to disrobe and proceeded to describe her most satisfying "voluptuous practices, the blood of 'Madame Colette's daughter' rebelled" (*MA* 108).

Colette suggests in her memoirs that the first years of her marriage passed like a confused dream, a half-conscious reverie whose details were plainly and fatally symbolic. But, she laments, "I was twenty-one and kept forgetting the symbols" (*MA* 34). Forty years later, she returns to the landscape of memory to reinterpret those richly textured signifiers whose meaning was clearly too painful for earlier elucidation. Incarcerated in a cluttered Parisian flat and treated like an invalid, the youthful Colette succumbed to traumatic symptoms of psychic numbing and emotional anesthesia by enacting the role of a sick and dying Camille. She glimpsed the shadow of mortality but eluded its threat by virtue of the loving ministrations of an anxious and attentive Sido. Colette recalls: "That wan *jeune fille* was near death, yet did not die" (*MA* 36).[10]

Recuperating her health, Colette reluctantly returned to her debilitating union with Willy. On holiday at Champagnolle, she offers a desultory portrait of their "room disgraced by a mildewed wall-paper, peeling off and dangling in liana-like strips, . . . and some nasty little curtains fit for wrapping up abortions" (*MA* 53). The sordid ambiance vividly alludes to an abortive sexual liaison. It evokes a repulsive image of Willy's genital imperialism occasionally relieved by furtive acts of libidinous gratification. The landscape of Colette's memoir evinces, in the mode of absence, Willy's curiously disembodied phallic potency, strangely detached from both love and procreation. "Perhaps," Colette remarks, "what I needed, without knowing it, was a child born of my own body" (*MA* 54). Her marriage to Willy was obviously doomed to sterility.

Not only was Colette prohibited by Willy from giving birth to a child, but she was forced to play the diminutive role of his surrogate daughter. Creating the fictional Claudine in the image of Willy's pornographic fantasies, she added, at his behest, salacious details to scenes of her provincial education and collaborated in giving birth to a sensational alter ego popularly interpreted as a raucous female libertine. Describing the arduous process of coming-to-writing, Colette recalls M. Willy's imperious directions to "add a little spice" to her "childish affairs" and "dialect, lots of dialect" (*MA* 59). Willy's editorial acerbity apparently chiseled the prose of Colette's enthusiastic logorrhea. "Perhaps he enjoyed his acid, pedagogic prestige," she remarks. "Nothing will rid me of the conviction that he was a born critic, . . . a born monitor, incisive, quick to find the sensitive spot" (*MA* 77).

Paradoxically, it was the demonic Willy who hurt Colette into authorship when he incarcerated her in her studio, forced her to produce autobiographical fictions based on her provincial adolescence, then usurped the fruits of her labor as publications under his own name. Willy's reputed coauthorship of the *Claudine* novels will always remain a mystery, though some scholars have recently speculated that he was actually more of a collaborator than Colette was willing to acknowledge. In a 1909 letter, she dismisses Willy's plagiarism and exposes the duplicity of his editorial strategies: "In the days when Willy did me the dubious honor of signing my novels, he would occasionally insert into my texts a few words designed to gratify his personal spite. He called this collaborating" (*Letters* 10). The one character that Willy apparently did invent for the *Claudine* novels was the figure of "fat Maugis," a projection that satisfied his "obsession for self-portraiture" (*MA* 61).[11]

In his authoritarian relationship with Colette, Willy deliberately infantilized his wife until she resembled Claudine, her piquant fictional brainchild. Reveling in the gestures of mimetic doubling, he forced Colette to cut her long, snaky locks, then dressed both his wife and Polaire, the actress who played Claudine onstage, in identical little-girl costumes and took pleasure in "trotting out [his] two kids" (*MA* 98). Colette demurely acceded to this exhibitionist scheme because, she tells us, "I was thirty; I had had ten years training" (*MA* 98). She minimizes the humiliations of her marriage by claiming merely to have sacrificed a frivolous and expendable decade: "It is better not to haggle over ten years of your life . . . provided they are youthful years. Later it is well to be thrifty" (*MA* 122).

By virtue of testimonial life-writing, Colette could resurrect and redefine these tormented years as a period of expansion rather than enclosure, of voluntary discipleship rather than shameful bondage. In *My Apprenticeships*, she portrays herself not as Willy's slave, but as his wide-eyed protégée in the arts of love and literature. She sets out to re-create conjugal disappointment in the carnivalesque mode of Menippean satire. If, as a young wife, she suffered cruelty at the hands of her spousal captor, she also learned the difficult lessons of feminine survival—of secrecy and perspicacity, psychological observation, and perpetual self-discipline. Like a medieval theologian, Colette justifies suffering in the name of wisdom and insists that this harsh initiation "taught me my most essential art, . . . the domestic art of knowing how to wait, to conceal, to save up crumbs, to reglue, regild, change the worst into the not-so-bad, how to lose and recover in the same moment that frivolous thing, a taste for life" (*MA* 71).

Colette describes her domestic captivity as a time of apprenticeship to a "master/*maître*" whom she would eventually surpass in creativity and fame. The alternative to the docility demanded by *le maître* is, of course, the French homonym *m'être*—the desire to function as an autonomous subject. Colette's autobiographical writing balances on the intersection of *maître/m'être*, constructing an elusive subject-position that inhabits the amorphous space of silence between fiction and autobiography, historical confession and romantic fabulation. The persona that emerges in Colette's unique "autography" is neither obsequious disciple to the *maître* nor the isolated self implied by the dream of *m'être*, but that of an imaginary and elusive authorial presence that straddles the polarity and challenges the reader to disentangle its various historical/fictive skeins. Colette insists on subverting patriarchal gender/genre by constructing a second mirror image of the self shimmering in the eye of the (m)other, uttering the infantile echolalias of a mother tongue, and gaily celebrating a semiotic discourse surreptitiously invoked in defiance of those rigid restrictions once imposed by a husband/father/*maître*.

III. *BREAK OF DAY*

From the evidence of Colette's life-writing, it seems clear that her marriage to Willy generated symptoms of psychic fragmentation and post-traumatic dysphoria well into middle age. Colette and Willy were legally separated in 1905 and formally divorced five years later. It was Willy who inaugurated divorce proceedings at the behest of Meg Villars, who threatened suicide if he did not marry her. "Colette instituted a countersuit on January 31, 1907, . . . claiming blatant infidelity" (Sarde 202). In 1909, Colette felt thunderstruck at the news that Willy had sold the rights to the *Claudine* novels for "next to nothing" to prevent her from claiming authorship. In a letter to Léon Hamel, she expressed shock that "these books which so entirely belong to me (morally speaking) are now lost to us both forever" and complained that "after three years of separation, I am still (and too often) discovering further betrayals" (*Letters* 11). The earlier renunciation of authorial rights to her first brainchildren "was indeed the most unpardonable act that fear ever made me commit" (*MA* 61).

Michèle Sarde speculates that Willy had remained, throughout his marriage to Colette, "anti-Semitic, antidemocratic, anticlerical, nationalistic, dandiacal and amoral" (Sarde 156). To this list might be added "misogynous" and "homophobic." One can imagine Willy's astonishment at the news of his ex-wife's lesbian liaison with the Marquise de Belbeuf ("Missy"), who became Colette's devoted companion, as well as her partner in the pantomime *An Egyptian Dream*. A scandalous kiss exchanged by the two women onstage brought down the house in roars of protest, which Willy found consummately amusing. He applauded boldly from his theater box and remarked that Colette's exhibition of her bisexuality at least had spared him the demeaning title of "cuckold."

In the solicitous arms of Missy, Colette found temporary respite from the conflicts she had come to associate with heterosexual domination. But in 1911 she met and fell in love with the handsome, charming, and egotistical Henri de Jouvenel. After a melodramatic encounter with his long-term mistress Isabelle de Comminges (alias the "Panther,") Colette and Henri (alias "Sidi") were married in December 1912. Two months earlier, Sido had died. Six months later, Colette's only child, "Bel-Gazou," was born. The unexpected joys of maternity seemed a midlife miracle to the woman who had claimed a "male pregnancy" (*R* 279) and felt obvious trepidations about the responsibilities of parenthood: "I remember welcoming the certainty of this late child—I was forty—with a considered mistrust. . . . I was worried about my maturity, my possible ineptitude for loving. . . . Love . . . had already served me ill in monopolizing me for twenty years in its exclusive servitude" (*R* 275-76). Colette would later celebrate her daughter as the greatest of her prolific creations.

Michèle Sarde observes that although "Colette had written 'One only dies from the first man,' . . . the second was also to kill her" (273). Colette's marriage to Henri de Jouvenel seems to have repeated earlier patterns of victimization initiated in her disastrous union with Willy. Hopelessly in love, she again felt captivated and resigned herself to the shackles of connubial dependency, explaining in 1911 letters: "I love this man, who is tender, jealous, unsociable. . . . I am mightily attached to him" (*Letters* 21-22). The attachment is echoed in the voice of Renée, Colette's fictional alter ego who, at the conclusion of *L'Entrave* (*The Shackle*), surrenders her freedom to the mysterious and elusive Jean, a lover modeled on Jouvenel. She responds with the "blind, primitive instinct of the animal crying frenziedly for its master" and welcomes Jean with the "meek, cringing gratitude of a bullied wife" (*The Shackle* 216-17). When Renée confesses that "the hand of my master fell heavily on me" (223), it is tempting for the reader to interpret the book's title as *"l'esclave"* rather than *"l'entrave."*

Tormented by anxiety over Jouvenel's military service in the 23rd Infantry Regiment during World War I, Colette made a hazardous journey to visit him at Verdun, then nervously awaited her soldier's return. But their postwar reunion proved wildly disappointing. The aristocratic Sidi was a jealous and domineering husband who compulsively engaged in extramarital love affairs. Colette often tried to cope with excruciating bouts of jealousy by adopting the curious strategy of befriending her husband's current or castoff mistresses. In 1924, the Jouvenels' conjugal charade finally ended. "I've been alone for a month," Colette confided in a letter to Madame Georges Wague. "He [Sidi] left without a word while I was on a lecture tour. I am divorcing" (*Letters* 66).

In deep shock over the failure of her second marriage, the fifty-one-year-old author determined to renounce romantic love and to heal herself through the narrative recovery of a world extinguished by her mother's death. When Sido died in 1912, Colette felt so traumatized by the news that she refused to engage in public mourning. "Mama died the day before yesterday," Colette wrote to Léon Hamel. "I don't want to go to the burial. I shall wear no visible mourning, and I am telling almost no one. But I am tormented" (*Letters* 28). Michèle Sarde remarks that, despite this stoic response, a "drawn-out period of mourning had begun" for Colette and "was to result in the books she explicitly dedicated to Sido" (287). In attempting to reconstruct an enabling myth of coherent identity, the mature author had recourse to scriptotherapy. Before she could come to terms with the traumatic resonances of conjugal abuse, Colette needed to reclaim the spirit of Sido as matriarchal muse. Her autobiographical texts that focus on this lost maternal territory defy the limits of traditional genre. Combining fact and fiction, memoir and fabulation, they capture the spirit of biomythography by incorporating myth and fantasy into aesthetically crafted life-writing.

In *My Mother's House* (1922), *Break of Day* (1928), and *Sido* (1929), Colette returns to the world of feminine fertility, the "cult of the little blue saucepan" (*BD* 132) associated with the earthly paradise of Saint-Sauveur. Life in Provence allows her temporarily to re-create the secret garden of her youth as part of a natural landscape that proves both nurturant and salubrious. In *Break of Day*, Colette finds sanctuary in La Treille Muscate, which she proudly describes as a dwelling "without a master" (*BD* 15). Her beloved friend Maurice Goudeket, later to become her third husband, is master neither of the house nor of her; he serves, instead, as a loving companion whose presence enriches her life, but whose absence does not diminish it.

Deliberately isolated in middle age, Colette determines to write herself into an autobiographical narrative of psychological recovery. It is Sido's enchanting letters that she takes as her germinal text in *Break of Day*—a meditation that has long been gestating in her heart and mind. At the outset of Colette's partially fictionalized memoir, the author recalls a letter in which her strong-willed mother refuses an invitation to visit because she anticipates the blossoming of her precious pink cactus, *"a very rare plant"* that *"flowers only once every four years"* (*BD* 5). Sido dares, at the age of seventy-six, to choose personal satisfaction over conventional family obligations. Although she continues to love her daughter Colette, she loves herself more and, until her dying day, manifests the joyous and incomparable gift of astonishment.[12]

Colette re-creates in *Break of Day* a *locus amoenus* that can, in some sense, revive her edenic memories of Saint-Sauveur. She regains not only the imaginary landscape of childhood but its precious spiritual independence. The mature author feels that she can at last emulate her mother's provincial ethic of autonomy and care. Metaphorically, she describes herself pregnant with Sido's spirit: "I felt stirring at the root of my being the one who now inhabits me, lighter on my heart than I was once in her womb" (*BD* 93). The imagery reverses the process of gestation. The adult narrator conceives and brings forth the sanctified memory of her mother, just as Sido once gave birth to the infant Gabrielle. In this filial persona, Colette is laboring to create a newly independent self liberated from the perennial conflicts of heterosexuality. She is struggling to realize, simultaneously, the image of her mother as creative artist and that of herself as liberated creator.

Romantic love, as an exercise in marital/martial combat, still pervades the author's dreams but no longer encroaches on her waking life. In a lyrical paean to the pleasures of middle age, Colette celebrates her newfound freedom from threats of emotional despair. "The love-sick, the betrayed and the jealous all smell alike" (*BD* 20), she remarks sarcastically. Love between men and women seems to be inscribed in cultural consciousness as a ritual battle, a psychological affliction from which Colette recovers only with the help of solicitous friendships. "Surely I ought to have thrown off that sordid domination?" she asks rhetorically. "It was all in such deplorable taste" (*BD* 22).

At this stage of her life, Colette tries to embrace a compensatory spirit of fraternity with the opposite sex: "Come, Man, my friend, let us simply exist side by side! . . . What you see emerging from a confused heap of feminine cast-offs . . . is your sister, your comrade: a woman who is escaping from the age when she is a woman" (*BD* 18). Colette takes as her premise Sido's philosophy that romantic love, as defined by the popular imagination, "is not a sentiment worthy of respect" (*BD* 22). This impassioned narrator welcomes the climacteric as a new phase of experience, "the season for sensual affection, . . . the only vintage time" (*BD* 30-31). She takes joy in thinking, writing, meditating, and discovering the authentic self so long diminished by amorous obsession. Protesting that the most intimate life of a woman does not focus on sexual liaisons, Colette refuses to capitulate to the seductions of a fictional suitor, Valère Vial. In her confrontation with this lovestruck young man, she recognizes a desire for conquest couched in chivalric devotion. Vial, in some sense, suggests a less invidious version of Monsieur Willy—an emotional vampire disguising his need for domination in the traditional rhetoric of courtly love.

Colette insists firmly that the anonymous but ubiquitous "*he*," the phallic shadow that has so long preoccupied both waking life and nocturnal dreams, must now, finally, be "no one" (*BD* 113). Renouncing sexual obsession, she embraces a different kind of passion—more dignified and tempered, restrained yet enduring. No longer craving the blind devotion of an *amoreux*, the mature narrator prefers to welcome man as her "dearest friend" and fellow traveler on the road to spiritual enlightenment. In this midlife memoir, Colette becomes the elusive aesthetic object that she so ardently aspires to create. Eschewing the kind of infatuation that twice elicited traumatic conjugal histories, she envisages a utopian future characterized by a life of wisdom, emotional stability, and sensuous delight.[13]

At the end of her poetic meditation, Colette testifies to spiritual (and emotional) conversion. She rejects the masculine sphere of rivalry, obsession, jealousy, and appropriation and chooses, instead, the beneficent philosophy fantasmatically embodied in the shade of her maternal muse. Sido knew and has now taught her daughter "why the true name of love, that suppresses and condemns everything around it, is 'frivolity'" (*BD* 133). Summoning the ghost of her mother as a tutelary spirit, Colette invokes the rhetorical strategy of prosopopoeia to give voice to the ecstatic vision articulated in Sido's final letter—an enigmatic message that points to an elusive but tantalizing earthly paradise regained. This mystical, hieroglyphic epistle gives Colette faith that it is "not too much to be born and to create each day" (*BD* 141). Relinquishing Vial as an inappropriate love object, she amalgamates his seminal image with the colors of dawn to fashion an imaginary figure that will be transmuted into a new birth of consciousness—an age of rejuvenated passion that dares to devote itself to all the spiritual treasures harbored in that secret garden once glimpsed by Colette as a child, but long since abandoned for the pleasures of erotic enchantment. Perhaps, in this final paean to her mother, the artist/daughter manages to retrieve that ever-elusive mother-infant bond whose fantasy of psychic wholeness always remains at the center and secret heart of female creativity.

So poignant is Colette's invocation to Sido as maternal muse that readers have tended to interpret this powerful mother-daughter bond in the context of what Marilyn Yalom terms "an unbroken stream of primary love" (quoted in Hirsch 103). Marianne Hirsch is one of the few critics to argue that the mother-daughter plot of Colette's narrative "pulls disquietingly in two different directions" (104). Initially constructing a fictive scenario of emotional estrangement in *Break of Day*, Colette fashions a story of separation that "fulfills the same function as Hades' rape in the Demeter myth by creating the space that makes plot possible" (105).

Throughout her memoirs, Colette inscribes in the scene of writing the nostalgic fantasy of an earthly paradise locked in the sealed world of the Lacanian imaginary, "a world of which I have ceased to be worthy" (*MMH* 6). It is a fairy-tale landscape of long ago and far away, a dream of preoedipal satisfaction that reconstructs a childhood reminiscence of integrated subjectivity—a moment of prelapsarian bliss shattered by the oedipal trauma of masculine seduction/abduction and heterosexual union. The historical Sido, cast as mythic (m)other, functions as both mother and incestuous lover to the infant psychologically sealed in a primary emotional bond with its matriarchal protector. The mother's de/faced image, tropologically engendered through prosopopoeia, emerges as a figure of totalizing self-presence whose loss imbues Colette's autobiographical texts with the gaps and fissures of unattainable desire. The space between wholly beneficent (and fantasized) maternal nurturance and the oedipal drama of frustrated libidinal need creates a psychic wound that spurs the adult narrator toward the kind of emotional suture offered by art.

As Marianne Hirsch has theorized, without an initial traumatic fall from maternal grace—and from the subvocal iterations of semiotic discourse—the female artist cannot experience the always-already absent locus of desire necessary for the recuperative act of writing. Without the intrusion of heterosexual desire through the metaphorical rape of Persephone by Hades, the mother-daughter plot would be unnarratable. For the woman writer, dreams of preoedipal beatitude function as the irretrievable center and focal point of unattainable homoerotic bliss. Nostalgia for a protective continuum of mother-daughter affiliation necessarily screens the Freudian threat of oceanic engulfment and regression to infantile, undifferentiated consciousness. It is precisely the wound of separation, the traumatic umbilical cut, that scars the psyche and spurs its creativity. Cut off from a fecund, compassionate mother, the child must initiate its own self-sustaining narrative of suture in the paternal or symbolic register and construct an autonomous subjectivity out of repressed longing for a semiotic mother tongue.

It is this imaginary fall from a state of primordial grace that motivates Colette to reconstruct the ambiance of (fantasized) infant omnipotence. In recuperating an infantile subject-position vis à vis a protective maternal and theological matrix, Colette paradoxically asserts her own authorial mastery at the same time that she protests failure, unworthiness, and vulnerability.

At least two Colettes emerge in the texts of *Sido*, *My Mother's House*, and *Break of Day*—a filial persona engaged in recollections of the painful, perplexing, and sometimes demeaning process of coming-to-knowledge in the hostile world of heterosexual conflict; and the mature artist implicitly seeking, at the dawn of middle age, a return to the idyllic world of infantile happiness, but spurred to creativity by the very space of desire she articulates so passionately.[14]

Throughout Colette's autobiographical oeuvre, Sido is portrayed as both goddess and demon-mother, wielding weapons of the garden—a pocketknife, a pair of secateurs—that figuratively cut the umbilical cord of dependence and wound the child-narrator into adult aesthetic consciousness (*S* 151). The scissors or secateurs are flaunted as instruments of traumatic rupture, severing infantile-maternal bonds and casting the daughter adrift in the realm of masculine discourse—the symbolic register of the law and the word of the Father, inaugurated at the moment of *Spaltung* or "splitting" during the Lacanian mirror stage. The space of insatiable desire informing the textual unconscious evinces the scene of Colette's elegiac writing practice.

The mature author metaphorically gives birth to her mother/lover as the irretrievable other, the always-already lost object of repressed libidinal and incestuous fantasy. The homosexual discursive matrix of such longing for undifferentiated affiliation informs Colette's autobiographical texts and structures her fantasies of mother-daughter communion. From memories of an earthly paradise, she fashions a sentimental dream of theological wholeness, a nostalgic reverie whose very inaccessibility evokes compensatory narration.

Through hybridized genres of autofiction and biomythography, Colette asserts a profound need to function creatively as *"m'être/maître"*—to reconstruct her own subjectivity in the symbolic register of the once idealized and inscrutable father. As author of an historical subject-position embellished through art, she fashions a mirror image of integrated selfhood reflected in the eyes of the (m)other and reiterated in the narrative skein woven by the author/daughter determined to give birth to herself through literary creation. Colette deliberately conjures the ghost of Sido as model or ground for the figure of her own development—as angel and goddess, protector and guardian, artistic collaborator and mystical muse. The romantic unconscious of the text fantasizes a sentimental oceanic communion reuniting Demeter and Persephone in the presymbolic realm of the imaginary.

The mother-daughter romance culminates in a lyrical, semiotic iteration that self-consciously defies the symbolic register by introducing into poetic language what Julia Kristeva would identify as a "*heterogeneousness* to meaning and signification . . . detected genetically in the first echolalias of infants as rhythms and intonations anterior to the first phonemes, morphemes, lexemes, and sentences" (*DL* 133). Sido's final epistolary communication ecstatically unfolds in the hieroglyphics of an ineffable mother tongue reproducing the rhythms, pulsions, and echolalias of preoedipal expression and setting the stage for more contemporary experiments in the art of *l'écriture féminine*. The mystery of this sacred maternal text resounds with insatiable desire couched in an embryonic language of ecstasy and affirmation—the language of *parler femme*.

> Two pencilled sheets have on them nothing more than apparently joyful signs, arrows emerging from an embryo word, little rays, "yes, yes" together, and a single "she danced", very clear. Lower down she had written "my treasure"—her name for me when our separations had lasted a long time. . . . It has a place among strokes, swallow-like interweavings, plant-like convolutions—all messages from a hand that was trying to transmit to me a new alphabet or the sketch of some ground-plan envisaged at dawn under rays that would never attain the sad zenith. (*BD* 142)

According to Marianne Hirsch, the significance of this letter "lies in its very resistance to interpretation. . . . As she vacillates between figure and ground, Colette reassembles the maternal body which has been fragmented, dispersed, and transfigured, merging with the landscape" (106-7). Colette's epistolary replication re-inscribes the body of the absent mother in a secret, mysterious, yet life-giving utterance reminiscent of Julia Kristeva's elusive *chora*—"unnamable, improbable, hybrid, anterior to naming, to the One, to the father, and consequently, maternally connoted" (*DL* 133). This semiotic disposition reproduces the split subjectivity implicit in mystical or poetic language by functioning through linguistic "constraints (rhythm, phonic, vocalic timbres in Symbolist work, but also graphic disposition on the page ['strokes, swallow-like interweavings, plant-like convolutions'] . . . accompanied by nonrecoverable syntactic elisions" that make the "meaning of the utterance undecidable" (134). Because language as symbolic function "constitutes itself at the cost of repressing instinctual drive and continuous relation to the mother," poetic language would be, in Kristeva's words, "the *equivalent of incest*" (136).

No longer fearing incestuous union with the forbidden mother/lover of her imagination, a mature Colette feels empowered to celebrate Sido's maternal message on this side of the grave. She can read her mother's semimystical communication as a presymbolic epistle that restores the "archaic, instinctual, and maternal territory" (*DL* 136) of artistic inspiration and offers metaphorical mediation (suture) between semiotic rupture and the symbolic register of phallocentric discourse. Kristeva explains: "To rediscover the intonations, scansions, and jubilant rhythms preceding the signifier's position . . . is to discover the voiced breath that fastens us to an undifferentiated mother, to a mother who later, at the mirror stage, is altered into a *maternal language*. It is also to grasp this maternal language as well as to be free of it thanks to the subsequently rediscovered mother, who is at a *stroke* . . . pierced, stripped, signified, uncovered, castrated, and carried away into the symbolic" (*DL* 195).

As she slips into immortality, Sido gives her daughter implicit permission to indulge in incestuous homoerotic fantasy and to identify with the maternal body on the brink of annihilation. The mother, as desirable object of filial longing and infantile cathexis, etiolates in Colette's "ex-centric" text, only to emerge as a Heideggerian "ek-static" subject swept beyond the boundaries of the transcendental ego (and the bounded text) by the lyrical tides and rhythms of visionary iteration. Her semiotic discourse erupts into *parler femme*, into what Hélène Cixous would identify as the process of "writing the body," creating a feminine textuality that expresses a female libidinal economy heretofore repressed by patriarchal culture ("Castration" 53). But challenging the symbolic register and disrupting the thetic voice of the master by asserting continuous relation to the body of the mother is, for the artist, dangerous indeed. What happens when the mother-daughter dyad takes precedence over the oedipal family romance implicitly positioned at the center of male master narratives? "To repeat the question: . . . what about this 'space' prior to the sign, this archaic disposition of primary narcissism that a poet brings to light in order to challenge the closure of meaning?" (Kristeva *DL* 281).

At the end of *Break of Day*, Colette's erstwhile romantic quest is left unfulfilled in its cosmic and aesthetic metamorphosis. Her artistic project is magically transformed into "an open and unending book," the first installment of which we are currently reading. The dream evinced by the biomythography's textual unconscious is a fantasy of incestuous love and maternal plenitude poised forever on a lyrical note of open-ended possibility rather than of amorous or filial satisfaction.[15] Might Sido's love for all that blossoms and has life, for a burgeoning pink cactus whose effulgence obscures all other passions, now be attained by her daughter through the heterosexual attachments she renounces and transforms? Might interpersonal love take on cosmic import and lead to wisdom and enlightenment? Colette's final peroration in *Break of Day* would suggest that such a dream might be so: "The ambiguous friend who leapt through the window is still wandering about. He did not put off his shape as he touched the ground. He has not had time enough to perfect himself. But I only have to help him and lo! he will turn into a quickset hedge, spindrift, meteors, an open and unending book, a cluster of grapes, a ship, an oasis" (*BD* 143).

Perhaps, like the cactus rose, the author's own fantasies must flower and change, as she invites to the inner sanctum of this fertile imaginary world the male presence heretofore shunned by both mother and daughter. There seems to be little room for heterosexual conflict in such an edenic bower. Nonetheless, the male suitor might be admitted if he agrees, like Maurice Goudeket, to assume the double visage of androgynous twin and solicitous helpmate—to become, in short, a matric male.[16] Soon after meeting Maurice, Colette wrote to her friend Marguerite Moreno: "Last night Goudeket and I had one of those talks that begin at ten minutes to midnight and go on until four twenty-five in the morning. . . . How it satisfies me . . . to find that my partner is on the right wavelength" (*Letters* 78).In another letter she concludes, "That boy is exquisite" (*Letters* 80).

In Maurice Goudeket, Colette found a collaborative partner willing to support and cultivate her literary genius. One has only to read Goudeket's memoir, *Close to Colette*, to understand the role of this devoted companion in creating a salubrious environment for a gifted and sensitive artist whom he treated with the same awesome reverence that Sido had once displayed toward her fragile, budding cactus. Celebrating his life with Colette, he offers this personal assessment of *Break of Day*:

> If ever a novel appears to be autobiographical, that one does. . . . Colette puts herself into it, describing herself in minute detail. Never has she pushed self-analysis so far. The transparent allusions to her past are authentic. . . . Everything is there, except that *La Naissance du Jour* evokes the peace of the senses and a renunciation of love, at the moment when Colette and I were living passionate hours together, elated by the heat, the light and the perfume of Provençal summers. (45)

"Colette," observes Mary Kathleen Benet, "may have found love easier to renounce in books than in life because the male characters she created were much less interesting than those she married" (232). But perhaps there is another reason why the author chose to renounce love in her literary memoir and joyously to embrace a May-December union in the second part of her life. Goudeket's epicene qualities implemented the resurrection of a fantasmatic earthly paradise relinquished in youth but imaginatively rediscovered in middle age. Unlike the fictional Vial, Maurice could provide an antidote to Willy's brutal mastery of a younger Colette by serving as emotional surrogate for the beloved mother earlier displaced. For an aging Colette, egalitarian fellowship with someone like Maurice enabled her to get beyond an obsessive-compulsive rehearsal of psychosexual enslavement to the kind of bullying partners that had twice captivated her heart.

Master of herself and of her own creative impulses, Colette could reconstruct in *Break of Day* a more pliable subject-position with the full confidence of recuperated subjectivity—a sense of agency and psychological empowerment that released her from haunting dysphoria. By reenacting her demeaning subservience to Willy in *My Apprenticeships*, she at last felt free to testify to earlier trauma in a coherent autobiographical narrative that allowed her to reconfigure the script of amorous infatuation. Maurice Goudeket's spousal devotion generated a safe emotional space for the author's experimental practice of *parler femme*. Toward the end of her life, Colette would write the feminine body on the sexual and textual tapestry bequeathed her by a dying but immortal Sido and sanctioned by an extraordinary and loving partner. In *My Apprenticeships*, she tells us that her later novels "dwelt most persistently upon love. . . . I brought it back into my books and found pleasure in it when I had recovered my respect for love—and for myself" (*MA* 85).

IV. POSTSCRIPT

One of Freud's central insights, says Cathy Caruth, is that "history, like trauma, is never simply one's own, that history is precisely the way we are implicated in each other's traumas" (*Unclaimed Experience* 24). Like so many modern authors who lived through the vicissitudes of two world wars, Colette was not spared the repercussions of historical trauma. During World War II, she was permanently scarred by her confrontation with anti-Semitic violence. Married to a Jew during the Nazi occupation of Paris, Colette would continue to reiterate in all her later writings the shock of Maurice Goudeket's brutal abduction to a German detention camp. That fateful knock on the door by the Gestapo in the early hours of December 12, 1941, made an indelible impression on her consciousness.

In a series of fraught communications with friends, an anxious Colette described Goudeket's removal and imprisonment:

> Maurice was arrested last Friday at 6:30 a.m. . . . He left very calmly for I don't know where, charged with the crime of being a Jew. (*Letters* 168)
>
> And I'm waiting. That's the hardest part. . . .
>
> This is the twelfth day. There is *no* correspondence of any kind allowed. (*Letters* 169)

> Since the 12th of December, he's been a hundred kilometers away, at the Compiègne camp. . . . Impossible to write or make contact. (*Letters* 169-70)

In "Evening Star," Colette carefully details the trauma of Goudeket's arrest, as well as the anxiety evinced by the unthinkable threat of his deportation to a Nazi concentration camp. After three months of near-starvation in freezing winter temperatures, Maurice still refused to cooperate with his captors. His reprieve, Colette sardonically implies, was a function of the inefficiency of early German efforts to exterminate the Jews, since the Nazi killing machine had not yet developed its full technological capacity. "Uncertainty still reigned over those first batches, those massive round-ups, and the jailers themselves seemed inexperienced" (*R* 215). On February 6, 1942, Maurice was released from prison but spent the rest of the war in hiding.

Goudeket's arrest inaugurated a "perfect and classical nightmare of absence" (*R* 164) for both husband and wife. Colette's own post-traumatic stress reaction was so severe that she continued to live in a permanent state of hyperarousal. For the rest of her life, an unexpected knock at the door or a surprise visit would immediately give rise to traumatic flashbacks. In "Evening Star," she describes her chronic vulnerability: "A ring at the bell still afflicts me, to a lesser degree, with nervous shock, a twitch of the mouth and the corner of the eye, of the shoulder raised to the ear." Autobiographical testimony had enabled Colette to resolve the pain of domestic violence and emotional abuse, but nothing could mitigate the impact of Nazi aggression. "Will one never get over it?" she wonders, noting soberly that "many women who suffered the same experience at the same time change so as to obliterate these reflexes." "But I," she concludes, "I'm too old to get over it" (*R* 163-64).

T W O

H. D.: Psychoanalytic Self-Imaging

You can go round and round in circles. . . . Or your psyche, your soul, can curl up and sleep. (*TF* 31)

I. *THE GIFT*

The last chapter of *The Gift*, a text H. D. described as "autobiographical fantasy" (*DA* 189), begins with an evocation of childhood trauma—Charles Doolittle's skull-snapping accident and the ten-year-old Hilda's swooning impotence: "'What is concussion, Mr. Evans?' I said. But . . . then the floor sank. . . . I would sink down and down and all the terrors that I had so carefully held in leash during the great fires and the terrible bombing of London would now break loose" (*G* 131).

In 1943, the 57-year-old author vividly recalls the bewilderment she felt as a prepubescent girl, watching her stunned and bleeding father and curiously trying to comprehend the meaning of a "blow to the head" that she feared might prove fatal. Amidst the seemingly endless horror of the London blitz, an adult H. D. again finds herself helpless and waiting, unable to handle the shock of concussion/bombing/fire/apocalyptic conflagration. The traumatic experiences of civilian life under siege during World War II release a flood of repressed memories aesthetically controlled through the narrative frame of scriptotherapy. Produced in the context of H. D.'s "dread of and obsession with being bombed," *The Gift* was generated as "a hybridized text. Precariously, it unfolds between the contours of the past, as H. D. intermittently and imperfectly recalls it, and the present, which is a state of continual imperilment" (Fuchs 88-89).[1]

Suddenly confronted with the possibility of being "burnt to death" during an air raid, H. D. embarks on an autobiographical re-creation of the past evinced, in effect, as a "repercussion of the blast" (*G* 133). The repressed memory of Charles Doolittle's mysterious accident had been disinterred initially from Hilda's unconscious during her psychotherapy with Mary Chadwick in London some 35 years after the event. H. D. wanted further to explore the resonance of "this submerged, long-delayed shock" with Sigmund Freud, to whom she depicted the experience in Poe-esque imagery as the sensation of being "Buried Alive" (*TF* 139). It is not entirely clear why her father's injury should have had such a momentous impact on the ten-year-old Hilda. For a coherent explanation, one must look to H. D.'s own self-analysis in *The Gift*—an autobiographical testimony that lays bare the psychic landscape of childhood fantasy at the very moment that its beleaguered author is struggling to survive relentless wartime air raids.

Bombs exploding over H. D.'s Chelsea flat in 1943 evoke an earlier psychological bomb-burst associated with uncanny fears of death by conflagration and with the fires of her grandmother Mamalie's secret ecstasy—a narrative shared with the prepubescent Hilda, but long obliterated by the shock of her father's accident. "I understood . . . a memory of my grandmother's or her grandmother's—a lost parchment, terror that led back finally to the savages, burning and poisonous arrows" (*G* 134).

Like an initiate of Mamalie's fantasized *Wunden Eiland*, H. D. declares: "I had passed the flame" (*G* 136). But even the supposedly comforting religious hymn *Abide with Me* resuscitates traumatic memory. "[N]ow that I was overstrung, undernourished, it all came back" (*G* 137), the author testifies. The aporia in this confession might well reside in H. D.'s hypothesis of malnutrition as a child, since nothing in *The Gift* suggests a lack of physical nourishment in the Doolittle household. Surely this allusion represents, metaphorically, the profound spiritual and emotional hunger of Hilda's early life, characterized by a tenuous and inscrutable relationship with a cold, remote, idealized scientist father and a complicated desire/demand for infinite nurture from a somewhat timid, malleable, and preoccupied mother: "It is *she* who matters for she is laughing. . . . *If* one could stay near her always, there would be no break in consciousness" (*TF* 33).[2]

Hilda evidently feels cheated of her mother's loving solicitude and her father's reassuring affection—emotions complicated by sibling rivalry with her elder brother Gilbert. Do her casual remarks about malnutrition imply a tendency toward anorexia nervosa, a disease first diagnosed at the turn of the century? Or is H. D. simply trying to reinforce the mystical sensibilities she wants to ascribe to her precocious persona as a young Moravian virgin? The utterance surfaces as a perplexing riddle at the heart of a fragmented text and is later reinforced by an allusion to emotional starvation in "H. D. by *Delia Alton*" (*DA* 194).[3]

Describing the 1943 London blitz, H. D. expresses amazement that the entire civilian populace "hadn't all gone raving mad." Perched on the brink of madness, the author faces trauma head on and throws herself mentally into "this worst of all trials" (*G* 138). What saves her is long acquaintance with the Freudian world of the uncanny and with ghost stories that must be resurrected from the unconscious as tales told in the dark to ward off incipient terror. She must deliberately infantilize herself and embrace, once again, the tenuous subject-position of juvenile helplessness. Like a child whispering nocturnal secrets, she reconstructs a coherent life-story that ends with resurrection and rebirth. The magical iterations of *The Gift*, H. D. tells us, "abracadabraize something." "They are the words of the spell . . . that in a sense . . . *keep me alive*" (quoted in Fuchs, 90-91).

What might be the symbolism of a nameless girl "burnt to death at the seminary . . . where our grandfather was principal" (*G* 1)? H. D.'s autobiographical fantasy begins with female conflagration and male impotence, despite the proliferation of masculine authority in the double(d) patriarchal figures of Papa and Papalie. Where are the mothers? The author's childhood reminiscences are characterized by maternal absence, female erasure, and a spectral patriarchal presence. Even the Christmas tree, an ancient pagan icon appropriated by Christianity as a symbol of seasonal regeneration, is eerily transfigured into an agent of female sacrifice. The tree, symbolic of light and winter renewal, becomes the source of a tragedy precipitated, in part, by the Victorian female garb of hooped skirt and stifling crinoline set alight by Christmas tree candles. H. D.'s memory of her grandfather's story resonates with Freud's analysis of the "dream of the burning child." The child's invocation in the Freudian dream, "Father, don't you see I'm burning?", is a paradigmatic "call by which the other commands us to awaken . . . to a burning" (Caruth *Unclaimed Experience* 9)—or to a repressed history of infanticide attributable to paternal negligence.

Hilda's girlhood reminiscences are littered with the corpses of dead girls and deceased women: her sister Edith and half-sibling Alice (by a dead Lady, Martha, Charles's first wife); and, of course, Mama's legendary sister Fanny. A flood of monosyllabic words, along with the prolific use of hypotaxis, contributes to the impression of infantile breathlessness and perplexity in the face of a confusing adult world, where mourning for the long-dead Fanny has become a lugubrious family ritual mimicked by the Doolittle children. "Why was it always a girl who had died?" Hilda wonders, shamefacedly confessing that the "crying was frozen in me" (*G* 4).

Alvin, Charles Doolittle's elder brother, had died of typhoid fever during the Civil War, and it was Charles who suffered a guilt of survivorship exacerbated by his mother's disappointment that Alvin, not Charles, had succumbed to the devastations of a bloody struggle among brothers fighting to subjugate a decadent southern aristocracy. What was left for Charles but stoic emotional retreat? A half century before Freud's invention of the talking cure, Charles Doolittle remained silent. Heroic in his efforts to demarcate the northern boundaries of a Union he had defended at the price of fraternal loss, Charles found his vocation in astronomy and took sanctuary in the exploration of distant planetary orbs.

Hilda's stargazing Papa seems an inscrutable figure with a mission defined by nocturnal pursuits. He goes "out to look at the stars at night" and is sheltered in a "little domed house" resembling an Eskimo hut (G 6). Charles/Papa is a denizen of an icy world habitable by none but Nietzschean hyperboreans, those legendary supermen reputed to live beyond the North Pole. His private domicile is a sacred, Olympian territory beyond the Lehigh River. This twentieth-century priest of science is magically "gifted" with a special night vision that reveals a cosmos invisible to the naked eye. When the curious children peer into Papa's sacred telescope, their daytime perusal of the heavens proves futile: "we would see nothing . . . only a white glare" (G 7).

Hilda "can not say that a story called *Bluebeard* . . . actually linked up in thought . . . with our kind father" (G 7). And yet she *does* say it, in the very breath that she denies the possibility of thinking the ineffable. In a brash, but tentative flirtation with prohibited iteration, she dares mentally to accuse her father of gynocide. Why, otherwise, would he be associated with so many female corpses planted in the cemetery—"Edith and Alice and the Lady" (G 7)? Hilda voices the unutterable idea that Papa, with his jet-black beard, is an avatar of the legendary Bluebeard—a murderer of his first wife and two female children.

If Papa is not Bluebeard, then perhaps he is God. Like Adam in the book of Genesis, he functions as a primordial "name-giver" to his daughter by arbitrarily, even casually, fingering an alphabetical list of female names in the family dictionary. His paternal finger can ostensibly vivify or kill: "Had he put his finger on Alice?" Hilda wonders (G 8). His supernumerary digit symbolizes a prehensile manifestation of arbitrary power—life-giving or death-dealing, but definitely incomprehensible in its whimsical vagaries. In her typescript of *The Gift*, H. D. notes that Papa "was like God in a robe in the garden on the first page of the illustrated Bible" (*G Ts* Box 40/Folder 1035/p. 9). "It was presumed that I loved my father. Perhaps love is not the word for it. Or shall we say, if each of us, individually is a sun, the soul-centre of the personal microcosm, following the laws of the macrocosm, that Papa was in that circle of life and being, not so much Jove or Jupiter or Zeus-Pater, God the father, as Saturn, Time, father-time" (7).

Stealing out of the house "like a thief," the wily astronomer resembles the Greek god Hermes, as he cunningly searches the heavens for secrets of the universe. The God of stars blesses the godlike astronomer who peers into a sky illumined by moonlight (in contrast to the maternal lamplight that warms the hearts of his children). He studies the great world and the world outside that world, the universe of stars rife with awesome cosmic mysteries. Charles Doolittle appears to his adoring progeny in the patriarchal manifestation of the Moravian "Our Father," conflated with God the Father in the Lord's Prayer and spiritually endowed with the powers of magical surveillance of every snowflake or sparrow that falls (*G* 60). The specular gaze of the all-seeing "Our Father" suggests an embodiment of the panoptical vision described by Foucault in *Discipline and Punish*, as well as the omnipercipient attributes of a Christian deity. It is the father's perpetual (en)vision(ing) that psychologically sustains his dependent offspring and inscribes them into the symbolic register of logocentric discourse.

The Professor imposes a tremendous emotional burden on his only surviving female child when he names her the "one girl . . . worth all his five boys put together" (*G* 42). Hilda, he implies, is precocious and gifted. Singled out for attention and affection, the young girl is tacitly implicated in a veiled metaphorical seduction. Sons may be autonomous, but the daughter is expected to function as Papa's particular favorite and to live up to his extraordinary demands on her person. "It made a terrible responsibility," Hilda observes (*G* 42).

Charles Doolittle is the figurative sun around which mother and children revolve, like planets in their singular orbits, spinning around the light and gravitational force emitted from the central radiance of the Father/God/Professor. A worshipper of those myriad intergalactical suns that function as his spiritual model, he reigns like a Sun God, Ammon Ra or Phoebus Apollo, over this domestic cosmos. Like Hermes, Professor Doolittle is guardian of secret and inaccessible knowledge. Hilda complains of total ignorance about her father's mysterious occupation, simply defined as "separate" and inscrutable (*G* 43).

If Hilda dare not imagine usurpation of the name and the word of the father, she nonetheless feels free to fantasize a transsexual twinship with her brother Gilbert that allows her to enjoy, in fantasy, an enviable masculine priority. When she sees a picture of Jack and Jill in a child's storybook, the French *Gil Blas* enables her to identify the male Gil with the female figure of Jill. If Hilda can metamorphose into Jill and finally become one with Gil, then Hilda/Deetie can appropriate with impunity the subject-position of an obnoxious brother who claims domestic privilege and does everything first. Hilda cunningly slips into the place of fraternal dominance by a deconstructive pun that usurps the power of naming and, through games of linguistic dissemination, sows the seeds for her transsexual identification with Gilbert.[4] Hilda's own name is, ironically, undecidable in the text, as it swerves through various metamorphoses: "Hilda," "Sister," "Deetie," and finally "H. D.," a name later selected for Hilda by Ezra Pound in the tearoom of the British Museum.

If names can be changed through powers of the imagination, then so can characters and personalities. The world offers endless possibilities in the manipulation of pliable discursive formations. *Uncle Tom's Cabin*, a text authored by a woman and reinterpreted as a histrionic theater piece, becomes for Hilda a paradigm of aesthetic transformation. "Little Eva came back after she was dead" (*G* 14), observes the awestruck child. Like religion, dramatic art can perform miracles that resurrect the deceased individual through prosopopoeia. In a moment of synesthetic epiphany, all the arts meld together and reveal to the impressionable girl a metaphorical horizon that unites her with the myths of Greece and Rome, pagan worship, and medieval Christianity. Dramatic mimesis evokes images out of the collective unconscious that allow an exhilarated Hilda to indulge in creative fantasy, until she concludes that "a play and to play were the same" (*G* 19).

In attempting theatrically to envisage the romantic landscape of her mother's distant youth, H. D. imaginatively re-creates the secret tryst shared by an ingenuous Helen Wolle with her first suitor, a South American Catholic. The adult author reconstructs a fictional dramatic monologue on the part of an infatuated Helen, who nostalgically recalls that Mr. Fernandez "sent me red carnations" (*G* 39). In the "Fortune-teller" section of *The Gift*, a mature and worldly-wise Hilda devises a melodramatic reenactment of her mother's first courtship. This authorial fantasy mythically replicates the archetypal abduction of Persephone: "like that Greek myth in the *Tanglewood Tales* . . . there was a girl who was raped away . . . by the darkness, by Dis, by Death" (*G1* 40). Embedded in the fortune-teller's inscrutable prophecy is Hilda's own emotional rendition of her mother's accession to sexual knowledge: "So far away, she had gone, the summer-house was wreathed in fragrant sea-weed and the jasmine-flowers were froth and pearls from the sea, and she was a mermaid, ageless, timeless, with a whole set of poetical and biological emotions that there were no names for, that were things having to do with the Tree of the Knowledge of Good and Evil" (*G1* 40). The mythic scenario portrays Helen as Persephone, abducted by Dis/Hades, seduced into the darkness of the unconscious, smothered by jasmine and wreathed in the blood-red flowers of pagan Catholicism—red carnations symbolic, perhaps, of either menstruation or sexual violation. Helen is cast as a perverse Madonna or a fallen Eve seduced by a Spanish-speaking "papist and heathen" despised by her puritanical Papa.

Where is Mimmie (Helen's mother) in this scene? She is invoked as the ominous voice of prophecy, warning of the black rose symbolic of female defloration and the threat of potential madness. The fortune-teller appears to Helen in the guise of a witch-woman gifted with second sight, but abetting a kind of psychological seduction dredged from repressed memories and brought to the focal point of Helen's consciousness by her hysterical response to the seer's hypnotic repetition of the word *carnations*. In the typescript of *The Gift*, Hilda reports hearing a cautionary parable about a young girl who "got some terrible disease because a passionate southerner kissed her" (*G Ts* Box 40/Folder 1035/p. 29). Helen Wolle Doolittle ominously warns her daughter "never to 'forget oneself'" (30).

In contrast to this seduction narrative gleaned from her timorous mother's memory bank, Hilda finds that discursive formations evoked by words, fairy tales, and iconographic representations reveal a magical treasure trove sequestered in the racial unconscious. The child-narrator feels symbolically betrayed by a mother who cunningly substitutes the Greek myths of the *Tanglewood Tales* for the tattered but beloved pages of Grimm, "the children's Bible" (*G* 48). Wistfully, Hilda reminisces about a picture she remembers depicting a princess with "long hair and lilies in her arms" (*G* 48). While defensively insisting that she does not care about the Grimm loss, Hilda cares so passionately that her mother's insouciance provokes a resonant confusion concerning sexual difference, linguistic representation, and gendered subjectivity. *Grimm's Fairy Tales* serve as a sacred repository of linguistic and iconographic images that allow the girl to envision herself as a beautiful princess with long hair and a star emblazoned on her forehead. The sheer effort required to sustain her creative imagination in the face of Mama's insistent introduction of classical reality severely disorients the disappointed child.

Just as the princess holds lilies in her arms, so, too, is young Hilda bequeathed a single white lily by a mysterious stranger, a "General from the Old South" described by H. D. in *Tribute to Freud* (*TF* 121). This "grandfather, godfather, god-the-father sees the children" and favors the little girl over her brothers. His obsequious gardener, "a younger edition of himself," first snips the flower from "an Easter-lily or Madonna-lily" blossoming in the midst of winter (*TF* 120-21), then drives the sleigh that the old man commissions to collect the female child. Although Helen Doolittle has instructed her daughter to place the Easter-lily on Papalie's grave, the mother later denies any recollection of either lily or sleigh. And Hilda feels confused by her memory of the lily's blooming while the "streets were full of snow. It could not be worked out" (*G* 50).

The elliptical world of adult knowledge seems uncanny to the child, especially since, as Claire Buck points out, the dream sequence can be interpreted ambivalently—either as an expression of preoedipal desire for the mother/Madonna, or as a manifestation of "female penis-envy, and the disavowal of the mother's castration" (110-111). Hilda's ambiguous recollection occupies a liminal space between reality and vision, experience and dream. The lily is so overdetermined as a cultural and religious symbol of female virginity that one cannot but wonder if the floral bequest might conceal a repressed image of real or imagined sexual abuse.[5]

Screen memories of fantasized sexual violation in *The Gift* seem to cluster around figures of whiteness, purity, lilies, and snow; and the release of frightening libidinal energy is associated, in mysterious fashion, with either terrifying or exhilarating vehicular motion. (Compare Hilda's panicky leap from a milk wagon to escape an exhibitionist toward the end of *The Gift*.) This compensatory sleigh ride is apparently pleasurable, especially when shared with Mama and the boys, as Hilda sinks down into the womblike warmth of a luxurious fur rug. Fetishes of fur, however, also mark paternal power, as in the case of Charles Doolittle's fur cap and leather boots, which make him look Russian (*G* 33). It seems possible, then, that the southern General is a dream version of the remote and inaccessible father, and that the son/gardener serves as his apprentice in the task of symbolic castration.

Since the father is generally unavailable to Hilda and her siblings, the truncated lily could signify a repressed image either of the primal scene of parental copulation or of the daughter's own fantasmatic sexual abuse. Charles Doolittle might well allow his only daughter metaphorically to ride in his sleigh or to share his icy abode as an incentive to serve Daddy's pleasure with unconditional filial devotion. The question, however, of who has given what to whom, under what circumstances, and for what price, remains ambiguous in this series of half-remembered images that might simply evoke vivid infantile fantasies in the economy of father-daughter libidinal exchange. When H. D. recounts this resonant anecdote in her analysis with Freud, she confesses: "I don't know if I dreamed this or if I just imagined it, or if later I imagined that I dreamed it" (*TF* 123). "It does not matter," Freud reassures her. "The important thing is that it shows the trend of your fantasy or imagination." "The old man was obviously, he said, God" (*TF* 123).

And what if God takes the form of the Greek god Apollo rather than Our-Father God? What if he manifests his phallic potency in images of snakes and caduceus symbols that haunt the consciousness of a prepubescent child and accost her with transparent psychosexual images? Hilda dreams or fantasizes that a monstrous phallic serpent with "great teeth" crawls onto "Papa-and-Mama's bed" and begins "drinking water out of a kitchen tumbler." Still another snake, coiled on the floor nearby, "rears up like a thick terrible length of fire hose" and strikes at the panic-stricken girl (*G* 56).

Although this daydream/nightmare has been read by Dianne Chisholm as a symbolic search for knowledge on the part of Hilda, it seems evident that, on the most primitive Freudian level, it constitutes an image of the primal scene of parental intercourse.[6] The snake fitting itself into a tumbler of water suggests a transparent phallic representation. The nightmare evokes Hilda's residual terror of sexual violation, with the serpentine "fire hose around the legs of the bed" (*G* 56) threatening her own legs and poised for vaginal penetration. Paradoxically, the hose cannot release water to quell the libidinal fires that inspire this epiphany, nor can it connect with the fertile female presence recumbent on the bed.[7]

Overwhelmed by the sensory delirium of a fantasy rife with sexual symbolism and illicit desire, Hilda rejects the metaphorical significance of double snakes' heads and leaps in her imagination to a metonymically related scene associated with an illustrated copy of the *Arabian Nights*. She tries to work out the mechanics of gender construction, as well as the duplicitous culture-coding associated with oriental veiling. "This is a girl," she insists, when first presented with a picture of Aladdin, who seems to be garbed in female dress (*G* 56). Yet Hilda is assured that despite his epicene appearance, he is indeed a boy whose genitals are veiled but nonetheless potent in terms of sexual difference. Although he wears a dress and "has long hair in a braid and a sort of girl-doll cap on his head," Aladdin "is not a girl" (*G* 57). His gender is determined negatively, as the opposite of the female he so curiously resembles. "Is it only a boy who may rub the wishing-lamp?" Hilda wonders (*G* 57).

Perhaps the veiled phallus/snake/firehose endows its owner with powers beyond the cognizance of the vulnerable girl-child searching for clues to the mystery of a sex/gender system predicated on male mastery and female subservience. Patriarchal authority is somehow allied with the tactile pleasure of rubbing a female genital/lamp that evokes the fantasy of wish-fulfillment in a male-dominated world. The girl is victimized by the hole in the scopophilic economy of the father that labels her own genital/gender negatively, as the "nothing to be seen." But even when the male sex cannot be seen, it still retains the power of the seeable and the touchable to rub a lamp, make a wish, and inherit patriarchal authority as a biological or cultural right.

A terrified Hilda graphically describes the fantasy of being attacked by a malevolent phallic serpent who bites the side of her mouth with equine teeth. "I will die soon of the poison of this horrible snake," she fears (*G* 57). Hilda's snake-stung mouth evinces a veiled allusion to displaced genital eruption—perhaps a fantasy embodiment of prepubescent fear of clitoral and labial development, or of sexual violation by the phallic serpent imagined earlier. It is surely significant that the snake threatens the child's mouth, a site emblematic of speech, art, creativity, and oral communication. This mythic monster stands in for a father-lawgiver punishing the female word-shaper. The symbolic logos becomes sacrilegious and profane when subversively uttered by a transgressive feminine mouth. By rubbing two (oral or vulval) lips together in aesthetic iteration, Hilda has dared to rub the wishing lamp whose privileges have historically been reserved for males. Since H. D. must have known Freud's work on "Creative Writers and Daydreaming," the notion of art as wish-fulfillment could not have been far to seek. If Hilda usurps the garb and the prerogatives of an artist-creator, she must be punished by the phallic serpent who serves as a patriarchal gatekeeper prohibiting female entrance into the exclusive male temples of art and science.[8]

A beleaguered Hilda, wounded and panic-stricken, summons matrilineal ghosts to her aid: the memory of Mama and a "much-beloved, later, dark Mary" (*G* 57), who at first appears to be a family servant or governess, but who might also embody Hilda's maternal great-grandmother Mary, the initiator of a long line of gifted females: Elizabeth Wolle, Helen Wolle Doolittle, and Hilda Doolittle. "Dark Mary," a healing witch figure, prescribes mother's milk as an antidote to snake's venom. She orders Hilda to "eat things you do not like" (*G* 57) in a diet of ill-tasting foods to cleanse the palate of the girl-child threatened by a serpent's poison. (Ironically, *das Gift* means "poison" in German.)

Another possible unraveling of this skein of screen and remembered images might, however, like Poe's purloined letter, be fairly transparent. The snakes erupting from the textual unconscious could be construed as either benevolent or demonic. And the dual serpents in the first scene might embody the snakes depicted on the medical caduceus symbolic of health, empowerment, and integrity. "It was Asklepios of the Greeks who was called the *blameless physician*," H. D. notes in *Tribute to Freud*. "The *T* or Tau-cross became caduceus with twined serpents" (*TF* 101).[9]

Finally, the toothed serpents could, at some level, disguise memories of fantasmatic sexual abuse. The snake strikes lips that displace the symbolic fragility of the daughter's developing genitalia. The serpent overwhelms a vulnerable virgin, who cannot articulate the bodily disgust aroused when her vulval lips are stung and her hymen irreparably damaged. In retreat from the knowledge implied by this fantasy of sexual violation, the girl sinks back into the womb of maternal security to drink milk and ingest the ill-tasting food of exile. The dark Mary of this scene seems to mimic the advice of nineteenth-century nerve doctors who urged female patients to take to their beds, follow a steady diet of milk and bland foods, and relinquish any aspirations toward creativity.

Hilda further recounts her nightmare: "The monster has a face like a sick horrible woman. . . . It is a snake-face and the teeth are pointed and foul with slime" (*G* 58). As Dianne Chisholm observes, this frightening fantasy suggests a broader association with the Jungian collective unconscious and with racial memories that link the toothed serpent with the Greek god Apollo, the sacred python who transmits visionary wisdom. Sexually molested in a nightmare, Hilda identifies her phantasmic dream husband with Apollo in the incarnation of a python and remarks enigmatically: "All little girls are not virgins" (*G* 59).[10]

It is not surprising that this particular nightmare blends with a graphic illustration excised by Hilda's mother from a children's book called *The Simple Science*. The censored, but vividly imagined picture offers a convenient cover-up for repressed memories of violation. According to this iconographic representation of the pseudoscientific "Nightmare," the perpetrator of sexual abuse is not the male scientist/father, but the female night/mare/witch who acts as surrogate husband in rites of virginal defloration in primitive societies. The metaphorical nightmare is illustrated by a picture of a young virgin lying on a bed and attacked by a snarling witchlike creature who, Hilda fears, is "going to stick the little girl right through with her long pointed stick" (*G* 59).

It is safe, perhaps, to censor the memory in tricks of sex/gender reversal and recast the male member in terms of a witch's phallic broomstick—a synecdoche that relieves the child of responsibility for remembering the father's implicit seduction, since the alluring patriarch is displaced by a genderless night/mare whose sex was once female, but who now wields an instrument of penetration/violation that the male scientist (author of *The Simple Science*) himself envisages. The potential perpetrator creates a female witch as a scapegoat for his own libidinous urges, then sends the haggard crone flying abroad to violate little girls who risk physical or psychic defloration every time they go to sleep and entertain the night/mare or father/stallion from an unsimple scientific landscape.

Alluding to the threat of madness, Hilda cryptically observes: "It is terrible to be a virgin because a virgin has a baby with God" (*G* 60)—as did Mother Mary, who now, in a contemporary incarnation, sanctions mother's milk over Papa's poison. The deflowered virgin risks conception of the divine son through the aegis of God-the-Father—Our Father who art in heaven, our father who art in the observatory charting the heavens, our father who neighs like a horse (a night/mare?) when he laughs, our father whose gaze keeps snowflakes floating and sparrows flying and little girls safely tucked in their lily-white grave beds or beneath fur rugs on sleigh rides in the snow.

In a tableau imagined in *Tribute to Freud*, H. D. explicitly positions herself and her father in the iconography of the Freudian family romance: "A girl-child, a doll, an aloof and silent father form this triangle, this family romance: . . . *Father*, aloof, distant, the provider, the protector—but a little un-get-at-able, a little too far away and giant-like in proportion, a little chilly withal; *Mother*, a virgin, the Virgin, . . . adoring, with faith, building a dream, and the dream is symbolized by the third member of the trinity, the *Child*, the doll in her arms" (*TF* 38). H. D. echoes Freudian theory so accurately in this passage that her configuration of images resembles psychoanalytic pastiche. The virginal Hilda sits silently at the foot of her impassive Papa, gazing in awe at the progenitor whose phallus is deliberately veiled. She fondles a doll/baby in displaced longing for the child/penis that the father fantasmatically might engender.

In another recollected scene of rare intimacy with her father, Hilda is taken by Papa out in a boat onto the great maternal lake whose genital blossom is the water-lily—the lotus of inspiration and wonder, the flower that symbolizes beatific vision. Charles Doolittle resembles Moses among the bulrushes in a dream recounted by H. D. in her analysis with Freud: "The name of this picture is *Moses in the Bulrushes*. . . . Am I, perhaps, the child Miriam? Or am I, after all, in my fantasy, the baby? Do I wish myself . . . to be the founder of a new religion?" (*TF* 37).

The young Hilda is blessed by a beneficent patriarch with a magical moment of being, an epiphany among the water lilies (water roses) that reaches back to Egyptian history and Old Testament myth, then leaps forward to a Jungian suggestion of the Dantesque multifoliate rose of paradise. Charles Doolittle clearly functions as the presiding deity in the heaven of Hilda's childhood. This reverie out of time and excluded from history explodes in a transcendental moment of being that reveals to the author her future artistic vocation. She feels so ecstatic that emotions meld together until pleasure and sorrow, laughter and tears, all join forces imaginatively to burgeon in the mind and heart of the incipient artist. "Can one cry because one is happy, Mama?" (G 72), she asks. The childish question goes unanswered. Could one be crying and happy or laughing and sad at the same moment that the father/navigator/savior/Moses is initiating his daughter into unutterable creative mysteries?

In *The Gift*, it is women who ultimately prove to be the sacred priestesses of Eleusinian rites.[11] The secret of mystical joy has been carefully sequestered from the gaze of puritanical fathers by the matriarchs of Hilda's Moravian heritage. It is the (grand)mothers of the tribe who have remained repositories of laughter and sensuous pleasure, of devotional ecstasy and passionate faith. The secret of *Wunden Eiland* (*Isle of Wounds*) is communicated to Hilda by her feverish grandmother Mamalie, whose mind wanders over the nebulous terrain of the past—her own first marriage to Christian Henry Seidel and the Moravian heritage that has now been suppressed by disapproving Church Fathers. "Christian had left the secret with me" (*G* 79), she confides. The secret ostensibly revealed is somehow allied with faith in the biblical promise of Christ, *"lo, I am with you always, even unto the end of the world"* (*G* 84). Yet this simple utterance fails to bear the weight of sacred mystery it purportedly connotes.

The confused child tries to piece together disparate strands of Mamalie's story, like a mosaic or quilt emerging from the elderly woman's feverish, perhaps senile iterations. Hilda will later find herself psychologically united with the Moravian initiates when she witnesses her father's accident—a shock so powerful that it precipitates traumatic amnesia. After exposure to paternal powerlessness at the age of ten, the young girl so successfully represses her grandmother's colloquy that the narrative becomes a secret even to herself. It is only when the "shooting stars" of World War II make England figuratively a wounded island that H. D.'s repressed memories are suddenly liberated. The German blitz recorded in *The Gift* symbolically disinters the buried tale of Moravian mysticism.

The sacred text reconstructed by Mamalie, and later by Hilda, apparently refers to a scroll of flexible deerskin containing esoteric lore annealed on leather in Greek, Hebrew, and German characters. The scroll describes the "Ritual of the Wounds," a life-transforming ceremony so meteroic that it "burnt up" its initiates. "The laughter ran over us" (*G* 87), exclaims Mamalie, echoing the historical document. The Holy Spirit of Christianity, elided with the Native American Great Spirit, inspires extraordinary transports of rapture in the Moravian disciples.

When the ceremony culminates in a ritual exchange of women (Morning Star, wife of Paxnous, and the Moravian Anna von Pahlen, initiated into pagan mysteries by the "savages"), such maverick behavior is mistaken for witchcraft. The ecstatic brethren are accused of "extravagances," as the church elders forbid the ritual worship of Christ's wounds, "wide and red and blood dripping" (*G* 96). Did the secret ceremony involve sadomasochistic self-mutilation, or merely religious ecstasy? We do not know. We learn only that Christian Henry Seidel was himself "burnt up" with zeal and devotion, and that the massacre of Christians at *Gnadenheutten* put an end to the Moravian sect's fraternization with Native Americans.

The secret lore of this primitive sect is transmitted to Hilda by her grandmother in a flood of dissociated reveries. The epiphany functions as a mystical gift virtually walled off, or buried alive in Hilda's unconscious after her father's life-threatening accident. When Professor Doolittle becomes a symbolic martyr, a Christ figure battered and bloodied by an accidental fall from a streetcar, Hilda takes psychological refuge in strategies of denial and repression.[12] H. D. confesses to Freud:

> The cause of my father's accident always remained a mystery. He might have slipped off the old-fashioned steam tram or the local train engine might have backfired. . . . When we finally went to his room he was propped up, . . . but his hair and beard had turned white. It was another father, wax-pale, a ghost.
>
> I think I was ten years old at that time. I had "forgotten" this until I began my work with Miss Chadwick.
>
> I had "forgotten" my father's accident for thirty-five years. (*TF* 138-39)

In *The Gift*, H. D. recalls vividly that when she ran outside to greet her wounded father, she "found blood on his head, dripping" (*TF* 138). The ten-year-old child feels thoroughly startled to encounter Charles Doolittle's unseeing eyes, glazed over and unresponsive to her presence. The father's sudden anonymity, his impaired sight and limp limbs, apparently shatter Hilda's confidence in the integrated and coterminous self constructed by the scopophilic gaze of her father/priest/protector. Without Daddy's implicit mirror acknowledgment, she can no longer maintain the reassuring illusion of coherent identity.

H. D. recounts in *The Gift* her childhood recollections of ministering to her injured father with cloth and washbasin, a symbolic chalice for the blood of the suffering Savior, whose "beard was thick with blood" (*G* 107). Because the wounded patriarch resembles the crucified Redeemer portrayed in a painting by Guido Reni, Hilda associates his injury with the Moravian injunction against the ritual worship of Christ's wounds. Charles Doolittle, with flesh exposed and bleeding, endures a symbolic castration that evokes his daughter's subsequent terror at the "nothing to be seen" of veiled phallic power: "he did not seem to know us and . . . his eyes went on looking and looking" (*G* 107). If the father's gaze is empty and unseeing, then the panic-stricken child feels threatened with a loss of her filial subject-position and a psychological reduction to virtual anonymity.[13] With broken collarbone and fractured skull, Professor Doolittle has been symbolically feminized and decapitated, like a failed Scheherazade. His blank, decentered stare suggests a terrifying loss of mind, sight, mental lucidity, and patriarchal authority. If the godlike patriarch is capable of slipping into ordinary mortality, then his phallic power dissolves in a cracked façade. As clocks strike relentlessly in the Doolittle household, we are reminded that the order of Chronos, the logocentric order of the father, has been violently rent asunder.

By the time the 57-year-old H. D. set out to compose *The Gift*, she was looking back almost five decades. She had been analyzed by Sigmund Freud and would have been familiar with Freud's seduction theories, his elaborate symbol system, and his analysis of infantile sexuality. Why, then, does the author project onto her own childhood consciousness vivid dreamscapes that suggest fantasies of paternal seduction? One can only assume that she was deliberately writing autofiction in the context of scriptotherapy.

Throughout *The Gift*, H. D. self-consciously manipulates a variety of Freudian tropes—figures of serpents, witches, vulnerable virgins, Easter lilies, carnations, roses (red and black), water lilies, snow and ice, heroes and princesses, paper-cutters and broomsticks. She plays with words and with symbols, parodically depicting images of paternal seduction that Freud first credited, then relegated to the category of filial fabrication. H. D. remarks about her analysis with Freud: "But it is true that we play puss-in-a-corner, find one angle and another or see things from different corners or sides of a room. . . . We play magnificent charades" (*TF* 119-20).

Although H. D. complains that the Professor (a title denominating both Daddy and Sigmund Freud) "was not always right" (*TF* 101), she engages in a magnificent charade as she spins out psychoanalytic games with the doctor/healer/father/priest/confessor who marveled at her bisexuality and broadly hinted that her problem was one of classic female penis envy and preoedipal attachment to the phallic mother.[14] Playing the role assigned her by the master, H. D. assumes the subject-position of analyst and refashions her childhood memories on the model of Freudian self-imaging. She both loves and hates Daddy/Bluebeard and, at some repressed level of sexual desire, longs to have a baby with Our Father God. Her desire for the father evinces fantasies of seduction generated by the Lacanian imaginary—a lumber-room that houses an archetypal Father/God growing Easter lilies in his edenic garden, offering gifts and exhilarating sleigh-rides, but hovering in shadows replete with symbols of sexual danger.

At every stage, Hilda acknowledges the fantasmatic nature of her imaginary projections. Freud, after all, continually assured her that fact and fantasy bear equal weight in the world of the unconscious.[15] For once, H. D. asserts mastery over the master of psychoanalytic game-playing when she deliberately embraces a Freudian map of the unconscious and sketches explosive patterns of filial desire. Her childhood hunger for nurture and for love is laid bare in melodramatic schemata that implicitly enact scenes of paternal seduction and filial connivance. Playing with the fire of childhood fabulation, she beats Freud at his own analytic game by deliberately exposing oedipal paradigms of father-daughter incestuous attraction.[16]

By constructing a narrative of fantasmatic seduction, H. D. is implicitly blaming her father not for physical or sexual abuse, but for the kind of emotional deprivation so regularly practiced in nineteenth-century households that it went largely unnoticed in bourgeois society. As Janice Haaken observes, a variety of "developmental factors can underlie abuse memories, including dynamics associated with emotional deprivation, which can be elaborated intrapsychically as sadomasochistic fantasy." This dynamic might very well have been played out in H. D.'s own life narrative, since emotional "neglect and abandonment themes are even more difficult to construct through the narrative of memory than are abuse experiences. It is easier to struggle against a demonic presence than a perniciously absent one" (Haaken 1087).

Having once lived in awe of Charles Doolittle, a larger-than-life scientist/Father/God, Hilda feels psychologically traumatized when a concussive blow renders him temporarily sightless—unable to valorize the identities of his worshipful progeny, and butting his blind and bloodied head against the inexorable doors of eternity. Hilda, it seems, feels emotionally seduced and betrayed by an idol whose feet of clay and skull of glass challenge her childhood faith in patriarchal authority, as well as the illusion of a coherent, coterminous self constructed in the eye of the omnipotent father.

Definitely molded in the shadow of a genius Daddy, H. D. rebelled against his logocentric, scientific world view by embracing a bohemian life of literature and poetry, of illicit love affairs, divorce, single parenthood, and lesbian relationship. In the course of reconstructing her autobiographical narrative in *The Gift*, she works through the trauma of her father's accident and begins to think back to the repressed religious ecstasies of *Wunden Eiland*. She embraces a mystical mother tongue, in proud defiance of her progenitor's logocentric discourse. By therapeutic recuperation of childhood reminiscence, Hilda sloughs off the horrors evoked by the *Simple Science* nightmare and liberates herself from the enthralling gaze of a wounded Father/God whose chilling regard once held her transfixed. At the age of ten, the young girl confronts the vacuous stare of a failed redeemer and feels traumatized by his inability to shelter her from the perils of mortality. After all, Freud defined paradigmatic disavowal (*Verleugnung*) as "a mode of defense which consists in the subject's refusing to recognize the reality of a traumatic perception. . . . The denial of castration is the prototype—and perhaps even the origin—of other kinds of denials of reality" (Gallop *Feminism* 17-18).

In terms of Hilda's Moravian heritage, Our Father has descended from heaven and taken the place of Christ the Savior, whose blood and wounds are symbolically associated with virginal defloration. "In phallic fantasy," explains Jane Gallop, "the solid-closed-virginal body is opened with violence; and blood flows. The fluid here signifies defloration, wound as proof of penetration, breaking and entering, property damage" (*Feminism* 83). The uncanny sight of blood initiates what Luce Irigaray would identify as an eerie "mechanics of fluids" that threatens masculine power/solidity and calls into question sex-role attributions. If Our Father can fall into the feminized subject-position of Christ the Son and victimized redeemer, then the initiation ceremony of Mamalie's *Isle of Wounds* is metonymically associated with paternal castration. The father slips from his dominant subject-position to that of the Lacanian *objet petit a*, the unattainble object of filial desire always-already sightless and fallible. The figure of the wounded patriarch, symbolic of radical lack, must be violently repressed by the traumatized daughter, along with the Moravian secret of mystical, ecstatic worship.[17]

By resuscitating and working through earlier traumatic experiences, a middle-aged Hilda could use her recovered memory as a wedge into the unconscious and recuperate the matrilineal supplement to (de-authorized) phallic authority—the story of a Moravian rite suppressed by puritanical church fathers, but kept alive by the ongoing gift of female oral tradition. As Dianne Chisholm concludes, Hilda rediscovers through her maternal ancestors the "therapeutic efficacy of masochistic *jouissance*" (155).

In adult life, H. D. would look beyond the Christian Father/God for other saviors—to Freud and psychoanalysis, to the Greek god Apollo and the Egyptian deities of pre-Hellenic worship and, most important, to the Great Mother/Goddess Isis/Mary/Maia of ancient lore. It is only when she confronts the traumas of childhood and writes out the convoluted tale of her self-exile from the sustaining gaze of the Father/God/progenitor that H. D. feels free to embrace the matrilineal heritage of her mother Helen and her grandmother Mamalie, of Christian (not Francis) and his secret cult of mystical worship that allies itself with the Indian Great Spirit and with Native American reverence for Mother Earth.

For the Moravians of *Wunden Eiland*, the Holy Spirit is female, and the Comforter is called Mother/*Mutter* (Augustine 12). Though Mother England be a wounded island, bleeding and besieged, her children continue to sing hymns of glory that will resurrect a female Mother/Goddess/Isis (and a Father/God/Osiris) from the ashes of Hitler's earth-shaking holocaust.

Hence H. D.'s reverent orison in the typescript of *The Gift*: "Beneath every temple to Zeus, . . . there was found an excavation . . . of some primitive temple to the Earth Goddess, to Gaia or Maia or whatever name she had. Beneath the . . . polished pilasters of intellectual achievement and inheritance, is the deeper layer, the deeper temple, the cell or cella dedicated to the first deity, the primitive impulse, the primitive desire, the first love, Maia, mama, Mutter, Mut, mamalie, mimmie, madre, Mary, Mother" (*G Ts* Box 40/ Folder 1035/p. 10).

II. ADULT TRAUMA AND THE *MADRIGAL* CYCLE: *ASPHODEL* AND *BID ME TO LIVE*

If in *The Gift* H. D. defined as traumatic Charles Doolittle's mysterious accident and her own subsequent repression of Mamalie's Moravian spirituality, biographical evidence reveals more severe emotional struggles in the course of early adulthood. Hilda's late adolescence was dominated by a short-lived engagement to Ezra Pound, as well as by a turbulent infatuation with Frances Josepha Gregg. A devastating series of personal and cultural traumas circulated around H. D.'s maturation during the Great War: her precipitous marriage to Richard Aldington, followed by an unexpected pregnancy in 1914 and a shattering stillbirth in 1915; the death of her brother Gilbert in combat at Thiacourt in 1918; her father's sudden death from a stroke soon afterward; a second unplanned (and "illegitimate") pregnancy; a life-threatening bout with influenza; and the dissolution of her troubled relationship with Aldington after the birth of Perdita, Cecil Gray's child, in 1919. As Albert Gelpi observes in "The Thistle and the Serpent," the period of World War I proved for H. D. "so critical and traumatic that she would spend the rest of her life mythologizing it: rehearsing it in verse, in prose, in direct autobiography and in historical and legendary persona, again and again seeking to unriddle her destiny" (7).

H. D. fictionalized the tale of her ill-fated adolescent love for Frances Josepha Gregg at least three times in transparently autobiographical texts: *Paint It Today*, which she composed in 1921; *Asphodel*, probably drafted around 1921-22 and revised a few years later; and *Hermione*, which she worked on in 1926-27. She needed to articulate this powerful obsession not so much to get it right, but simply to get it out and get clear of it psychologically. Haunted by traces of a lesbian passion that rarely spoke its name, H. D., alluding to Frances, declared in a 1935 letter to Silvia Dobson: "Love terrible with banners only emerges or materializes once or twice in a life-time" (Guest 228).[18]

According to Barbara Guest, H. D. "had intended to tell the story of her life in four books: *Paint It Today, Asphodel, Her,* and *Madrigal*" (34), all of which were generated by the traumatic resonances of World War I. This original plan, however, had to be abandoned: "*Madrigal* emerged as her autobiography, entitled *Bid Me to Live. Asphodel* was written during a bitter and sometimes distraught period of her life, after the marriage to Aldington had broken up" (Guest 34). The composition of both autobiographical texts, thinly disguised renditions of H. D.'s experiences immediately prior to and during the Great War, seems characterized by traumatic obsession.

As in the case of Colette, only the impetus of severe trauma could fully explain H. D.'s continued efforts to revise, reiterate, and reinterpret her World War I experiences. As late as the 1950s, she was still trying to work through with Erich Heydt at Küsnacht Klinik the "repressed emotion centered on the birth of her stillborn child in 1915" (S. Friedman *Psyche* 21). It seems clear that pregnancy-loss, followed by spousal abandonment in the context of wartime deprivation and political upheaval, so disturbed H. D.'s psychological balance that it provoked symptoms of post-traumatic stress disorder that would slowly be unraveled over the next several decades through the healing mechanism of scriptotherapy. H. D. delineates the process in her *Delia Alton* essay: "*Madrigal*: this story of War I was roughed out, summer 1939, in Switzerland. . . . I had been writing or trying to write this story, since 1921. I wrote in various styles, simply or elaborately, stream-of-consciousness or straight narrative. . . . I had expected at first sight of the torn and weathered MS, to destroy *Madrigal*. . . . On re-reading the typed MS, I realized that at last, the War I story had 'written itself'" (*DA* 180). *Madrigal*, she reiterates in a letter to Richard Aldington, "was literally on the hob for 30 years. I added and subtracted and worked and destroyed till I got the 'perfect formula'" (Zilboorg 2:194).

It was Freud who specifically prescribed scriptotherapy as a cure for the infamous writer's block that tormented H. D. in 1933 and 1934. Overwhelmed by a "flood of war memories" evinced by reading the recently published letters of D. H. Lawrence, H. D. was ordered by her psychoanalyst to combat symptoms of dysphoria and psychic fragmentation by attempting to articulate the trauma narrative in a therapeutic autobiographical text. In a 1933 letter to Bryher, she confesses: "Evidently I blocked the whole of the 'period' and if I can skeleton-in a vol[ume] about it, it will break the clutch. . . . the 'cure' will be, I fear me, writing that damn vol[ume] straight, as history, no frills" (quoted in Friedman *Psyche* 30). *Madrigal*, the roman à clef composed in response to Freud's directives, was eventually published as *Bid Me to Live*, the draft of which seemed to release H. D. from the stranglehold of post-traumatic stress disorder.[19]

In *Bid Me to Live*, shock waves echo through two entirely different wartime arenas—the male world of military conflict and the female world of vigilance, patience, emotional helplessness, isolation, impotence, and fear. "Oh, the times, oh the customs!" H. D. exclaims sententiously. "Times liberated, set whirling out-moded romanticism; Punch and Judy danced with Jocasta and Philoctetes" (*B* 7). Mores and moral action seem to hinge on problems of epistemology, as H. D. betrays a classical nostalgia for origins and order, for generic roots that will ascribe philosophical meaning to both heroic and villainous action. Thrust into a vertiginous discursive whirlpool of classical allusion and literary lamentation, the reader is presented with the same indeterminacy of genre that torments the author. If the protagonist is enacting an historical drama, then what is the genre of the story? Is it a comedy, a Punch and Judy puppet show? Or a serious classical (or Renaissance) tragedy, filled with intrigue and melodrama, "gallant and idiotic Sir Philip Sidney-isms"? And how is one to *act* in this baffling tragicomedy if the nature of the script be undecidable? The narrator acerbically remarks: "They did not march in classic precision, they were a mixed bag. Victims, victimised and victimising" (*B* 7).

In writing through the gaps of historical drama, H. D. deliberately leaves holes in her narrative to create a palimpsestic parchment that shows signs of erasure—a smooth surface rubbed clean of pain, with a text doubling back on itself in a gesture of radical repression. The war leaves people haunted by an unending stream of stories—tales told by idiots and compulsively repeated until they assume illusory shape and mythic meaning. "What was left of them was the war-generation, . . . not blighted, not anaemic, but wounded, but dying, but dead" (*B* 8).

What H. D. envisages so poignantly in *Bid Me to Live* and *Asphodel* is the implicit analogy between the text of woman's body, scarred and mutilated by the physiological stress of childbearing, and male narratives of war wounds and heroism. "Men were dying as she had almost died to the sound . . . of gun-fire. . . . The guns had made her one in her suffering with men" (*A* 114). Hilda/Hermione/Julia feels equally trapped by political conflict and female physiology: "Was there nothing else in the world? Men and guns, women and babies. And if you have a mind what then?" (*A* 115). As Rachel Blau DuPlessis notes, "*Bid Me to Live* and its study of the rupture of coequal genders because of the masculinist values derived from war exemplifies the consideration of militarism which is a unifying theme in H. D.'s work as a whole" (*H. D.* 106-7).

Julia Ashton, the H. D. figure in *Bid Me to Live*, has been traumatized by a stillbirth that leaves her shell-shocked and grieving. Her own personal battle will be with the forces of life and time that make love a perilous expression of intimacy and sex a dangerous battleground. The pain of pregnancy-loss has gouged a "gap in her consciousness, a sort of black hollow, a cave" (*B* 12) suggestive of constriction and psychic numbing. "She had lost the child only a short time before. . . . A door had shuttered it in, shuttering her in" (*B* 12).[20] At the beginning of *Bid Me to Live*, Julia is apparently suffering from traumatic dysphoria, a symptom of post-traumatic stress disorder characterized by "confusion, agitation, emptiness, and utter aloneness. . . . Depersonalization, derealization, and anesthesia are accompanied by a feeling of unbearable agitation" (Herman 108-9). In a mood of emotional hysteria, H. D.'s alter ego identifies with the "horror of a flayed saint" pictured in the Louvre: "He [Rafe] was right . . . when he said 'You don't feel anything'" (*B* 37). "It was annihilation itself that gaped at her" (*B* 13).

In *Asphodel*, pregnancy-loss is similarly rendered in terms of psychic shock followed by unspeakable emotional torment: "The state she had been in was a deadly crucifixion. Not one torture . . . but months and months when her flaming mind beat up and she found she was caught, . . . like a wild bird in bird-lime. . . . No one would ever know it for there were no words to tell it in" (*A* 113).[21] Hermione/Julia suffers the numbing loss of affect characteristic of both melancholia and post-traumatic stress disorder. She meticulously delineates experiences of hyperarousal and the sense of emotional paralysis associated with traumatic constriction. "Long after the danger is past," explains Judith Herman, "traumatized people relive the event as though it were continually recurring in the present. They cannot resume the normal course of their lives, for the trauma repeatedly interrupts" (*Trauma* 37).

In *Bid Me to Live*, life-shattering trauma elicits obsessional anger displaced and directed against H. D.'s husband Richard Aldington/Rafe Ashton, who returns from France belching "poisonous gas and flayed carcasses" (*B* 39). "Rafe's nightmares . . . have spilled into her unconscious, just as traces of poisonous gas are transferred from his body into hers when they kiss" (T. Tate 29). Morbidly depressed, Julia cannot imagine resurrection from the marriage bed that she identifies as a virtual deathbed: "Sheets, a bed, a tomb" (*B* 18). Julia, writes Trudi Tate, "is a civilian war neurotic" who "suffers from dissociation" (31). She is "threatened to the point of severe neurosis by the war's reshaping of subjectivity" (32).

Julia writes her memoirs out of melancholia and mourning, to compensate for an object-loss interpreted by the psyche as an ego-loss. The self has been schizophrenically divided, and a mental projection of maternal subjectivity seems torturously extinguished. "Melancholia," Freud tells us, "behaves like an open wound, drawing to itself cathectic energies, . . . and emptying the ego until it is totally impoverished" (*SE* 14:253). Julia recalls

"1915 and her death, or rather the death of her child. Three weeks in that ghastly nursing-home. . . . How could she blithely face what he called love?" (*B* 24-25).[22]

In a gesture of affection before parting, Rafe entrusts Julia with his military watch encased in a cage of wire netting—a visible symbol of the palpability of time during war, when every leave-taking may augur a final sundering. Julia's mind, relentlessly ticking with intrusive flashbacks, resembles a bomb about to explode. Everything, from temporality to the human spirit, seems brutally caged and imprisoned, and Rafe's watch becomes a symbol of time metaphorically held prisoner but defiant of human mastery. Julia feels keenly aware that women left alone on the home front during wartime suffer an agony of temporal suspension. Moments balloon into eternities of mental endurance, and nothing remains but absence, though the absent lover is all the more present for his constant unattainability. His figure becomes a sacralized image buried at the heart of desire, encased in the powerful myths of idealized presence constructed by the psyche to compensate for loss. "He would be almost nearer, once he had gone" (*B* 24), Julia remarks wistfully. "The wrist-watch was a stone, scarab weighing her to this bed" (*B* 36).

Clutching the gift of Rafe's cast-off timepiece, Julia remains silently watching and awaiting her husband's return. The sense of impotence associated with stillbirth gives rise to agonizing emotional torment. Julia suffers irrational guilt because her life-blood failed to nurture the tendril blossoming from a love now threatened with extinction. Frantically, she deals with symptoms of hyperarousal and constriction by telling herself that "like a tight-rope walker, she must move tip-toe across an infinitely narrow thread, a strand, the rope, the umbilical cord, the silver-cord that bound them to that past" (*B* 24). She remembers the harsh curse of a gloating matron: "'You know you must not have another baby until after the war is over'" (*B* 25). In the face of such misery, romantic platitudes echo through the void. "Between us we might make an artist," Rafe had promised (*B* 34). But marriage as an idealistic project of aesthetic collaboration has proven abortive. Gone is the lyrical season of Keatsian "*mists and mellow fruitfulness*" (*B* 35) earlier portrayed in *Asphodel*.[23]

In *Bid Me to Live*, Julia Ashton desperately pastes together a collage of romantic memories to ease her sense of bereavement and melancholia over the loss of her husband, her child, her lover, and her poetic collaborator. All have vanished. Her writing functions as a compulsive exercise in scriptotherapy, etching the marks of discursive displacement that will give aesthetic shape to intrusive, unendurable flashbacks. This "agony in the Garden," Julia insists, "had no words. . . . I had my crucifixion. I can't go back, step over my own corpse and sweat blood, now that you are what you are" (*B* 46). "Go, Orpheus, look not back" (*B* 54).

Scorning Rafe as a "great, over-sexed officer on leave" (*B* 47), a failed Orpheus with bronze head and late Roman physique, Julia/Eurydice relinquishes her testosterone-driven lover to the voluptuous Bella Carter. "Fighting not so much a losing as a lost-battle, she went on" (*B* 49). How could amorous desire, she wonders, flourish in the midst of physical fear? If every act of intimacy might engender a life that potentially threatens one's own, then fear of accidental pregnancy would surely stifle any physical expression of love.[24]

"I couldn't help being . . . paralysed—with fear" (*B* 133), Julia confesses. Bella Carter's apparent insouciance toward her own aborted child merely exacerbates Julia's wounds, as a naive and victimized Bella protests her inability to "have educated ut [*sic*]" when she found herself accidentally pregnant in Paris (*B* 100). Her pathetic plight reminds Julia of the "biological catch" that sex necessarily entails for women: "Why this vaunted business of experience, of sex-emotion? . . . It might be all right for men, but for women, any woman, there was a biological catch and taken at any angle, danger. You dried up and were an old maid, danger. You drifted into the affable *hausfrau*, danger. You let her rip and had operations in Paris (poor Bella), danger" (*B* 135-36).

"I love you, I desire *l'autre*" (*B* 56), Rafe protests, echoing Richard Aldington's letter of self-justification to Hilda on May 20, 1918. Explaining his liaison with Dorothy "Arabella" Yorke, Aldington continues: "Really I can never be happy without you; and very often it seems I couldn't be happy without her" (Zilboorg 1:55-56). Two weeks later, he cauterizes the wound by confessing that "my body hungered for a woman who was earthy like me" (1:66). His affair with Arabella, Caroline Zilboorg tells us, was evidently inaugurated "with H. D.'s knowledge" and tacit consent and "was consummated . . . in the Aldingtons' own bed curtained off at one end of H. D.'s large room" (1:38).

In *Bid Me to Live*, (Ara)Bella Carter is obviously intended as a caricature of Aldington's wartime lover and postwar companion, Dorothy Yorke, who later complained that H. D.'s fictional portrait reduced her to the status of "an illiterate bunny-brained whore" (Zilboorg 1:227). In H. D.'s roman à clef, Bella's magnetic sensuous presence offers Rafe temporary escape from battle fatigue and the constant fear of mutilation and death. This femme fatale serves as *l'autre* of male fantasmatic desire—the projected object of psychological need that ostensibly obliterates wartime terror. Whereas Julia forces Rafe to remember, Bella mercifully helps him to forget. She seems to embody the goddess of Rafe's libidinal imagination and provides an illusory anodyne to the nightmare of trench warfare.

The hapless Julia, in contrast, is doubly alienated and ironically forced to play the role of *l'autre* to her husband's *l'autre*. "The funny thing was that facing Bella, Julia felt that she was looking at herself in a mirror" (*B* 103). Bella/Dorothy and the D. H. Lawrence persona, Frederico, are balanced as binary opposites in a highly charged melodrama, both tugging in different directions at the collapsing marriage of H. D./Julia and Richard Aldington/ Rafe Ashton.[25] When rejected by Rafe, Julia turns to Rico as an artistic soulmate and, though fascinated by his intellectual brilliance, ultimately refuses to dance to the puppeteering maneuvers of his genius (*B* 164).

Sequestered in the enchanted natural landscape of Cornwall, Julia begins mythically to identify with ancient Druidic spirits that seem to inhabit the land. "She was Medea of some blessed incarnation, a witch with power. A wise-woman" (*B* 146-7). Taking Rico's somewhat flippant and derogatory Dionysiac advice, she manages to kick over her "tiresome house of life"—to destroy the walls of emotional security and urban consciousness by embracing the pantheistic, healing powers of nature residual in the magical environs of Cornwall. Idealizing Rico in the guise of King Arthur, she rewrites the Camelot story by choosing a Sir Galahad figure, Cyril Vane, in lieu of the heroic and legendary king. In this version of the narrative, Cyril (Cecil Gray) emerges as Hilda/Julia's temporary savior. Playfully, he addresses his artist compatriot by the androgynous epithet "Person," a nickname interpreted by Julia as the French word "*Personne*, Nobody" (*B* 172). "But I will find a new name," she defiantly proclaims. "I will be someone" (*B* 176).

Rico's artistic genius, Julia believes, is born of a furious (and maddening) "desire to create [his] mother" (*B* 181), a compulsive but egotistical need to function in the simulated role of matric male. In imaginary dialogue with the absent Father/God/artist, Julia chooses a creative independence that protects her from incineration in the phoenix holocaust of Rico/Lawrence's voracious ego. "I could not be your mother," she explains. "I need a great-mother as much as you do" (*B* 182). "Perhaps I caught the *gloire* from you," she speculates romantically, insisting that the modern artist must occupy both male and female subject-positions. Defiantly, Julia challenges Rico's earlier critique of her poetry: "I could be Eurydice, . . . you said, but woman-is-woman and I couldn't be both. The *gloire* is both" (*B* 176).

Julia's own dreams of aesthetic creation are emblematically encoded in Rico's symbol of pure possibility, the "*gloire*": "The child is the *gloire* before it is born" (*B* 177), she postulates. And it is this potential child that symptomatically functions as the repressed textual unconscious of *Bid Me to Live*—the mysteriously germinating seed of an ineffable future that transcends male-female gender polarities. At the end of the novel, Hilda/Julia vows to mother the nascent artistic potential in herself, but H. D.'s second pregnancy is left unrepresented. In this particular autobiographical fiction, Perdita's conception has been conceptually erased from the text. Cyril Vane/ Cecil Gray is ironically portrayed as savior and guardian angel; whereas, on the historical stage of H. D.'s own wartime biography, this redemptive function was propitiously transferred to Bryher (Winifred Ellerman).

The intertext for H. D.'s introduction of the amorphous notion of *gloire* might, in fact, be buried in *Notes on Thought and Vision*, a document that amalgamates a female, subterranean experience of "womb consciousness" with a mythic masculine "over-mind": "Into that over-mind, thoughts pass and are visible like fish swimming under clear water. . . . I first realised this state of consciousness in my head. I visualise it . . . centered in the love-region of the body or placed like a foetus in the body" (*Notes* 19). When speculating about the relation of this overmind to gender construction, H. D. remarks: "For me, it was before the birth of my child that the jelly-fish consciousness seemed to come definitely into the field or realm of the intellect or brain" (20). In other words, the artist must function as both mother and father to her/his aesthetic progeny by combining the imaginary subject-positions of phallic mother and matric male.[26]

Bid Me to Live ends on a note of expectancy and resurrection, although H. D.'s imminent expectation of a child is conspicuously absent from the text. It was only in the manuscript of *Asphodel* that H. D. felt free to articulate the dilemmatic choices surrounding her daughter's birth. Her decision to carry this second pregnancy to term evidently involved an unconscious effort to relive and "correct" the earlier trauma of stillbirth. In *Asphodel*, Hermione Gart, H. D.'s alter ego, awaits a sign from the gods when a swallow (sister/Procne?) flits through her window in Cornwall, and she interprets the omen as an auspicious augury of future maternal joy. "If a swallow flies straight in, now without any hesitation, just in here to me," she tells herself, "I'll have it [the child]" (*A* 154).

Barbara Guest conjectures about the unconventional strategy played out in H. D.'s decision: "Should she have the child? She had been called a 'pagan mystic' by admirers of her Imagist poetry. Now she would behave as one. She decided that if a swallow flew into her room it would be a sign that she should give birth. The necessary bird accomplished its flight" (95). If the story of Hilda's romantic obsession with Frances Gregg is repressed in *Hermione* and treated more graphically through lyrical encodings of transgressive desire in the intertext of *Paint It Today*; the heroic choice of illegitimate maternity, repressed in *Bid Me to Live* and *Paint It Today*, is more fully portrayed in *Asphodel*. The palimpsest of H. D.'s wartime experiences seems to get absorbed by an infinite deferral of textual traces that both reveal and conceal autobiographical dimensions of her tenuous emotional survival.

In *Asphodel*, Hermione Gart self-consciously identifies with Morgan le Fay, a powerful and fetishistic witch figure of Arthurian legend. The *gloire* suddenly erupts with redemptive force, filling the "black hole" at the center of her suffering consciousness and engulfing her with the ecstatic light/life earlier extinguished by traumatic loss. A joyous Hermione feels magically protected by the developing embryo she harbors: "Men could do nothing to her for a butterfly, a frog, a soft and luminous moth larva was keeping her safe. She was stronger than men, men, men—she was stronger than guns, guns, guns. . . . The body within her was a mysterious globe of softly glowing pollen-light" (*A* 162).[27]

In the context of H. D.'s own compromised conjugal situation, her search for spiritual refuge in matrifocal mythology is clearly understandable. Her lover, Cecil Gray, fled Cornwall to avoid military conscription, then abdicated paternal responsibility and left his partner to deal with the trials of illegitimacy on her own. Although Richard Aldington initially connived in his wife's adulterous affair with Gray, his passionate declarations of love from the trenches abruptly ceased when, in August 1918, he learned of Hilda's pregnancy.

Aldington's first response was remarkably solicitous. "You seem to be in rather a devilish mess, and in a way I am responsible," he writes on August 3, 1918. "I will accept the child as mine, if you wish, or follow any other course which seems desirable to you" (Zilboorg 1:118). The next day, however, his stance alters considerably, as he lectures Hilda under "two main headings: Natural and Social" and calls on the laws of nature to establish Gray as her consort (1:119). Three weeks later, Aldington again changes course and tries to reassure Hilda: "Be brave, be strong, have your child and I will try to care for it for your sake" (1:131). On August 31, he implores her not to consider abortion and resolves "to break with both of you [Hilda and Arabella] and go live by myself" (135). In case she has not yet gotten the message, he brutally reiterates his point the following day: "It is all over, napoo, fini—understand? Neither of you. I can do without you" (136). Later, he advises: "Get from Gray what you want or what you can; and call on me in any emergency. I shall not fail you" (160). In the end, however, he did fail her, and his spousal rejection proved profoundly traumatic for Hilda.

It is unfortunate that H. D.'s own letters to Aldington have not survived, but her emotional resolve in the face of social disapprobation can be traced in fictional renditions of the crisis. In a therapeutic effort to work through trauma, H. D. recontextualizes her experience of maternity in exclusively feminine terms. In *Asphodel*, a deliberately chosen pregnancy promises redemption from wartime suffering and a renewed sense of universal sisterhood with a panoply of women throughout the ages of human history. Casting aside Cyril Vane/Cecil Gray as a used-up messenger of the gods, a "wax angel," and paternal imposter (*A* 166), the H. D. figure Hermione identifies with Mother Mary, who "had a baby with God." "I said yes, . . . bowed my head like Magdalene, like Mary and said yes and I know that God makes me one, one with trees, with the sea" (*A* 170).

Donna Hollenberg notes that "H. D.'s account of Hermione's second conception in this magical setting stresses its importance to her as a virgin birth, a divinely ordained reparation for the narcissistic injury caused by her first loss" (38). This second pregnancy "has a marked parthenogenetic quality," in keeping with Hermione's "need to incorporate an omnipotent idealization of herself" and "a wish for psychic reintegration, for an unconflicted conception of herself as both mother and creator" (38-39). *Asphodel*, a detailed and explosive autobiographical text, marks an end to H. D.'s own private war; or, in terms of psychoanalytic working through, at least a provisional ceasefire.

Facing trauma head on in *Asphodel*, H. D./Hermione deliberately reenacts her earlier physiological struggle. "[Y]ou are risking your life again like any soldier" (*A* 170), she assures herself. The risk, however, is not for the sake of imperial or political prizes that accrue to *miles gloriosus*, but for the spiritual reward of *gloire*: "Hermione was a cocoon, a blur of gold and gilt, a gauze net that had trapped a butterfly" (*A* 179). "I am alone like Madonna," she realizes (*A* 187). "You never know what will, what is going to save you" (*A* 189). As H. D. explains in a 1929 letter to Ezra Pound, she felt deeply wounded by Aldington's rejection of both her and Perdita in 1919, despite his earlier promise to care for her and the child. "I put down a lot of myself after Perdita's birth. I loved Richard very much and you know he threatened to use Perdita to divorce me and to have me locked up if I registered her as legitimate. This you see, was after he had said he would look after us" (Zilboorg 1:206).

When Aldington appeared at Hilda's London flat in the company of Dorothy Yorke, demanded a divorce, and threatened his wife with arrest if she were to register her daughter under his sacred patronymic, H. D. felt that she "was literally 'dying.' I mean, anything in the way of a shock brings that back and I go to pieces" (quoted in S. Friedman *Psyche* 27). In a statement drafted shortly after Aldington's divorce petition in 1937, H. D. assessed the trauma in melodramatic terms: "I have lived with a subterranean terror, an octopus eating out my strength and vitality for almost eighteen years. . . . I was frozen . . . as a deer in a forest or a rabbit or hare is frozen. . . . I was dead. Richard did not injure me or hound me. . . . He killed me" (Zilboorg 2:63). The birth of her daughter Perdita evidently healed, in part, the war-wound that had earlier destroyed H. D.'s sense of coherent identity and effective agency in the world. She would eventually recover from the most deleterious effects of post-traumatic stress disorder, but only through protracted experiments in scriptotherapy whereby she wrote and wrote again, in various autobiographical forms, the narrative of those life-shattering experiences that led to her first serious breakdown in 1919.[28]

It is interesting that, in her *Delia Alton* essay, H. D. employs the metaphor of the goddess Isis seeking out and reconstructing the fragmented body/text of her brother Osiris and, in so doing, redeeming the dissociated fragments of herself in mystical postures of hermaphroditic wholeness.

> She knows . . . that "women are individually seeking, as one woman, fragments of the Eternal Lover." As the Eternal Lover has been scattered or disassociated, so she, in her search for him. In *Madrigal*, she seeks for him in contemporary time. . . .
>
> She knows that to keep him, she must lose him. . . . She can not know that she knows this, until she has . . . redeemed not so much the fragments of Osiris, as of his sister, twin or double, the drowned or submerged Isis. (*DA* 181-82)

Both Susan Stanford Friedman, in *Psyche Reborn*, and Deborah Kelly Kloepfer, in *The Unspeakable Mother*, offer convincing arguments for H. D.'s gradual self-healing from the Great War's traumas through a creative resurrection of the archetypal Mother/ Goddess in her writing. Rediscovering the mother tongue once denigrated and long denied, an adult H. D. was able to excavate semiotic hieroglyphs that could unite her with preoedipal history, as well as with occult aspirations of the race. "Textualization," Kloepfer tells us, is "the way H. D. heals herself and the world: writing in images . . . replaces the symptom" (114).

I find arguments for what Rachel Blau DuPlessis terms a "subtext of persistent matrisexuality" (*H. D.* 44) compelling and not necessarily antithetical to my own palimpsestic interpretation of H. D.'s complex aesthetic and psychological development. I have suggested in this chapter the addition of still another layer to the matrifocal poetic vision of the adult author, whose "mother fixation" made Sigmund Freud more than a little uncomfortable. As Angela Moorjani has argued in *The Aesthetics of Loss and Lessness*, H. D. manages to preempt Freud's mother fixation with "the father-mother-home integration, the (impossible) ideal against which loss, disintegration, and exile are measured" (130). "The house in some indescribable way," says H. D., "depends on father-mother" (*TF* 146). Contiguous with the manifest mother fixation that continued to dominate H. D.'s consciousness, there lay a repressed obsession with what Julia Kristeva would call the "father of personal prehistory"—the preoedipal paternal imago originally identified as the object of maternal desire.

As Claire Buck has suggested, the resolution of the Freudian dilemma of feminine insufficiency "promises to be bisexuality" (103). In searching for the fantasmatic phallic mother, Hilda was figuratively confronted with the threatening image of a feminized and castrated father. The oedipal patriarch's phallic insufficiency, once exposed to filial consciousness, undermines Papa's valorizing gaze and thrusts the female child into a condition of epistemological uncertainty. She will, in turn, have recourse to the rhythms and echolalias of a semiotic mother tongue, the bond of discourse and sympathy that predates the father's law and implicitly undermines the oedipal triangle—and that returns her, simultaneously, to phantasms of an integrated and hermaphroditic male-female progenitor.[29]

Although the de-authorized patriarch may be associated with trauma and disappointment, his impotent figure might nonetheless be recuperated through art in the guise of a matric male. A strong matrifocal heritage, passed from (grand)mother to daughter and granddaughter, eventually proves spiritually sustaining to the artist H. D. who, in the experience of becoming a mother, symbolically gives birth to herself, her daughter, the phantasm of a matric male, and the *gloire* that generates a future life of poetic creativity. The mysterious Lady of H. D.'s aesthetic mythology amalgamates the figures of both mother and daughter, Demeter and Persephone, when she appears as a modernist muse in *Tribute to the Angels* and bears in her arms a sacred, mystical text, "the unwritten volume of the new"(37).

"This Isis," says H. D., "takes many forms as does Osiris" (*DA* 221)—as does the recuperated subject of the fantasmatic imagination, reconstructed in the guise of a perfect male-female creator. "I am on the fringes or in the penumbra of the light of my father's science and my mother's art," notes H. D. (*TF* 145). "Isis is incomplete without Osiris," she cautions, but adds, more whimsically: "Judy is meaningless without Punch" (*TF* 150). In *Bid Me to Live*, the author sardonically compares the Great War to a Punch and Judy puppet show, whose carnivalesque enactment of domestic violence might expose the absurdity of both conjugal and international hostilities. Now, as master puppeteer, H. D. revels in the sense of control aesthetic expression offers her and implies that veiled autobiographical narrative has, indeed, effected a therapeutic recovery from the haunting resonances of wartime trauma.

THREE

Anaïs Nin's Interior Cities:

Incest, Anxiety, and Father-Daughter Loss

I was bound and bandaged by my traumas like a mummy. (*D* 2:86)

I believe one writes because one has to create a world in which one can live. (*SM* 12)

I. FATHER LOSS AND INCEST

If Hilda Doolittle fantasized the emotional landscape of paternal seduction, Anaïs Nin enacted the fantasy in adult life. The central traumatic event of Nin's childhood was apparently the loss of her father at the age of ten, when Joaquin Nin y Castellanos deserted his wife and children to take up residence with a younger woman. The figure of the absent father dominated Nin's development and was incorporated into the self as a harsh, implacable parental imago that haunts much of her diary, as well as her autobiographical fiction. Anaïs constantly had to confront and attempt to propitiate a stern superego symbolic of the law and the word of the absent Father/God.[1] In late adolescence, she confided in her journal: "To me, 'Father' is a mystery, a vision, a dream. What infinitely beautiful stories I have wound around the magic name. . . . Father! All my life has been one great longing for you" (*ED* 2:87). In January, 1933, the adult diarist exclaimed: "If only I could be freed of this quest for the father. Father? Savior? God?" (*D* 1:165).

On her journey from Barcelona to America in 1914, the young Anaïs began to write entries in a journal that masked long, passionate love letters to Joaquin Nin in a desperate attempt to impress him, to woo him, to seduce him, and to win him back. The diary, she tells us, served as a "substitute for the absent father" (*WS* 157), "to make him share our life, think of us, want to join us" (*D* 6:100).[2] As Anaïs poured out a flood of intimate disclosures in an adolescent document of self-revelation, she was highly conscious of writing for an implicit audience. "Every act related to my writing," she confesses, "was connected in me with an act of charm, seduction of my father" (*D* 6:109). What is revealed in the diary is not the pure, unmediated, private self, but a self-conscious literary persona generated by an intense desire for love and admiration—first from the absent parent of childhood fantasy, then from a worldwide audience of devotees who might reinforce the insecure subject-position of a vulnerable, abandoned child.[3]

Like both Colette and H. D., Nin was haunted by an obsessional need to gain control over personal (and oedipal) trauma. Her journal allowed her to name and to analyze the painful incidents of her past, to assert aesthetic and psychological mastery over chaotic historical events. Constantly weaving quotidian experiences into a coherent narrative web, Nin became the Penelopean artist of an intriguing confessional tapestry. "I relive my life," she tells us, "in terms of a dream, a myth, an endless story" (*D* 1:89). "I was telling myself the story of a life, and this transmutes into an adventure the things which can shatter you. It becomes the mythical voyage . . . through the labyrinth" (*WS* 193).

At the age of ten, the young Anaïs felt herself suddenly expelled from a domestic Garden of Eden. In her *Early Diary*, she describes "Villa Les Ruines" in Arcachon, where "Father left us, apparently on another concert tour, but having planned never to return" (*ED* 2:88). In *Nearer the Moon*, Anaïs acknowledges that the "paradise of my childhood was already an invented one, because my childhood was unhappy" (*NM* 62). She refers to Joaquin's betrayal as an utter "catastrophe" (*NM* 63) and, in *Fire*, questions the long-term effects of trauma: "Could a sorrow alone, a shock, cause blindness, deafness, sleepwalking, unreality?" (*F* 145).

Like many children who lose parents at an early age, Anaïs judged herself emotionally responsible for paternal desertion in a scenario far beyond her control: "If my father left, . . . it must have been because I was not lovable" (*D* 1:91). Unconsciously, the young girl accused herself of an original sin of filial desire, a primordial transgression that drove Daddy away. Like Hilda Doolittle at a similar age, she virtually apotheosized the absent father in her childhood imagination, transforming him into a godlike figure of authority and judgment, a paradigm of the "Enormous Parent" (*D* 5:40).

Interpreting her father's abdication of responsibility in archetypal patterns of recrimination, Anaïs asks in the first volume of her *Diary*: "Can a child's confidence, once shaken and destroyed, have such repercussions on a whole life? Why should my father's insufficient love remain indelible?" (*D* 1:76). At the age of eleven, she proclaims: "I have decided it is better not to love anybody. As soon as you begin to love, it is time to leave" (*D* 5:227).[4]

Later, in analysis with Dr. René Allendy, Anaïs confesses to severe psychic fragmentation precipitated by "the first and ineffaceable pain of [her] Father's abandonment" and describes a "distorted, morbid, neurotic fear" of rejection, as well as pathological symptoms that might be interpreted in terms of post-traumatic stress disorder: "I feel that an initial shock has shattered my wholeness, that I am like a shattered mirror. Each piece has gone off and developed a life of its own" (*D* 1:103). In a more depressed mood, she writes: "There is a fissure in my vision, . . . and madness will always push in and out" (*I* 21).

According to Jessica Benjamin, "the failure of the idealized father of rapprochement to provide a recognizing response is often a pivotal issue in a girl's self formation. This idealized figure is maintained internally even though the real father may increasingly reveal his faults and weaknesses to the child" (119). An adult Anaïs perspicaciously observes: "The old legends knew, perhaps, that in absence the father becomes glorified, deified, eroticized" (*D* 1:203). Nin's devotion to the absent father seems to have crested during adolescence, and the first volume of her *Early Diary*, *Linotte,* reveals sacrilegious fantasies of Joaquin as the Christ figure embodied in the Catholic sacrament of the Eucharist: "At the moment of Communion, it seems more as though I am kissing and hugging Papa, rather than receiving the body of Christ" (*ED* 1:27).

A full realization of the circumstances surrounding her father's desertion strikes Anaïs rather belatedly, when she interrogates Rosa in a 1919 conversation: "He deserted us? Oh, but I thought it was you who took us away from Arcachon. Tell me how it happened, will you?" Rosa feels compelled to remind her daughter that Joaquin "was very brutal. He would lock me up in one room so as to be able to beat you. . . . You must remember many scenes of brutality, don't you?" (*ED* 1:365). A sixteen-year-old Anaïs seems thoroughly to have repressed negative memories of her father and can only nod weakly in assent to her mother's promptings.

Nin's psychological obsession with her father continued well into adult life, ambiguously colored by a passionate longing for erotic union with the Father/God/lover of her dreams and a fierce disdain for Joaquin's emotional frigidity and physical violence. "Father was fond of spanking us," Anaïs writes in her *Early Diary*, at the age of seventeen. She describes great battles and violent scenes between her quarreling parents, dramatic conflicts that sometimes reduced her to fits of hysteria. Joaquin would first batter his obstreperous wife, then lock her in a bedroom while he forced the three children to march to a secluded attic room for ritual spankings. "He was a strict father to us," Anaïs remembers. "I would do anything to keep him from lifting my dress and beating me" (*ED* 2:85-86).

In the first volume of her *Diary*, Anaïs reveals to Dr. René Allendy her deep-seated fears of male irascibility: "[T]he fear of cruelty has been the great conflict of my life. I witnessed the cruelty of my father towards my mother, I experienced his sadistic whippings, . . . and I saw his cruelty towards animals (he killed a cat with a cane)" (*D* 1:72). When Dr. Allendy diagnoses a lack of self-confidence behind the bravado of her "quadruplicities in love" (*I* 103), Anaïs acknowledges emotional insecurity provoked by paternal criticism: "My father did not want a girl. He said I was ugly. . . . I never remember a caress or a compliment from him" (*HJ* 115).

It was not until the composition of "Seduction of the Minotaur," the final novella in *Cities of the Interior*, that Anaïs would acknowledge, under the veil of autobiographical fiction, the full ramifications of her father's brutality. Toward the end of this continuous novel, Nin's alter ego Lillian Beye recalls a bewildering confusion of pleasure and pain in response to corporal punishment: "As if the spankings, while hurting her, had been at the same time the only caress she had known from her father. Pain had become inextricably mixed with joy at his presence, the distorted closeness had alchemized into pleasure" (*CI* 566-67). As Freud explains in "The Economic Problem of Masochism," "the wish, which so frequently appears in phantasies, to be beaten by the father stands very close to the other wish, to have a passive . . . sexual relation with him" (*SE* 19:169).[5]

Such latent fantasies of sexual union are exposed by an adult Anaïs when she attempts to explore the injuries caused by paternal abuse through a dramatization of repressed memories, real or imaginary, in *Nearer the Moon*:

> *I imagine this:* My Father has taken me up to the attic room to spank me. He takes my pants off. He begins to hit me with the palm of his hand. I feel his hand on me. But he stops hitting me and he caresses me. Then he sticks his penis into me. Oh, I enjoy it. . . . In and out, . . . he takes me from behind. But my mother is coming up the stairs. . . . I have a violent orgasm.
>
> I believe this really happened. I do not believe my Father penetrated me sexually, but I believe he caressed me while or instead of beating me. (*NM* 207)

Nin's only physical and emotional intimacy with her father took place under the guise of ritual punishment or pornographic photo sessions. Joaquin Nin shared some of the scopophilic obsessions of Lewis Carroll: "He liked to take photos of me while I bathed. He always wanted me naked. All his admiration came by way of the camera" (*D* 1:87). Anaïs's girlish self-image is constructed in the pedophilic gaze of the artist-father who admires her slender, nubile body. Doubling the Lacanian gaze through photographic specularity, Joaquin replicates the fantasmatic desire to deflower his virgin daughter by posing, shooting, developing, and framing her tantalizing figure. The implicitly incestuous scenario, enacted in covert patterns of childhood sexual abuse, sows the seeds for the prepubescent daughter's idolatrous and sadomasochistic longing for her father. Objectified by Daddy's bespectacled gaze, Anaïs is conditioned to display her naked body as an aesthetic object of lascivious enjoyment. The signature of the father marks the daughter, the photograph, and the iconic image that channels his libidinal drives into the framework of pornographic art. The graphic suggestions of the photographic negative encode the father's lust onto the body of his victimized daughter and reinforce his paternal right/rite of filial possession.[6]

Posing nude, the helpless girl-child tries to envisage her father's gaze doubly distanced and shielded by thick glasses and a camera lens. She feels shame elicited by the humiliating intrusion of Daddy's photographic instruments. From these early modeling sessions, Anaïs ascribes to the eye of the camera powers of voyeuristic exposure. "An exposure of what?" she asks in the *Diary*. "Of the desire to charm, of coquettishness, of vanity, of seductiveness" (*D* 1:88). The camera represents her father's ever-present gaze of recrimination: "Eyes of the father behind a camera. But always a critical eye. That eye had to be exorcised, or else like that of a demanding god, pleased." Joaquin assumes the intimidating shape of "Photographer God and Critic" (*D* 5:52).

Unjustly deserted by Daddy, Anaïs apparently tried to compensate for this initial narcissistic injury by a powerful reaction formation. Unable to *possess* the absent father, she was forced, psychologically, to *become* him. Elyce Wakerman notes in *Father Loss* that, in cases of father absence, "a fantastic idealization is likely to occur, and Oedipal longing, based on that idealization, intensifies rather than resolves. The girl is engulfed in a lifelong commitment to the perfect lover, a fierce dedication to the man that got away" (67). Frequently, the deserted daughter will attempt to ameliorate "the pain of her loss by incorporating some of her father's characteristics into her own identity" (113). Jessica Benjamin argues that women rejected by their fathers during the identificatory process of developmental rapprochement often seek surrogate paternal figures in the form of heroic sadists. The woman's masochistic acts of self-abnegation in such relationships are "meant to secure access to the glory and power of the other" (117).

Hence the source of Nin's apparently sadomasochistic obsession with Henry Miller who, in the early 1930s, invaded the bourgeois monotony of her connubial life with Hugh Guiler in Paris in the guise of a seductive Prince Charming directly out of the pages of *Bubu de Montparasse*: "he kisses me and awakens me, I who have been sleeping one hundred years" (*HJ* 97). Despite the apparent mutuality of their sensual exhilaration, Anaïs is so infatuated that, like Colette in the company of Willy, she feels perpetually infantalized by the master who manifests gargantuan sexual appetites and courts her with artistic braggadocio. Simultaneously fascinated and repelled by Henry's love of ugliness, vulgarity, sordidity, and slang, Anaïs admires his devotion to literature and is beguiled by his treasure trove of salacious tales: "When I listen, I am a child, and Henry becomes paternal. The haunting image of an erudite, literary father reasserts itself" (*HJ* 128). She describes Miller as a "Rabelaisian figure" and exults in the "absolute dissolution of myself into him" (*I* 52, 47).

In her relationship with Henry, Anaïs virtually prostrates herself before the heroic sadist worshipped on the altar of paternal devotion: "I want to give up my life, my home, my security, my writing, to live with him, to work for him, to be a prostitute for him, anything, even to be fatally hurt by him" (*HJ* 127). In *Incest*, she waxes ecstatic in her description of erotic subjugation: "I want a man lying *over* me. . . . I want to be dominated" (*I* 57). "I see men as sadists," Anaïs confesses when Dr. Allendy culls from her dreams a "consistent desire to be punished." The Freudian analyst warns her of deeply embedded masochistic tendencies: "This comes from a sense of guilt for having loved your father too much. . . . And now you seek punishment" (*D* 1:82).

A particularly bizarre dimension of Nin's emotional masochism gives rise to an almost paralyzing timidity that forces her to suffer the frustrations of frenzied sexual activity without orgasmic release. An erotic initiate, Anaïs only discovers the pleasurable effects of clitoral stimulation when treated to a lesbian exhibition at a Paris brothel in March 1932. She watches enthralled as a "fat, coarse Spanish-looking woman" reminiscent of her mother brings a "small, feminine, almost timid" consort to climax through the skillful performance of cunnilingus: "The big woman reveals to me a secret place in the woman's body, a source of a new joy, . . . that small core at the opening of the woman's lips, just what the man passes by" (*HJ* 70-71)

The "terrible secret" Anaïs finally shares with Dr. Allendy is that she has been faking orgasms with Henry in order to hide her purported frigidity: "I am thinking that with all the tremendous joys Henry has given me I have not yet felt a real orgasm" (*HJ* 130). During passionate hours of amorous abandon, Anaïs ignores her own sexual pleasure because emotional insecurity and fear of rejection dictate a sadomasochistic script.[7] She believes, in fact, that: "Women are masochists" (*I* 140). "To be violated is a need of woman, a secret erotic desire" (*NM* 52). When Dr. Allendy chooses to play the comical savage by enacting a stylized sadomasochistic pantomime, Anaïs is startled to discover a subliminal attraction to the toy fetish he uses to titillate her senses. "After all, I liked that whip" (*I* 148), she coyly remarks. "Masochism. The word is out. My concept of love as sacrifice" (*D* 3:248).[8]

By thoroughly repressing the abusive dimensions of both Henry's egotism and Joaquin's pathological brutality, Anaïs tends to idealize the absent father and, simultaneously, to denigrate her ineffectual and impotent mother, whom she irrationally holds accountable for the trauma of father loss.[9] It is not surprising that, although Anaïs praises her mother in several of her early diaries, she later recoils in strong-willed rebellion against Rosa Culmell Nin for investing so much faith in an unfaithful husband and sacrificing her own emotional life for the sake of her troubled offspring. In therapy with Dr. Allendy, Anaïs confesses: "I have always been afraid of becoming one of those women who are hopelessly dominated by one man." "My mother," she explains, "only had one love in all her life, my father. . . . When he deserted her, her love turned to hatred" (*D* 1:110). Horrified by Rosa's emotional and economic desperation, Anaïs resolved to avoid the traditionally feminine fate of the exploited wife left to fend for herself and her children as a single parent, embittered and impoverished in the new world. After Rosa's death in 1954, Nin reflects on her conflicted relationship with her mother:

> While she was alive, she threatened my aspiration to escape the servitudes of women. Very early I was determined not to be like her but like the women who had enchanted and seduced my father, the mistresses who lured him away from us. . . .
>
> During her life she condemned my freedom. . . . I fought her influence, and she fought in me the kind of women who had displaced her. (*D* 5:182)

If the mother has been devalued as a subject and stripped of both personal dignity and sexual agency, then the wounded daughter's "identification with this helpless mother is particularly insupportable" (Benjamin 119).[10] Unable to emulate the victimized Rosa, Anaïs determined to escape the bonds of womanhood by mimicking her absent father—by imbibing his fierce sexual independence, along with his aesthetic sophistication. Although she describes Joaquin Nin as a dandy in the first volume of the *Diary* and protests that *"I had always lived not to be my father"* (*D* 1:209), Anaïs later suggests to Otto Rank that, in all her love affairs, she was following in the footsteps of her Don Juan Daddy.[11] In the course of adolescence, she explains, "I *became* my father. I was the intellectual adviser of my mother. I wrote. I read books" (*D* 1:281). It was only in the realm of music that Anaïs rejected her father's influence, since she felt that his "severity barred the way to [her] becoming a musician" (*D* 7:80). If Joaquin Nin had been an accomplished pianist, then his daughter would flaunt her physical beauty as an exotic Spanish dancer. If he had been celebrated as a world-renowned musician, she would devote her energies to the creation of art in another medium, making words dance on the page until they sang with poetic resonance.

Paradoxically, Anaïs seems to have inherited her father's gifts for both artistry and dissimulation. From early childhood, she began fabulating alternative versions of reality in tall tales that Rosa disdainfully labeled the "Nin lies," but which Anaïs construed as "necessary . . . fairy tales" (*I* 109). "When I told a lie it was a *mensonge vital*" (*I* 235), she explains. *"Lying is the only way I have found to be true to myself, to do what I want, to be what I want with the least possible pain to others.* To sustain illusion I have to lie" (*F* 58). Her father, Nin recalls, "by deception, lies, inventions and a gift for illusion improved upon reality" (*D* 5:130).

In the context of father loss, Nin's diary functions both as an autobiographical text and as a work of skillful fabulation, highly crafted over years of revisionary editing. Throughout the original seven volumes of the expurgated *Diary*, Nin self-consciously fashions the idealized persona of an independent artist who is refined, sensitive, nurturant, and compassionate. The narcissistic wound of paternal desertion inaugurates a lifelong gesture of aesthetic compensation, as Anaïs reconstructs her personality in the mode of art before an implicit audience of spellbound admirers. She creates herself anew in a guise that will be acceptable first to her own father, then to a long line of lovers whom she must please and placate as surrogate Daddy figures.[12]

It is not surprising that at the end of the first volume of her *Diary*, when the adult Anaïs is finally reunited with her biological father in 1933, the meeting proves disastrous. With shock and dismay, she realizes that the object of her adolescent devotion is neither God nor devil, but an egotistical dandy—frail, narcissistic, a bit silly, and totally dependent on younger women for nurture and for praise. The painful epiphany comes, however, only in the wake of her tremulous submission to Joaquin's incestuous seduction—an event cautiously omitted from the published *Diary*, but described in vivid detail in the unexpurgated volume *Incest: From "A Journal of Love."*

After two decades of separation from her remote and idealized father, the thirty-year-old Anaïs confesses in her journal that a desperate desire to win Daddy's love prompts her to connive in his bohemian proposal of incestuous union. These two "satanic" libertines first share titillating tales of sexual excess, of flamboyant adventures and voluptuous delight. They seal an "ironic pact of similarity" by trading intimate secrets, including Joaquin's vituperative denigration of Rosa as a "spider, voracious, bestial" (*I* 206-7). After extravagantly praising Anaïs as an ideal woman who synthesizes the most desirable traits of his many past lovers, he mourns the tragedy of their blood relationship and curses the futility of his daughter's magnetic attraction.

Anaïs, in turn, is overwhelmed by Joaquin's demand for erotic consummation and cajoled into satisfying his narcissistic fantasies. Desperately in love with Daddy and conditioned from infancy to please the authoritarian father, she sincerely believes herself a complicitous partner in this "fantastic, unique" adventure (*I* 210). Deirdre Bair graphically reconstructs the scene of father-daughter incest when she reports that Anaïs and Joaquin "exchanged caresses upon their bare flesh while he cautioned that they 'must avoid possession.' In the meantime, he made her nipples harden and inserted his finger in her vagina until . . . she lifted herself, threw off her negligeé, and mounted him" (174). The issue of who seduced whom and under what circumstances remains somewhat ambiguous in this highly charged drama. In the very act of sexual consent, Anaïs feels a sensual exhilaration psychologically compromised by a powerful surge of fear and "revulsion" (*I* 209).[13]

What I find most troubling in this admittedly perplexed portrait of father-daughter incest is Nin's apparent illusion of autonomy and control.[14] Oblivious of her father's disguised strategies of early sexual humiliation, she first idealizes him, then finds herself beguiled by the intensity of his passionate imprecations. Certainly, Anaïs cannot imagine rejecting the man who promises compensation for two decades of unrequited love. Conniving in her father's implicit seduction, the adult daughter rationalizes his coercion by attributing the guilt of temptation and arousal to herself—by assuming that it is she who is choreographing this volatile encounter, and that she has finally achieved mastery over the master of her heart.

Virtually mesmerized, Anaïs elevates her Don Juan Daddy to the vaunted position of an experienced professor presumed to know erotic secrets he alone can bequeath. He will initiate her into the mysteries of amorous expertise, though the price be "continuous excitation" without release, a "dim, veiled, unclimaxed joy" (*I* 212). Acknowledging a passion founded on awe, Anaïs adopts the inevitable role of altruistic mistress. Aware, too, of the biblical parable of Lot and his daughters, she is split between Joaquin's continued infantilization of her as amorous partner and his melodramatic orgasmic cry, *"Toi, Anaïs! Je n'ai plus de Dieu!"* (*I* 209). The father conveniently holds his daughter morally responsible for what he construes as their incestuous perdition.[15] Claiming to have been ensorcelled by a taunting, irresistible temptress, Joaquin cries out ecstatically that he has "lost God" in the orgasmic discovery of his daughter's forbidden genital (w)hole. By casting Anaïs in the subject-position of inaccessible phallic mother, he takes refuge in the sanctuary of her lubricious vaginal spaces and reduces her to a mirror(ed) reflection of his own narcissistic need. Anaïs must have felt overwhelmed by his erotic demands and by the force of his implicit phallocratic authority.

Congratulating herself, nonetheless, on her sexual liberation from the cloying societal law of the Father, Anaïs dances to Joaquin's erotic choreography in order to free herself from a lifelong obsession with the absent Father/God. She apparently hopes to demystify his figure by meeting him in bed as an ordinary, vulnerable male, and not the bagful of divinity she has worshipped since childhood. But her strategy predictably backfires in its obsessive-compulsive repetition of unacknowledged patterns of earlier sexual abuse. Anaïs tries to approach and conquer the arrogant patriarch she remembers as cruel, authoritarian, judgmental, and emotionally inaccessible —a figure screened by the fetishistic veils of eyeglass lens and camera lens, cold and remote in his emotional self-absorption. In her 1936 *Diary*, she will judge Joaquin "tender and lying," a "pathological and incurable mythomane" (*D* 2:114). In language worthy of Sylvia Plath, she describes him as "egotistically, egocentrifugally, egocentripetally delightful and clear and clean as a Frigidaire" (*D* 2:114). She visualizes her father almost entirely without affect, in an atmosphere of "floating icebergs," so remote as to belong to a "non-human species" (*D* 2:63).

After the first trauma, perhaps there is no other. All subsequent narcissistic injuries reinforce and resonate with the concussive blows of primordial shock, with that first sense of infantile abandonment experienced in relation to the father of personal prehistory. The traumatic wound of Daddy's desertion cannot be healed by the masquerade of reenactment. By consenting to participate in a love affair with her father, Anaïs has fallen headlong into the Freudian trap of repetition compulsion. Involved in one of the most abnormal situations imaginable, she tries to rationalize uncanny sensations that contaminate the union, but she cannot help feeling that her father's "sperm was a poison" (*I* 210).

Rather than validating the integrated and coterminous sense of self she so desperately seeks, incest doubles the daughter's emotional bondage. By fantasmatically seducing the debilitated patriarch, by manipulating him through gifts of pleasure and amorous satisfaction, Anaïs hopes to conquer the man who has dominated her imagination and then, by rejecting this besotted lover, to free herself from filial obsession. Playing the role of a seductress who triumphantly spurns her wounded admirer, Nin tries magically to reverse the original trauma of paternal abandonment.

The scheme fails disastrously, as Anaïs reconstructs the elusive Prince Charming in ever more idealized images. She portrays him as the French *Roi Soleil*; Apollo, the god of light and clarity; and finally, the crucified redeemer who has sacrificed all in the name of love. In a moment of filial empathy, Anaïs manages to reverse the gift-giving economy of sexual exchange by interpreting her father's incestuous longing in the register of paternal altruism. Clearly, she connives in Joaquin Nin's perversion (*père-version*) of culturally inscribed gender codes. "I used to identify myself to my father," Anaïs notes acerbically, "but I acted like my mother, the sacrificed one" (quoted in Bair 285).[16]

Clarification and emotional lucidity after the incestuous encounter would eventually come, but only with time, psychoanalytic therapy, and self-analysis through journals, confessional writing, and autobiographical fiction. It was not until Joaquin's death that Anaïs began accurately to assess the truncated oedipal drama that scarred her life: "My father died this morning, in Cuba. The hurt was so deep, the sense of loss so deep, it was as if I died with him. . . . I wept and felt the loss in my body, this terrible unfulfilled love. . . . I cannot accept his death. It will never heal. Because it was an incomplete, an aborted, an unfulfillable relationship" (*D* 5:51).

How could an adult Anaïs deal with the incestuous repetition of childhood narcissistic injury? One way, apparently, to keep from going mad, was to record the narrative as closely and meticulously as possible in a private journal whose pages would be shared only with trustworthy psychoanalytic confidantes. By confessing the incestuous liaison to Dr. Allendy in explicit detail, Anaïs may have felt temporarily absolved of sexual guilt. By sharing her intimate journal with Dr. Otto Rank early in 1934, she evidently captured his interest and inaugurated his therapeutic care. Nin even reports that Dr. Rank prescribed the self-conscious abandonment of her father as a healthy antidote to Joaquin's initial desertion.[17] "Rank said, 'Hurt him. . . . Abandon him as he abandoned you. Revenge is necessary. To re-establish equilibrium in the emotional life. It rules us, deep down. It is at the root of Greek tragedies'" (*D* 1:307). Nin judged herself vindicated by this advice and explains: "It made me feel that I was balancing in myself the injustices of life, that I was restoring in my own soul a kind of symmetry" (*D* 1:313).

For much of her career, Nin continued to write out the shock of her incestuous encounter with her father in fictional forms—in *House of Incest*, for instance, where the narrator plunges into the realm of the unconscious to confront "THE FISSURE IN REALITY" (*HI* 37). Although father-daughter incest seems unutterable, it remains representable in art, if not nameable in life. At the heart of Nin's incestuous habitation hangs a portrait of biblical debauchery, "Lot with his hand upon his daughter's breast while the city burned behind them" (*HI* 52). The painting suggests an ambiguous representation of unutterable transgression couched in surrealistic images of urban devastation and infernal torture. "DOES ANYONE KNOW WHO I AM?" (*HI* 26) the narrator pleads hysterically. "If only we could all escape from this house of incest, where we only love ourselves in the other" (*HI* 70).[18]

By the time she composed "Winter of Artifice," Anaïs concealed her unspeakable secret in palimpsestic layers of stylistic obfuscation. Readers familiar with the unexpurgated volume *Incest: From "A Journal of Love"* will recognize Nin's novelette as a thinly veiled autobiographical sketch of her incestuous relationship with her father. At the heart of this dense, sometimes inchoate narrative, the father-daughter dyad emerges in all its obsessive dimensions: love (filial, paternal, and amorous), idealization, resentment, disillusionment, fury, vengeance, and disdain. The stage setting has been transposed directly from the *Incest* journal to a small town in southern France, where a fastidious Don Juan nurses a case of lumbago and flagrantly courts his infatuated daughter. Even the script is borrowed from the unexpurgated diary, as the father mourns his daughter's conjugal inaccessibility and celebrates her as "the synthesis of all the women I loved" (*WA* 59).

The author titillates her audience, leading us closer to the breathless moment of incestuous seduction, but stops just short of scandalous revelation. At precisely the point of erotic climax, the eye of the camera shifts to a freeze-frame tableau, and the prose swerves into italicized interior monologue. Extravagant symbols replicate sexual orgasm, as the protagonist metaphorically becomes her father's mystical bride. Nin's potentially pornographic prose gives way to an avalanche of surrealistic images and experimental streams-of-half-conscious reverie. The conclusion of this story remains indeterminate, the coupling of father and daughter veiled in a mist of lyrical obfuscation that evinces a strangled cry for filial "*absolution*" (*WA* 62).[19]

As the protagonist begins to analyze her father/lover, she is startled to discover that his face is hidden behind a mask tainted with blood, a carapace of lies and prevarications: "Lost in a cold, white fog of falsity" (*WA* 84). The father is a papier-mâché figure trapped behind a fishbowl façade, an object of ridicule and pathos. In abandoning her pusillanimous suitor, the daughter can at last feel that she is "restoring in her own soul a kind of symmetry. . . . Mystical geometry . . . impelled this balancing of events" (*WA* 75-6).

If Nin rehearses, throughout her early journals, the narcissistic injury of paternal desertion, then feels doubly betrayed by her father's incestuous seduction, she finally wreaks the kind of revenge purportedly prescribed by Otto Rank when she elaborates the narrative of Joaquin's emotional failures in a work of fiction that fully exposes his narcissism, duplicity, cruelty, and moral corruption. She has portrayed herself as both victim and avenger, gaining moral stature and artistic self-aggrandizement by mining traumatic experience for incendiary materials that explode in surrealistic prose poetry. In the process of typesetting the text on a small handpress, Anaïs insisted that she was "erecting the last monument to [Joaquin's] failure as a father" (*D* 3:192).

After composing "Winter of Artifice," a mature Anaïs could recognize Joaquin as a zombie or death-in-life figure—"a mummy, a dried-up soul." Later, she would bitterly reflect: "Meeting my Father was no salvation but a test, an ordeal" (*F* 392). *Nearer the Moon*, Nin's 1937-39 unexpurgated journal, reeks of filial invective. When Joaquin is divorced by his second wife, Maruca, Anaïs accuses him of "soullessness, vanity, shallowness, feebleness." The theme of her recriminations is blind, insufferable egotism: "Every word a selfish one—a narcissistic one" (*NM* 253). Joaquin's confessions of monstrosity and self-abasement alternate with elaborate exercises in self-justification, but his blatant hypocrisy is simply "not forgivable" (*NM* 271). "By a miracle," Anaïs concludes, "I escaped from my father's burden . . . because he killed my love" (*NM* 291).

II. DAUGHTER LOSS AND MATERNAL ANXIETY

> In man the father I feel an enemy, a danger. (*I* 382)
>
> Father returned . . . like a thorn in my side, . . . and he is the great abortionist. (*I* 340)

The 1993 publication of the unexpurgated journal *Incest* exploded like a bomb on the feminist community, many of whose readers felt shocked by the frank portrayal of Nin's incestuous relationship with her father and startled by the discovery that the poignant account of her stillbirth in the first volume of her *Diary* was, in fact, based on a third-trimester abortion.[20] Apparently, Anaïs had been assured by a physician that her introverted womb would make conception impossible (*I* 367). In analysis with Dr. Allendy, she confessed "that when I found pleasure in sexual intercourse with Henry I was afraid of having a baby. . . . But a few months ago a Russian doctor told me it could not happen easily; in fact, if I wanted a child I would have to subject myself to an operation" (*HJ* 176). Somewhat skeptical, Dr. Allendy provided Anaïs with a diaphragm, which she flamboyantly brought back to his office: "I returned to him a rubber *préventif* he advised me to wear. . . . I wanted to show him I was in a mood of repentance for my 'loose life'" (*HJ* 194).

How, one wonders, could Anaïs have treated the issue of contraception so casually? Once aware of her pregnancy, why did she place so much faith in the unskilled and obviously flawed techniques of a Parisian *sage femme*? Why does her journal bear witness to such a repressed emotional response to this kind of life-transforming event? And how was Anaïs able to muster sufficient sangfroid to carry on a love affair with Otto Rank in the course of a pregnancy that saw her body burgeoning with Henry Miller's potential child?[21]

What seems clear from the very beginning of Nin's pregnancy narrative is the ambivalence she feels about such a powerful, confusing, and overwhelming physiological experience. She confesses to a "terrible mixture of emotions" aroused by vivid fantasies of a "little Henry" and finds herself, by turns, "sad, elated, hurt, bewildered" (*I* 329). In mid-August, she celebrates the intense excitement of gestation and proclaims maternal love for the ripening "seed" developing in her body (*I* 367).

Yet, in a colloquy with the unborn child, Anaïs rationalizes her decision to terminate the pregnancy by arguing that it would be better for the fetus to be annihilated than for a son or daughter to be born into a fatherless environment. The rhetorical strategy again reflects Nin's obsessive preoccupation with father loss. Elaborating on the stoic aphorism that "happiest is he who has never been born," she insists that prenatal obliteration would be preferable to the agony of paternal desertion. Her rhythmic, semiotic incantation is part lyrical meditation, part prayer for absolution, as she tells the "half-created child" about to be "thrust back into the *néant*," "You ought to die because you are fatherless" (*I* 373-74)

Addressing the fetus directly, Anaïs pronounces what appears to be an eloquent exercise in self-exoneration. Even as she ponders the issue of termination, however, she torments herself by personifying the fetus and by labeling the abortion an act of murder. Although a lapsed Catholic, Anaïs still exhibits a powerful sense of guilt in this dialogue, as well as in the multiple confessions made to her journal, her analyst, her lovers, and her readers. She expresses a sincere desire for absolution, both before and after committing the terrible "sin" of which she accuses herself.

In seeking love and emotional validation from a partner as egotistical as Henry Miller, Anaïs has inadvertently repeated the original scene of childhood betrayal. She has sought the impossible father/lover who will, once again, abandon her in crisis. Henry, she believes, is himself an overgrown "child—not a father, not a husband" (*I* 331). Unconsciously reenacting the trauma of filial rupture, Anaïs leaps to the conclusion that Henry would surely abdicate paternal responsibility should she defy his wishes and carry her pregnancy to term.[22] She feels convinced that the self-centered artist is constitutionally incapable of fidelity and nurturance, and that her nascent son or daughter would have to endure a devastating rejection. Directly addressing the fetus in her womb, she angrily predicts: "You would be abandoned, and you would suffer as I suffered when I was abandoned by my father" (*I* 375).

In an outburst that approaches hysterical logorrhea, Anaïs passionately tries to convince herself that a baby would simply be a fetter to her artistic freedom. Claiming that she is destined by nature to play the exotic role of aesthetic muse, she represses her own deep-seated fear of emotional betrayal by representing herself as the virginal Bilitis (*I* 382). In the unconscious guise of sister/lover, Anaïs can nurture without blame, seduce without guilt, and copulate without issue. She offers her lovers a nonthreatening erotic union that represses the phallic copula and provides a tantalizing simulacrum of preoedipal bliss. Without a child as a visible sign of the threatening maternal body, Anaïs can continue to occupy the subject-position of innocent ingenue seduced repeatedly by father figures who are searching for a recrudescence of their youthful potency. "I am the mother of the dream" (*F* 312), she insists. At one point, she compares herself to the Egyptian goddess Isis on a mythic quest to refashion the butchered body of her lost brother/lover: "I am going to piece my Osiris out of fragments whenever I find them" (*I* 94).

Paradoxically, the role that Anaïs feels compelled to play well into middle age is that of the pliable, accommodating, nonthreatening daughter offering filial service to dozens of Daddy surrogates. She repeatedly describes in her diary her own experience of sexual intercourse as an act of "birthing" the male artist. In a metaphorical celebration of sexuality that conflates vagina and womb, Anaïs compares her partner's phallus to an embryo floating in amniotic fluid: "When man lies in her womb, she is fulfilled, each act of love is a taking of man within her, an act of birth and rebirth, of child-bearing and man-bearing" (*D* 1:106).

This lyrical paean to the joys of sexual rebirth is suffused with Lawrencian language that celebrates love in terms of uterine imagery and the ecstatic transfer of electrical energy. As in the case of the Gudrun-Gerald relationship in *Women in Love*, however, it is the infantilized male who emerges symbolically revitalized. The woman, in her role as *magna mater*, feels depleted of emotional resources. Lovemaking leaves her exhausted and empty, as she sacrifices herself by "creating a uterine world for the man in which he can live" (*F* 78).[23] When Nin poetically personifies her lover's penis in discursive odes to erotic joy, she unconsciously invokes a Freudian conflation of phallic member and emergent embryo. If Anaïs experiences sexual activity as metaphorical maternity, then what role might childbearing play in her phallocentric and filially positioned psychic landscape? She dreads the kind of self-sacrifice traditionally associated with motherhood and fears that female masochism is rooted in the "maternal instinct. . . . It is like the masochism of people brought up in the Catholic religion" (*D* 1:165).

Had Anaïs carried her pregnancy to term, Henry Miller almost certainly would have renounced responsibility for his progeny, and Hugh Guiler might have guilelessly provided for the illegitimate offspring, despite its uncanny resemblance to a well-known American author. "I can't give Hugh a child of Henry's," Anaïs reasons (*I* 329). Her colloquy with the developing fetus reveals still another source of anxiety—a kind of sibling rivalry at the possible loss of her husband's exclusive solicitude. If Hugh were entrusted with the care of a needy infant, he might well be distracted from his essential role as nurturant, matric male, and Anaïs would feel, once again, like an emotional orphan. "My true ideal father is Hugh," she proclaims (*F* 153), "because he protects and forgives all things" (*NM* 145). This long-suffering, sympathetic partner serves as the "young sweet father" who, Nin believes, stabilizes her sanity and keeps her from "going crazy" (*NM* 92).

The unexpurgated text of *Incest* gives evidence that Anaïs rejects maternity out of a sense of anxiety and panic generated by an intense fear of assimilation to the body of the mother that she herself so insistently repudiates. It is out of sheer terror that she chooses to terminate such an ill-conceived pregnancy—terror of engulfment and absorption into the lost maternal territory of female subservience and ego extinction. She can only interpret motherhood as the "supreme immolation of [her] ego" (*I* 329). Rejecting the mother who ostensibly drove Daddy away by sacrificing feminine beauty to the harsh demands of parenthood, Anaïs cannot bring herself to consider the kind of domestic asphyxiation that destroyed Rosa Culmell Nin. She feels convinced that Rosa alienated her husband Joaquin by eagerly embracing maternity, and she dreads a similar fate in relation to Henry Miller. Anaïs believes that she must choose "between the child and Henry" (*I* 329).

Pregnancy, suggests Julia Kristeva, forces a woman to identify, in a powerfully regressive movement, with the body of the mother abandoned at birth. Returning to the preoedipal state of physiological symbiosis, the pregnant woman is both herself and not herself, in a unique subject-position that involves internal doubling and splitting, "the strange form of split symbolization (threshold of language and instinctual drive, of the 'symbolic' and the 'semiotic') of which the act of giving birth consists" (*DL* 240). This shared physiological identity bodes inevitable separation, since gestation must end in a (physically and emotionally) traumatic parturition. As Kristeva observes in "Stabat Mater," the culturally determined role of motherhood, with its "bio-symbolic latencies, . . . lays women open to the most fearsome manipulations" by society: "Silence weighs heavily . . . on the corporeal and psychological suffering of childbirth and especially the self-sacrifice involved in becoming anonymous in order to pass on the social norm" (*KR* 183).

Anaïs, renouncing her own mother as a physiological vessel who gave birth to a daughter only to be discarded by the husband who seeded and separated, finds herself ironically destined to fight a lifelong battle with self-doubt and insecurity—an enervating contest that condemns her to feel contempt for the earthbound, "uncultured" maternal body rejected by her ascetic and aesthetic father. Starving and pruning her own girlish physique, Anaïs complains of mammary insufficiency, but exploits her fragile figure in subtle seductive strategies. She takes advantage of her diminutive posture to gain access to the symbolic discourse of the father, "whereas a woman as mother would be, instead, a strange fold that changes culture into nature, the speaking into biology" (Kristeva *KR* 182).

Because entry into the symbolic register demands that the daughter repudiate attachment to the body of the mother, Nin feels she must sacrifice both mother tongue and maternal physiology in order to be admitted, as androgynous ephebe, into the heavily guarded world of art and paternal discourse. She must connive in the veiling of the father's phallus by stifling the possibility of amorous issue. The child, as phallic sign and threat to paternal dominion, must be banished from the erotic liaison between father and daughter. No mothers or sons are allowed to disrupt the incestuous dyad; no sibling rival need apply for admission to this fantasmatic paradise.

When Anaïs trusts a *sage femme*, a "wise woman" of French folk medicine, to rescue her from the physiological threat of maternity, a surrogate mother once again fails her. She is forced to announce her pregnancy to the multiple men in her life, to appeal to a male physician for aid, and to entrust her body to the alienating environment of a modern hospital equipped with technological instruments of torture that will finally deliver her: "I have to be operated on, and the child is six months old, and alive and normal. It will be almost a childbirth" (*I* 371). Comparing herself to Christ suffering on the cross, she reluctantly submits to a symbolic female martyrdom.

Nin's riveting description of her gruesome labor and delivery takes on the sacrificial tone of torture and bodily immolation. The beleaguered subject experiences a mythic life-passage through a "long, dark, tunnel" in this journey of painful initiation into womanhood. Surrealistic images flash through a semihysterical, tormented consciousness, as she imagines a "blazing white light" absorbing her body "in long icy threads" (*I* 379). Wracked with excruciating pain, and threatened with further violation by a fascistic German physician (Dr. Endler), Anaïs wonders: "Am I dying? The ice in the veins, the cracking of the bones, this pushing in blackness, . . . the feeling of a knife cutting the flesh" (*I* 379). Even now, she is emotionally split by conflicting desires "to keep and to lose, to live and to die" (*I* 380). The operation is a cruel mimicry of the hours she has spent in ecstatic lovemaking, as her "legs are twisted in pain and the honey flows with the blood" (*I* 380).

The birth process climaxes in a fiery eruption of sanguinary images suggestive of heroic struggle through a torturous death chamber in a battle fought with mythic valor and ending in spiritual triumph over superhuman obstacles: "There is blood in my eyes. . . . There is fire, flesh ripping, and no air." She feels her blood "spilling out" until the moment of "sudden deliverance" (*I* 381). Figuratively disemboweled, and balancing precipitously on the edge of possible extinction, Nin is writing the feminine body with meteoric intensity.

Anaïs has identified so completely with the father who abandoned her that she herself must reject her potential daughter/son in order to avoid betrayal by an egotistical lover. The child, she insists, "is a demon" that "lies inert at the door of the womb, blocking life" (*I* 380). Envisioning a filial replication of Henry Miller, she wreaks vengeance on all the father figures who have deserted her by "pushing out" the imaginary son that she mentally constructs in the guise of a "diminutive Henry" (*I* 382). The son, however, turns out to be gendered female: a daughter is (still)born in the wake of her anxious labors. Anaïs is shocked by her confrontation with the dead baby's female sex. The shrivelled child resembles a "doll, or an old miniature Indian. . . . I hated it for all the pain it had caused me, and because it was a little girl and I had fancied it to be a boy" (*I* 381).

Nin's ostensible callousness may cloak a more profound emotional response, since the dead baby's gender suddenly evokes an unexpected narcissistic identification with the lost daughter/self. The fantasmatic son could be envisaged in the mode of paternal aggression and demonic masculine threat. The daughter, in contrast, engenders such a powerful narcissistic bond that the bittersweet triumph of physiological separation must have traumatized the confused and exhausted Anaïs even as she pushed forth and delivered the baby whose life, she believes, would have threatened her own.

The dead child, which at first appears "perfectly made" and "completely formed," nonetheless has a "bigger than average" head that obscures fetal deformity: "One more day and the tumor in its head would have infected me," Anaïs observes coolly. "I would have died" (*I* 381). Deirdre Bair, among others, has expressed skepticism at the diagnosis of this inexplicable tumor. How, she wonders, could the baby have suddenly "metamorphosed into a monster" (202)? Under such intensely stressful conditions, the exhausted Anaïs, judging the six-month fetus by criteria appropriate to a full-term infant, must have felt startled by what seemed to be a disproportionately expanded cranium. She might, in fact, have misinterpreted the "caul" as a dangerous tumor, then inferred a medical judgment that would exonerate her of residual guilt. Alternatively, the obstetrical probings and surgical balloons introduced into her uterus could, indeed, have caused teratogenic deformity. The ominous brain tumor, whether real or imagined, symbolically synthesizes Nin's maternal anxieties and justifies, in her own mind, her decision to abort the pregnancy. Years later, a middle-aged Anaïs would continue to rehearse the injury she felt at Rosa Culmell's Catholic "belief in motherhood, so strong that in Paris when my life was in danger, she felt the child should have been saved even at the cost of my life, and would not listen to medical explanations that a child would always be strangled by old adhesions" (*D* 5:181-82).[24]

It is not surprising that Anaïs should marshal to her psychological defense every possible weapon against cultural constructions of maternal guilt. Even in the most horrendous of circumstances, the loss of a potential child through abortion or miscarriage can be emotionally difficult, if not traumatic, for the woman who suffers psychological conflict and a profound sense of personal bereavement. Ambivalence lies at the heart of a beleaguered subject whose body is physiologically colonized by the species, and whose mind must either accept or reject the subsequent doubling of personal/maternal subjectivity during a gestation process that will climax in the "ex-matriation" of the newly born infant as a separate individual. The experience of parturition necessarily splits a unified, integrated, and symbiotic maternal-filial subject-position whose uniqueness and mystery has yet to be theorized by a largely masculine philosophical tradition. Julia Kristeva's essay "Stabat Mater" offers a tentative articulation of the paradox: "What connection is there between myself, or even . . . between my body and this internal graft and fold, which, once the umbilical cord has been severed, is an inaccessible other? . . . No connection. . . . The child, whether *he* or *she* is irremediably an other" (*KR* 178-79).

There are probably as many responses to pregnancy and childbirth as there are reactions (often ambivalent) to maternity and child-rearing. Nin's was only one. And perhaps, considering the dire circumstances surrounding her third-trimester abortion, it evinced extreme feelings of guilt and remorse mingled, simultaneously, with a sense of relief and psychological liberation at the "glory of deliverance" (*I* 383). In reading *Incest*, I felt moved by Nin's confessional narrative and deeply troubled by the societal frustrations imposed on her by a coercive pronatalist environment. Denied easy access to medical assistance, she initially had recourse to a folkloric midwife who poked and prodded, but succeeded in doing little more than possibly damaging the developing fetus. Nin found herself in a dilemmatic situation, which she apparently handled largely through complex strategies of denial and repression. As Adrienne Rich insists in *Of Woman Born*, abortion "is violence: a deep, desperate violence inflicted by a woman upon, first of all, herself. . . . The absence of respect for women's lives is written into the heart of male theological doctrine, into the structure of the patriarchal family, and into the very language of patriarchal ethics" (273-74).

Carol Gilligan demonstrates in her study *In a Different Voice* that the decision to terminate a pregnancy proves, for the majority of women, a highly personal and conflicted choice between a passionate desire to care and a desperate need to survive. Most women approach this controversial issue not as an abstract ethical question of fetal rights, but as a moral problem situated in the larger context of long-term nurturance and commitment. In contrast to a plethora of stylized literary representations, the testimonials collected in a book like Mary Pipes's *Understanding Abortion* give evidence of numerous cases of post-traumatic stress disorder characterized by protracted mourning over the encrypted imago of a fantasized "lost one"—an always-already absent object of desire that may continue to haunt female consciousness long after the experience of pregnancy-loss. "Nin's loss," observes Diane Richard-Allerdyce, "whether stillbirth or abortion, is her loss," and the unexpurgated journal raises salient questions "about grief's lack of discrimination" ("Narrative and Authenticity" 83, 86).

The severe judgment leveled against Nin by her most recent biographer, Deirdre Bair, seems both intemperate and unsubstantiated. "The account of the birth in the diary," Bair claims, "is a portrait of monstrous egotism and selfishness, horrifying in its callous indifference. . . . There is no regret in her account, only a confused collection of excuses" (200, 202). No regret? After the immediate exultation of deliverance, a pensive Anaïs gives vent to an emotional deluge of "regrets, long dreams of what this little girl might have been." She clearly mourns the fate of her "first dead creation" (*I* 381). Never more Catholic in the configuration of her emotional life, Anaïs recites a virtual litany of self-laceration: "To protect Henry, to be free, I killed the child. Not to be abandoned, I killed the child" (*I* 382). In bitter lamentations, she craves the intensity of the unique "womb love" that she felt for the embryonic child, the "little Indian" whom she compares, in Freudian fashion, to a surrogate phallus, "a penis swimming in my overabundant honey" (*I* 382). She seems to feel that love for this potential daughter/self has been the most intimate emotional and physiological experience of her life.

What remains clear, to this reader at least, is that Nin's third-term abortion provoked psychological dysphoria and haunting flashbacks expressed in a compulsive need to narrate the birth story over and over again—to relive the pain of pregnancy-loss in revised aesthetic frameworks until the reiterated trauma could be mitigated, sanitized, and made acceptable to a tormented consciousness. The unexpurgated journal entries offer a riveting exercise in denial and repression, self-accusation, confessional remorse, and religious exoneration. It is precisely the gaps and interstices in the palimpsestic text of *Incest*—the startling contradictions and bewildering incongruities—that make it such a poignant testimonial to the trauma of pregnancy loss.[25]

Only a traumatic neurosis could explain Nin's compulsive need to describe the abortion experience as a "superb adventure" of heroism and endurance, a life-threatening initiation into womanhood that climaxes in mythic "joy at having escaped the great mouth of the monster" (*I* 403, 385). In this particular dramatis persona, Anaïs is at her most Catholic, learning the lessons of sainthood through the pain and suffering of a virtual martyrdom, then spiritually redeemed through epiphanic revelation. "I died and was reborn again in the morning," she proclaims, as she testifies to a mystical experience of "superhuman joy" (*I* 384). Like the blessed mother of Catholicism after the miracle of Christ's virgin birth, she has remained physically "intact, as if nothing had ever happened" (*I* 385).

Despite her aborted pregnancy, Anaïs vicariously participates in the obscure mysteries of maternal parturition. Having delivered to the world a dead daughter expelled from the womb like a potentially fatal viper, she feels temporarily exultant at the victory symbolized by this simulacrum of birth. "My life will always be a tragedy," she laments (*I* 371). And yet, the journal gives her the option of rewriting tragic (or traumatic) life history in the Dantesque mode of spiritual transcendence. "I melted into God," proclaims Anaïs the survivor. "I felt space, gold, purity, ecstasy, immensity, a profound, ineluctable communion" (*I* 384). It is not surprising that Nin's pregnancy evokes an uncanny (*unheimlich*) mystical response, since, as Julia Kristeva observes in "Stabat Mater," the "love of God and for God resides in a gap. . . . But it is there, too, that the speaking being finds a refuge when his/her symbolic shell cracks and a crest emerges where speech causes biology to show through: . . . the time of illness, of sexual-intellectual-physical passion, of death" (*KR* 184-85).

Without the aesthetic context of beatific illumination, Nin's intense physical pain and traumatic pregnancy-loss would have seemed meaningless, her excruciating ordeal wholly futile. Unable consciously to face the possibility of such bereavement, Anaïs calls upon a Catholic religious tradition that would label her an apostate and identifies herself as a new "St. Theresa of love" (*I* 348). She protests that she would not, in fact, have wanted to relinquish this "superb adventure" for the maid "Emilia's short abortion of two hours" (*I* 403).[26]

And yet, Nin's future would be plagued by emotional fragmentation and by nightmares resonant with images of interrupted maternity:

> I have terrible nightmares. I dynamited a city. I was in a room full of dead animals. I saw a baby who had been abandoned. I decided to adopt him. As I began kissing him, he began to look more and more like a baboon. (*F* 88)
>
> On the ship I had dark fantasies. Doctor Endler would be waiting for me on the pier. I would be taken back to the hospital and go through everything again. . . . Then I would recall every detail of the *fausse couche* [aborted pregnancy]. (*F* 92)

In a sensitive response to the revelations of *Incest*, Erica Jong expresses feminist sympathy for Nin's choice of termination under what must have been fairly horrendous physical and emotional circumstances: "With this act, Anaïs feels she has delivered herself as an artist. She has killed the woman in herself, committed female infanticide, both on her child and on herself. . . . With one act she has repudiated her mother, her father, Henry, Hugo, Rank, and all the men who want to possess her. She will never face abandonment again" (24).

III. NARRATIVE RECOVERY

In the 1960s and early 1970s, Anaïs Nin gave us a carefully selected, artfully crafted version of the sprawling, 150-volume manuscript that comprised the ur-text of her intimate journals. She spent most of her adult life as both fiction-writer and autobiographer, articulating various versions of her personal experiences in novels, diaries, and short stories—many of which were, in some sense, elaborate exercises in scriptotherapy in the interest of narrative recovery. In the pages of her unexpurgated journal *Incest*, she insists that diary-writing rescued her from the threat of "insanity" (*I* 217). Recalling the tormented months when Dr. Otto Rank, her therapist, forbade her to keep a personal journal, she confesses: "I wanted my diary as one wants opium. . . . But I also wanted to save myself. So I struggled and fought. I went to my typewriter and I wrote" (*I* 306).

In the original edited version of her *Diary*, Nin perfected an idealized persona—a luminous image of ethereal spirituality, of compassion and fragility, fortified by a stubborn willfulness, bohemian bravado, and inner moral strength. The painfully fragmented ego later revealed in the unexpurgated volumes *Incest, Fire,* and *Nearer the Moon*—that of a confused daughter, neurotic lover, and sexually traumatized woman—is re-created in Nin's art as a coherent, but amorphous and endlessly protean self. In *Fire* she laments: "I live on a hundred planes at once. . . . Desiring unity but incapable of it. Playing a million roles" (*F* 24).

Nin grew up as a radical individualist who placed implicit faith in the powers of personal will. As she attests in a 1971 interview, if the "*Diary* proves anything, it is that liberation comes first of all from within" (*Conversations* 71). She presents herself in her journals as an avant-garde artist living in valiant opposition to a hostile bourgeois establishment. Not until the last few years of her life did she begin to develop a nascent feminist consciousness and to associate her own marginal plight with that of other women struggling to emerge from the cocoon of the 1950s. She felt that she was contributing to the feminist movement by striving "to make a bridge between two ways of approaching liberation: one psychological and the other social" (*Conversations* 145). Like many successful women of her generation, Nin tended to see herself as a bisexual exception to the universal law of female oppression. She took as her role models independent figures like Lou Andreas-Salomé, who forged their own destinies largely by gaining acceptance in male-dominated professions or by forming strong attachments to influential men.[27]

"The nature of my contribution to the Women's Liberation Movement is not political but psychological," Nin insisted (*SM* 27). In the first volume of her *Diary*, she expressed the conviction that her published journals would give voice and courage to all those mute, inarticulate women who have taken refuge historically in female intuition: "*It is the woman who has to speak* . . . for many women" (*D* 1:289). By the early 1970s, she considered herself "politically an activist" (*D* 7:162). "I don't know what a 'radical feminist' is," she proclaimed, "but I *am* a feminist" (*WS* 35).[28]

What interests me most about Nin's diary is that it offers a consummate example of contemporary life-writing as scriptotherapy. And perhaps because her journals so meticulously examine the traumatized and fragmented subject, they more closely resemble the category of psychoanalytic case history than traditional autobiography. What separates Nin's life-writing from Freudian analysis is the ambiguity of the clinical case history she both delineates and revises. Apparently, Nin wrote so compulsively because she was driven by childhood traumatic injury to the point of lifelong obsession. And the strategies of autobiographical testimony that led her to become one of the greatest diary writers of this century most likely saved her from psychological disintegration.

Anaïs complains, for instance, in the autumn of 1933, of feeling "hellishly lonely" and describes herself as "ill with morbidities, obsessions, susceptibilities" (*I* 266, 272). At times, she appears to exhibit manic-depressive symptoms in a series of journal entries peppered with casual references to the possibility of suicide or mental breakdown. "I may go mad," she speculates on November 2, 1934, just five weeks after her first abortion (*I* 399). Shortly thereafter, she bemoans the "terrible algebra" of her chaotic lifestyle: "If I have not gone mad these days with all that has happened to me, I never will" (*I* 402-3).

Early in January 1936, Anaïs recounts a series of mental crises: "I lay on the bed and sobbed hysterically. . . . In place of my heart there seemed to be a hole in my body, the vital core missing" (*F* 193). She fears that her "disease is winning out. Melancholy is setting in" (*F* 196). Anxiety immediately prior to and during the course of her menstrual period seems to precipitate extreme emotional chaos for Anaïs, who frequently reiterates the feeling that "one week a month, . . . I am crazy" (*F* 174). During the "moonstorm," she feels her entire body "revolting, splitting, poisoned" (*F* 179), and compares herself to Christ being crucified on the cross (*NM* 203). She seeks relief by discharging, along with her menstrual flow, "all the turgid, dark, brooding elements into writing" (*NM* 76).

All sorts of evidence in Nin's diary suggests the possibility of what today might be diagnosed as post-traumatic stress disorder—or, at the very least, a defensive escape into illusion as a strategy for coping with traumatic personal history. Throughout her journals, Anaïs continually reiterates symptoms of psychological dysphoria. She reports battling "the most choking depression" (*F* 100). "As soon as I am alone a diseased flow of morbid images begins: self-torture, jealousy, obsession" (*F* 178). "I feel the danger of madness" (*NM* 54). "I find only suicide and despair" (*NM* 321). Dealing with suicidal fantasies and the threat of psychosis, Anaïs ascribes her tentative hold on reality to a healing engagement in therapeutic life-writing, an activity that allows her metaphorically to anneal the fragments of personal experience onto the holistic tapestry of her own (un)conscious integument: "Work has been my only stabilizer. The journal is a product of my disease, . . . but it is also an engraving of pain, a tattooing of myself" (*HJ* 207).

During her Rankian retreat at les Marronniers, Anaïs describes a panic attack that precipitates a "choice between . . . hysterical weeping—or writing." She articulates a genuine fear of madness, alleviated only by the decision to sit at her typewriter and give vent to psychic chaos through artistic transformation. In shrill, hysterical tones, she instructs herself: "Write, you weakling; write, you madwoman, write your misery out" (*I* 308). The graphic articulation of pain appears to be her sole remedy against suicidal depression. The "labor of creation," she insists, "is the only thing which makes life bearable" (*F* 170).

Scriptotherapy proved to be Nin's strongest defense, albeit partial and temporary, against the "monstrous enemy melancholia" (*I* 229). In January 1933, she wrote: "I feel splintered, blurred—floating. I want again to reintegrate myself by work" (*I* 87). Impulses toward destruction gnaw at her vitals like a serpent sequestered (Cleopatralike) in her breast (*NM* 69)—a viper that will kill her unless liberated through testimonial narrative. Every time she reaches a "new peak of tragedy," Anaïs finds sanctuary in "WORK. Marvelous work" (*NM* 152, 156). "The transmutation of art is imposed in the Nietzschean sense: Not to go mad" (*NM* 333). Writing, she tells us, is her "means of evasion, burrowing [her] way out to freedom" (*D* 4:70).

As Kim Krizan observes, Anaïs "viewed creativity as a salvation, . . . and in her case illusion acted as a defense against a harsh reality, but eventually became a bridge which led the way to objectivity" (22). Neurotic symptoms are ubiquitous in Nin's journals, but they are evidently held in check by a brilliant and powerful mind that plays out the fascinating possibilities of psychic fragmentation as masquerade or Bakhtinian carnival. Nin always remained tightly in control of her experimental scripts, both in life and in the context of literary representation. By the late 1930s, she could proclaim exultantly: "I am no longer neurotic" (*F* 374). "I truly believe that a perpetual season in hell can be exorcised" (*D* 6:385)[29]

In the fourth and fifth volumes of her *Diary*, Nin records the epiphanies evinced by a visit to Acapulco and a subsequent experience of tropical change, self-discovery, and rebirth. *Cities of the Interior*, her fictional rendition of the struggle for psychological liberation, anatomizes "the malady which makes our lives a drama of compulsion instead of freedom" (*D* 4:143). With a lens finely chiseled by the tools of psychoanalysis, Nin developed "a way of looking at . . . what defeats us as a monster created by ourselves, . . . and therefore dissolvable and transformable" (*D* 4:148). The trajectory of her personal journals would eventually intersect with a Proustian continuous novel delineating spiritual evolution "from subjectivity and neurosis to objectivity, expansion, fulfillment" (*D* 4:25). In the fifth volume of her *Diary*, Anaïs testifies to a conviction of personal recovery: "I feel now that the warring factions inside of me are slowly integrating, fusing" (*D* 5:235).

There is little question that Nin's half-century of journal-writing gave her an aesthetic sense of her life unfolding on a mythic stage in a powerful drama of self-revelation. The diary traces an intense and complex psychological journey toward emotional freedom and a regenerative "feeling of strength and cohesion" (*D* 6:315). As Anaïs insisted at the outset of World War II, the twentieth century would be forced to acknowledge the birth of a modern hero "who would master his own neurosis, . . . who would struggle with his myths, . . . who would enter the labyrinth and fight the monster" (*D* 2:347).

Nin's diary offers a meticulous anatomization of a prolonged struggle with life-shattering trauma eventually resolved through autobiographical testimony. When invited by Renate Druks to attend a masquerade party dressed as her madness, Anaïs, somewhat scantily clothed, covered her head with a birdcage spewing forth "an endless roll of paper" with "lines from [her] books," a simulated "ticker tape of the unconscious" symbolic of her efforts to escape neurosis through scriptotherapy (*D* 5:133). Throughout lectures and interviews in the early 1970s, Nin continually reiterated her own conviction of narrative recovery. She stressed the pivotal importance of journal-writing in reconstructing the bridge between herself and the social and political world. When asked by Keith Berwick in 1970 whether her "writing both in the diary and in the works of fiction" could be considered "a kind of lifelong therapy," she responded: "The results were that. The actual effect is simply that I feel that the pieces are all working in harmony" (*Conversations* 64).

Psychoanalysis, Nin testifies, helped her discover the oedipal plot that seemed to dictate neurotic replications of the pain of father loss in masochistic relationships with numerous father surrogates who invariably failed her. Once able to acknowledge the source of her obsessive-compulsive behavior, Anaïs, like Lillian Beye in "Seduction of the Minotaur," could explore the center of a convoluted psychic labyrinth and heroically confront the minotaur of her neurosis in the form of a judgmental Father/God whose severe recriminations had seriously undermined her fragile sense of agency and subjectivity. Initially shattered by her father's abuse and implicit betrayal, Anaïs was able to write out the shock of post-traumatic stress disorder in a protracted self-analysis that allowed her to lay to rest a haunting entourage of private demons. What she "was finally able to achieve in the later diaries . . . is a *refusal to despair*" (*WS* 6). The magical power of storytelling, she tells us, provides an "*anti-toxin*" to trauma, and narrative offers a sanctuary "in which to reconstruct ourselves after shattering experiences" (*WS* 182). Toward the end of her life, Nin apparently achieved peace of mind and emotional harmony, a state of contentment "free of anxiety and conflict. . . . A sense of deep fulfillment" (*WS* 262).

The mature Anaïs was finally able to realize, at least in part, the dream of emotional liberation articulated in *Henry and June*: "I am not the slave of a childhood curse. The myth that I have sought to relive the tragedy of my childhood is now annihilated" (*HJ* 234). "The quest for the father was only one phase of my life," she explains (*Conversations* 57). If psychoanalysis revealed to Anaïs the stifling neurotic patterns inscribed by early domestic trauma, it was the artistic process of reformulating experience through the medium of her journal that allowed her to achieve a sense of autonomy and freedom. "So my salvation somehow was always in the work" (*WS* 109), Nin testifies in the 1970s, as she proclaims that the habit of diary-writing, "acquired accidentally as the result of a psychic trauma," proved to be "a guiding element in [her] life" (*WS* 157). The "diary saved me," she insists. "It was my truth and my reality" (*D* 5:90).

FOUR

Janet Frame's *New Zealand* Autobiography: *A Postcolonial Odyssey*

> *And we walk like Theseus or an ashman in the labyrinth, with our memories unwound on threads of silk or fire; and after slaying. . . the minotaurs of our yesterday we return again and again to the birth of the thread, the Where.*
>
> (*Owls Do Cry* 52)

"Really, if you want to write you have to be desperate," Janet Frame explains in an interview with Elizabeth Alley. "The thing which prompts you to sit down and write must be something which haunts you" (44-45). Frame's three-part autobiography, *To the Is-Land*, *An Angel at My Table*, and *The Envoy from Mirror City* (collected as a single volume *Autobiography* in 1991), evokes a world of grinding poverty familiar to many who endured the Great Depression of the 1930s. Tales of hunger and pain, of life without household heat or indoor plumbing, imbue Frame's vivid description of New Zealand family life amidst debt, illness, and shocking domestic tragedy. A brother given to uncontrollable epileptic fits; an elder sister, Myrtle, drowned in the Oamaru swimming baths; and a second sister, Isabel, drowned a decade later in a grotesque repetition of the earlier tragedy: such was the fabric of Frame's haunted childhood. Just as her mother turned to religious faith and Victorian verse for comfort, Janet took refuge in the poetic imagination, creating a fantasy life that she would metaphorically envisage as an enchanted Mirror City.[1]

An autobiography in the shape of a *Künstlerroman*, Frame's life narrative unfolds as a poignant account of female artistic development in the face of harrowing physical and psychological vicissitudes. At the age of eight, Janet feels acutely aware of the repercussions of global economic depression, "with a large share of misery where there was no place to lay the blame" (*A* 37). Into this impoverished setting, the sensitive child projects philosophical questions of contingency and existential dread. "Why *was* the world?" she persistently inquires, but can find no comforting response anywhere in her environment. Instead, she is left with a residue of premonitions "which immediately gave the thought of *no world* and a feeling of everlasting depths from which one had to struggle to escape" (*A* 37).

Having witnessed "Grandma Frame's dying, . . . world-sad with everyone sharing" (*A* 22), as well as the gruesome demise of an aunt struck down by esophagal cancer, Janet faces a more powerful tragedy with the accidental drowning of her sister Myrtle in 1937. After a petty sibling quarrel one hot summer afternoon, the bookish Janet stays home to read while Myrtle slips off to the Oamaru swimming baths. A few hours later, a doctor arrives to announce the shocking news of the young girl's death. A stunned Janet can only absorb the communication by focusing on the word "morgue," a locution hitherto forbidden in domestic parlance. Gradually, the reality of absence begins to dawn on her shattered consciousness, as she realizes that Myrtle's death entails her "complete disappearance and not even a trial" (*A* 86).[2]

Utterly devastated by the loss of the vivacious and talented sister she had considered both a rival and a role model, the twelve-year-old Janet gradually withdraws into her own private imagination. Oblivious of the full psychological impact of trauma, she is plagued by symptoms of hyperarousal whenever she hears lyrical echoes of her sister's name. "Myrtle's death," she confesses, "was too much within me and a part of me" to be eulogized "*dreamily, poetically*," in sentimental verse (*A* 93). The experience of such overwhelming bereavement is far too shocking to be articulated in the stilted meta-language that the young girl associates with nineteenth-century elegy. Bereft of a literary genre to give voice to her grief, Janet must search for a tougher, more realistic prose vehicle to express her melancholy and mitigate her perilous sense of isolation. Eventually, the fluid and malleable discourse of autobiography would give vent to her long cry of repressed mourning.[3]

Frame's *Autobiography* calls to mind James Joyce's *Portrait of the Artist as a Young Man*, but with a difference. The rigidly delineated sex-gender system dominant in European culture in the first half of this century marks boundaries of experience rarely crossed in either the colonies of the empire or the dominions of the Commonwealth. Both Stephen Dedalus and the adolescent Janet Frame are portrayed as fiercely independent individuals—socially marginal and always seeking a private place or space that will define them as imaginative artists. Whereas Janet is constantly humiliated by her difference among the crowd of schoolgirls at Waitaki Junior High, Stephen revels in his rebellious distinction from the other boys at Belvedere College. He is convinced of the revolutionary rectitude of his artistic vision, though short of sight and emotionally diffident. Janet, seeing clearly, is self-conscious to the point of perpetual alienation. "I entered eagerly," she tells us, "a nest of difference . . . which I lined with my own furnishings" (*A* 110).[4]

Janet addresses her diary to "Mr. Ardenue," a phantasmic patriarch who embodies a godlike second-person projection of Frame's filial need for male approval. She perceives her own father as a "frail husband made strong only by his intermittent potions of cruelty" (*A* 220). Mr. Ardenue, in contrast, is "pictured as a kindly old man with a long, grey beard and 'smiling' eyes" (*A* 117). This male muse has a signature that seems vaguely French, but that also captures a homonym for the second-person pronominal "you" to suggest a mirror reflection of Janet's animus elevated to the role of paternal authority. "Are you there, Mr. Ardenue?" Janet seems to be pleading, with all the ardor of a new self constructed from fragmentary adolescent fantasies. "In the creation of Ardenue I gave a name and thus a certainty to a new inner 'My Place'" (*A* 117).

At the end of Joyce's *Portrait*, Stephen Dedalus, poised on the brink of emigration to Paris, begins keeping a diary that incorporates intimate confessional discourse into experimental narrative. Janet Frame confesses in *To the Is-land* that before leaving for Dunedin Training College, she incinerated her childhood diaries and notebooks: "Only in the *Truth* had I printed my real name, Janet Frame, by which I was now known, the old Nini and Fuzzy and Jean being discarded" (*A* 140). Painfully timid, the young girl suffers such low self-esteem that she feels wracked by an adolescent "homelessness of self" far beyond her years (*A* 110). Frame recalls an almost pathological introversion: "My only escape was within myself, to 'my place,' within an imagination that I was not even sure I possessed" (*A* 108). Unlike Joyce, who portrays Stephen Dedalus exuberantly welcoming an "envoy from the fair courts of life" (*Portrait* 172) at the climax of the seaside epiphany that reveals his vocation as a writer, Frame configures the artistic imagination as a Mirror City whose envoy will summon her to visions of alternative life-worlds. The utopia she fashions is analogous to a Platonic realm of ideal forms, a mysterious source of inspiration that invites welcome escape into the sanctuary of aesthetic fantasy.

As a female artist, Janet faces problems that the Irish Stephen Dedalus never envisioned. She must, for instance, cope with the embarrassing dilemma of menstrual hygiene. Too poor to buy sanitary napkins, she is forced to rely on awkward, unwieldy menstrual rags that have to be washed and recycled. "The bulk and the stink and the washing of the towels became a haunting distaste," she tells us (*A* 118). While boarding as a college student with her Aunt Isy and Uncle George in Dunedin, Janet has access to more efficient commercial products, but feels bewildered by the challenge of disposing of her mortifying menstrual pads. Ingeniously, she decides to destroy these signs of female corporality by symbolically burying them in the cemetery. Her choice seems appropriate if one recalls Julia Kristeva's theoretical association, in *Powers of Horror*, between menses and abjection. "The abject," Kristeva explains, "is the feeling of violence of mourning for an 'object' that has always already been lost" (15). "The *defilement* from which ritual protects . . . is the translinguistic spoor of the most archaic boundaries of the self's clean and proper body" (73).

If all corporeal waste products—feces, urine, sweat, and menses—can be seen in the context of physiological production, then the body provides its own natural symbols of creativity. By burying her menstrual tissue(s), Janet returns these physical secretions to the womb of Mother Earth, keeping them safe for natural decomposition. Too timorous even to cremate such evidence of female sexual difference in the family's weekly holocaust of rubbish, the sensitive young girl neurotically guards every product of either mind or body. Only later, through autobiographical candor, will she break the taboo that seals her in a prison of feminine abjection. In *An Angel at My Table*, Frame finally names these sanguinary excrescences and dares to expose the bloodsoaked rags that once humiliated her as a teenager.[5]

A Rilkean angel will, eventually, sit at her table and counsel peace. But during her first years at Dunedin Training College, Janet has no table at all. Morbidly self-conscious and painfully shy, she insists on consuming small vegetarian snacks alone in the scullery rather than partaking of communal meals served in the family dining room. Surely she is driven by masochistic motives, if not by a form of anorexia nervosa. Starving, the young girl survives by foraging in the sink for leftovers and secretly wolfing down bits of stringy meat cast aside as garbage. Pocket money is invested in caramel candy bars until Janet, emboldened by her younger sister Isabel, dares taste the secret cache of prize chocolates treasured by her aunt. The thrill of transgression titillates the appetites of these two ingenuous thieves, who lavishly indulge their palates in compensation for a childhood of sensual deprivation. A family feud ensues, a battle of words followed by an exchange of angry letters, culminating in the girls' shameful eviction from Aunt Isy's domicile. One marvels at the domestic mores of such times, when the younger generation could outrage its elders by trafficking in forbidden sweets, and the playful antics of a "cruelly innocent" duo could warrant such harsh punishment (*A* 158).

It was not, however, an innocent era. It was the time of World War II and the Holocaust, of a shrinking planet and an expanding global population. It was the beginning of the nuclear age. "Had I been a city," Frame remarks, "the shock of war would have torn apart all buildings, entombing the population. . . . I had never felt so shocked, so unreal" (*A* 121). In the month that Janet reached her majority, the first atom bomb exploded on Hiroshima, and her coming of age was marked by a ghastly "mushroom fire," a "spectacular illumination of the ceremonies of death" (*A* 187). It was a crucial historical juncture, both personally and politically.

In that same month, Frame wrote and published her first short story, "University Entrance." And in the same year, on the dreaded Day of Inspection, she begged to be excused momentarily from her classroom, then took a momentous walk out of the school and out of the teaching profession, never to return. She could no longer bear the false self-system so conscientiously displayed to a judgmental world—the persona of a "lovely girl, no trouble at all." The author observes that her social mask of feigned equanimity felt "cemented in place" to the point of emotional asphyxiation (*A* 188).

Rather than trouble anyone with her desperate need for intimacy and psychological support, the ostensibly perfect pupil swallows a packet of aspirin, only to rise from this failed suicide attempt rejuvenated by a new lease on life (*A* 189). The incident is imaginatively recounted in Frame's autobiographical novel, *Faces in the Water*:

> I will write about the season of peril. I was put in hospital because a great gap opened in the ice floe between myself and the other people whom I watched. . . .
>
> I was a teacher. The headmaster followed me home, he divided his face and body into three in order to threaten me with triple peril. . . .
>
> The headmaster flapped his wings; he was called a name that sounded like buzzard which gave him power over the dead, to pick the bones of those who lie in the desert.
>
> I swallowed a stream of stars. (*FW* 10-12)

One remembers Sylvia Plath's basement self-burial in *The Bell Jar*, followed by her torturous experience of electroshock therapy. In "Lady Lazarus," Plath boasts of a cycle of death and rebirth that mythically replicates religious patterns of spiritual resurrection. She dies and is reincarnated—like Lazarus, like Osiris, like Christ, or like a cat with nine lives. Janet Frame's own reprieve from the depression of an airless bell jar was short-lived indeed. Her suicide attempt resulted in a six-week hospitalization—the first of several incarcerations culminating in a disastrous misdiagnosis of "*Schizzofrenier*" or "*dementia praecox*, described as a gradual deterioration of mind, with no cure" (*A* 196). Frame recalls her alienating experience at Seacliff Hospital as a "concentrated course in the horrors of insanity" (*A* 193).

In 1947, Janet's younger sister Isabel accompanied their mother Lottie Frame on a special holiday trip to Picton, where "on the afternoon of February 17, Isabel, a strong swimmer, left a crowded foreshore and swam a considerable distance into the bay. Then the horrifying events of ten years before began to repeat themselves" (P. D. Evans 31). Fears that had dominated Janet's consciousness for the last decade now came to pass in a terrible repetition of the earlier nightmare: "Isabel drowned. It was almost ten years since Myrtle's death, and this new blow, like a double lightning strike, burned away our thinking and feeling" (*A* 207).

In the grip of traumatic constriction, Janet feels numb and emotionally anesthetized. Once again, she seeks comfort in the literature that she loves, but finds little solace in Eliot's *Waste Land* or Virginia Woolf's *The Waves*. When her own sense of domestic tragedy fails to discover an objective correlative in modernist genres, the bereft survivor takes refuge in self-protective isolation and retreats into psychological "hiding" (*A* 211). Terrified of the specular gaze of a hostile world, Janet succumbs to post-traumatic dysphoria: "Loss, death, I was philosophical about everything: I still had my writing, . . . and if necessary I could use my schizophrenia to survive" (*A* 212).

Frame's younger self curiously describes her purported schizophrenia as a performative mode of behavior—a persona that she can don, or doff, at will and use as a convenient excuse for seeking emotional sanctuary and psychiatric help. She ingeniously determines to exploit the "world of the mad" in order to survive (*A* 198). In conversations with the psychologist John Forrest (the historical John Money), Janet self-consciously feigns a "glazed look" and begins to represent "fantasy as if I experienced it as a reality" (*A* 201). When the amateur therapist diagnoses a melancholia reminiscent of Van Gogh and Hugo Wolf, his young poet-patient feels like a triumphant initiate into the company of deranged artists. "I was playing a game, half in earnest," Frame confides, "to win the attention of a likeable young man" (*A* 201).

Avidly exploring books about Freudian psychology, Janet discovers that some medical authorities have interpreted "*guilt over masturbation*" as a residual symptom of schizophrenia. She feels sufficiently intrigued to "investigate both meaning and deed" in an experiment which she proudly confesses to her analyst (*A* 202). Frame explains to the reader that "to *suit* the occasion, I wore my schizophrenic fancy dress" (*A* 203). Courting adolescent infatuation in the guise of therapeutic transference, she engages in a whimsical masquerade whose potential repercussions prove dangerous indeed.

When Forrest relinquishes his Freudian research and leaves New Zealand for a job in the United States, Janet feels grief-stricken and emotionally abandoned. Both death and the formal rhetoric of condolence, she speculates, can be perceived in terms of a "dramatic accomplishment of absence" (*A* 210). Her sister Isabel and her mentor John Forrest have precipitously vanished from her affective life-world. Suffering from depression, post-traumatic stress disorder, and the "horror of . . . decayed teeth," Janet turns on her "'schizophrenia' at full flow" (*A* 212-13). She appeals to Forrest's friend, Mrs. R., who advises immediate dental work and voluntary admission to Sunnyside Mental Hospital. Frame thus describes her shocking 1947 incarceration: "I woke toothless and was admitted to Sunnyside Hospital and I was given the new electric treatment, and suddenly my life was thrown out of focus. . . . I grieved for everything lost. . . . The years that followed, until 1954 . . . were full of fear and unhappiness. . . . I was fearful always, like a condemned person returning to the executioner" (*A* 213-14).

The startling dimension of Frame's description of mental illness is the great lacuna in her *Autobiography* when she attempts to depict traumatic memories of life in an institution. She endures it all—Park House, with its bestial, dehumanizing environment, where patients are "quickly transformed into living as animals" (*A* 216); electroshock therapy; temporary amnesia; and a total loss of freedom and self-esteem in a Dantesque inferno, where the prevailing mood is one of doomed resignation, "all hope abandoned" (*A* 216). Life imitates art when Janet's metaphorical sensibilities are interpreted by her doctors as evidence of mental aberration. Her epistolary quotation of the vivid phrase "peanut-buttery smell," which she attributes to Virginia Woolf, is judged ample proof of verbal schizophrenia, and she is "removed to the back ward," to become "one of the forgotten people" (*A* 213, 221). According to Frame's self-report, the so-called experts "had not spoken to [her] at one time for longer than ten or fifteen minutes, and in total time over eight years, for about eighty minutes" (*A* 221).[6] "I had seen enough of schizophrenia," Frame insists, "to know that I had never suffered from it" (*A* 224). In *The Politics of Experience*, R. D. Laing hypothesizes that schizophrenia might, in fact, be a strategy that an individual invents in order to cope with an intolerable situation.

A great deal of literary drama, after all, pivots on traumatic events and personal bereavement. Hamlet, Oedipus, and Orestes all grieved the murder of a male parent, and Oedipus faced traumatic revelations of parricide and incest, as well.[7] If Hamlet, impelled by spectral delusions, feigned madness; Orestes was driven to schizoid behavior by the haunting Erinyes. And Oedipus might well have suffered from temporary insanity when he masochistically blinded and symbolically castrated himself for the sin of unwitting copulation with his mother. Freud took great pains in his paper on "Mourning and Melancholia" to distinguish between normal mourning and neurotic symptoms of pathological melancholia. But where does melancholia end and madness begin? And what if the psychiatric community fails, as it did in the case of Janet Frame, to distinguish among manifestations of intense bereavement, post-traumatic stress disorder, and schizophrenia?

It is instructive to compare the characteristic symptoms ascribed to schizophrenia in the fourth edition of the *Diagnostic and Statistical Manual of Mental Disorders* with those associated with post-traumatic stress disorder; and, in turn, to examine both etiologies in light of the condition of *Bereavement*. Although Frame's doctors undoubtedly made use of somewhat different (and presumably less sophisticated) diagnostic criteria, a review of even the most current assessments of mental illness reveals alarmingly vague nosologies. According to the American Psychiatric Association, "positive symptoms" of schizophrenia can include delusions, hallucinations, disorganized thinking, and catatonic motor behaviors (APA 275-76). "Negative symptoms" are identified as "affective flattening, . . . with poor eye contact and reduced body language;" "alogia," or poverty of speech, and "avolition," or the "inability to initiate and persist in goal-directed activities" (APA 276-77).

Nowhere in her autobiography does Frame allude to or exhibit any of the positive symptoms of schizophrenia—delusions, hallucinations, grossly disorganized thought and speech, word salads, or catatonia. The authors of *DSM-IV* admit that it is almost impossible for the diagnostician to judge disorganized thought, so he or she must assess the subject's interlocutory abilities. But what serves as a valid criterion for discursive organization? Does poetic, lyrical, or metaphorical language immediately render the patient suspect? *Whose* organization is being honored in this binary struggle between logocentric thought and inappropriate emotional expression?

The negative symptoms of schizophrenia seem even more slippery and amorphous, as the mental health authority is asked to judge the vivacity and responsiveness of the patient's facial expressions, his or her "fluency and productivity of speech," and his or her ability "to initiate and persist in goal-directed activities" (277). But, one might ask, *whose* goals are being acknowledged in such an investigation? Clearly, the individual must be objectivized in this diagnostic session, and it is the specular acumen of the scientist that will indict or exonerate the patient on the basis of evidence provided by animated facial expressions and/or energetic linguistic exercises. Might "affective flattening" be a manifestation of either shyness or mourning? Might the patient's resistance to "goal-directed activities" signal, on the one hand, a self-conscious rejection of the vacuous or uninteresting goals prescribed by oppressive authorities; or, on the other hand, a further repercussion of either depression or melancholia? The ideological state apparatus of western medicine obviously dominates such diagnostic practices. Who is to be a worthy judge of "diminution or emptiness of affect" in a postmodern desert where the technological hegemony of cyborg culture drains the human subject of feeling, volition, compassion, and empathy, and establishes in place of affect a glittering simulacrum of dispersed emotional energies?[8]

Can a health professional always distinguish, with certainty, between the symptoms of schizophrenia and the emotional repercussions of post-traumatic stress disorder—between mourning or melancholia and madness? Evidently not, since Janet Frame's psychiatric caregivers appear to have confused the two. It is noteworthy that the repercussions of post-traumatic stress disorder can eerily mimic schizophrenic symptoms, especially those associated with disorganized behavior. The "[d]iminished responsiveness to the external world, referred to as 'psychic numbing' or 'emotional anesthesia'" in post-traumatic stress disorder might easily be confused with schizophrenic "affective flattening," especially since trauma victims frequently complain of "markedly reduced ability to feel emotions" (APA 425). Primary symptoms of post-traumatic stress disorder could be misdiagnosed as schizophrenic alogia, avolition, or anhedonia.

All of the above, we are further warned, might be misread by a clinician as symptoms of a "Major Depressive Episode," which in turn can be misdiagnosed in the case of a patient suffering persistent symptoms of bereavement after the loss of a loved one (323). Not a clinical disorder, the category of *Bereavement* merits but a single paragraph in the *DSM-IV*, in an appendix devoted to "Other Conditions That May Be a Focus of Clinical Attention." According to the American Psychiatric Association, "As part of their reaction to the loss, some grieving individuals present with symptoms characteristic of a Major Depressive Episode (e.g., feelings of sadness and associated symptoms such as insomnia, poor appetite, and weight loss). . . . The diagnosis of Major Depressive Disorder is generally not given unless the symptoms are still present 2 months after the loss" (APA 684).

It seems quite astonishing that the authors of the *DSM-IV* confine the appropriate period of grieving after the death of a loved one to approximately eight weeks—an extremely short time, when one considers that most religious practices acknowledge the necessity of a mourning period of one to two years after the death of a family member. "Loss of a loved person," says John Bowlby, "is one of the most intensely painful experiences any human being can suffer" (*Loss* 7-8). Bowlby repeatedly lays emphasis "on the long duration of grief, on the difficulties of recovering from its effects, and on the adverse consequences for personal functioning."

Healthy mourning, he insists, "has a number of features that once were thought to be pathological" (8).[9]

One can detect striking similarities between symptoms caused by severe bereavement and those associated with both schizophrenia and post-traumatic stress disorder. In other words, response to the death of a family member might evince either symptoms of normal bereavement or those characteristic of post-traumatic stress, depending on the circumstances and the emotional reaction of the individual. In either case, the bereft subject may present symptoms that suspiciously resemble those of schizophrenia. The negative symptoms of schizophrenia, the authors of the *DSM-IV* acknowledge, "are difficult to evaluate because they occur on a continuum with normality" (APA 277).

I have discussed these issues at length because I want to argue that Janet Frame's psychiatric case history gives evidence of abnormal bereavement and post-traumatic stress disorder, but no evidence whatsoever of schizophrenia. It seems obvious that one might read, with historical hindsight, the array of pathological behaviors exhibited by Frame as manifestations of post-traumatic stress disorder precipitated by the emotional shock of sororal loss. Evidently, Frame's aspirin overdose was interpreted by authorities not as an exhibition of grief or as a desperate cry for help, but as a suicidal disposition indicative of schizophrenia. One might well imagine an independent and self-willed artist like Janet Frame sitting silent and stone-faced before a medical authority reviewing her dishevelled appearance and inscrutable visage, her laconic speech and idiosyncratic bodily gestures, for telltale signs of affective flattening, alogia, avolition, and anhedonia. And what if the patient were to refuse demeaning goals, such as those required in occupational therapy: "to make baskets, to fill toothpaste tubes with toothpaste, and . . . to weave French lace" (*A* 223)? Surely such insolent behavior would be diagnosed as an obstinate resistance to goal-directed activities. Once the label of psychosis had been pasted onto Frame's traumatized emotional history, it conveniently stuck. Her subject-position was deconstructed and denied, her clinical identity resubjectivized in the abject category of incurable dementia. That way lay madness, and in its wake, the threat of surgical lobotomy.[10]

What is conspicuously absent from the heart of Frame's *Autobiography* is the schizophrenic subject whose "othering" by medical authorities virtually traumatized the authorial consciousness testifying to this ineffably painful period of her life. Her eight-year incarceration as a mental patient becomes the object of Frame's controlled and impassive (self)historical discourse, a tale schematically rendered in factoids that leave little room for personal affect. The autobiographical voice becomes attenuated and disembodied, as the narrator assumes a mask of scientific objectivity to record the horrors of medical error. The history of Frame's struggle to survive incarceration is fragmentary and leaves an elliptical black hole at the center of her life narrative that suggests the spectral presence of a decentered, disempowered, and suffering subject. "I experienced a feeling of nowhereness and nothingness," she confesses, "as if I had never existed. . . . I had somehow fallen into a crevice in time" (*A* 215). Her psychic location reveals temporal/spatial disjunction: "I felt painful humiliation, . . . an increased torment of not knowing where to *be*" (*A* 217). Her island of loneliness, a liminal state of suffering and uncertainty, "resembles that place where the dying spend their time before death" (*A* 213).

It was "writing that at last came to my rescue," Frame testifies. "It is little wonder that I value writing as a way of life when it actually saved my life," she explains. "My mother had been persuaded to sign permission for me to undergo a leucotomy [lobotomy]" (*A* 221). Assured that such an operation would make her normal again, the helpless Janet was thoroughly spooked by the sight of her own name on a list of patients scheduled for brain surgery.

Frame's frontal lobes and creative mind won a miraculous reprieve when she was honored in 1951 with a literary prize, the Hubert Church Award, for her first book of short stories, *The Lagoon*. What, one wonders, would have happened if *The Lagoon* had not been published at the behest of John Forrest (a.k.a. John Money)? Or if the hospital head, Dr. Palmer, had failed to notice the announcement of Frame's celebrity in the newspaper? In that antediluvian age "before the use of drugs, leucotomy was becoming a 'convenience' treatment" (*A* 222)—a socially acceptable way to pacify the insane, to control the deviant, and to impose a zombielike normality on disruptive or anarchic individuals.[11]

Frame's *Autobiography* is in many ways comparable to Sylvia Plath's *Bell Jar*, as well as to Frances Farmer's powerful but lesser-known autobiography, *Will There Really Be a Morning?* Frame's own account of life in a mental institution is far more restrained than Farmer's and more circumspect than that of the American poet whose work she would later emulate. In the interest of psychological survival, Frame consigns the experience of madness to the borders of her autobiographical text. She erases unbearable scenes from both mind and written memory. Only the protective mask of fiction, donned in *Faces in the Water*, would liberate her testimony and give her permission to expose the horrors of institutional abuse.

Frame's autobiographical voice in *An Angel at My Table* tempers the terror and reduces it to a cerebral report of emotional desperation. The trauma of physical, emotional, and psychological torture, combined with virtual imprisonment, defies confessional articulation. Frame can speak passionately, but laconically, about the "two hundred applications of unmodified E.C.T. [electro-convulsive therapy]" that virtually shredded her memory and destroyed her self-confidence, until she considered herself a freak, "officially a non-person" (*A* 224). All the rest is judiciously consigned to silence.

Her autobiography offers a striking example of a double-voiced discourse, with the smooth, controlled, authoritative iterations of an adult narrator deliberately masking the mental chaos imposed on a younger self by institutional dehumanization. The author refuses to give utterance to feelings of hysteria, though symptoms of post-traumatic stress disorder are everywhere present on the margins of the text—repressed, muffled, mitigated, and contained. As narrator of her own life story, Frame valiantly battles with her purportedly deranged persona in order to assert aesthetic control over an earlier, fragmented, and inadmissible image of the self. That self-image is, of course, the schizophrenic subject virtually produced by the matrix of institutional discursive practices that reiterate a set of regulatory norms in a clinic that serves as both spiritual sanctuary and virtual prison. As Michel Foucault observes in *Discipline and Punish*, it is the "very materiality" of the institution of incarceration that functions "as an instrument and vector of Power" to objectivize the body of a patient or prisoner (30).

Within the confines of the clinic, Janet is socially constructed as a schizophrenic subject, an abject being whose behavior thrusts her into an ineffable "zone of uninhabitability," described by Judith Butler in *Bodies That Matter* as "the defining limit of the subject's domain" (3). This state of "disavowed abjection" functions as the delimiting outside of an exclusionary matrix that defines the boundaries of normative identity. As both Foucault and Butler make clear, the schizophrenic subject is not simply laden with a persona that can be shed as easily as a social mask. The abjected outsider—prisoner or patient—has been resubjectivized through incarceration and materialized in the body of a "stranger" to the earlier normative self. What the long journey from ostensible madness to social normality entails is not only a redefinition of the self, but a virtual reconstruction of the discursive subject denied power, agency, and individual autonomy.

When finally judged sane and released from the hospital, Janet finds herself so disoriented that she must undergo further psychotherapy in order to reverse the dire effects of an inaccurate diagnosis that reduced her to "being and feeling a nothing and nobody" (*A* 224). Tormented by persistent nightmares of incarceration, she feels naked and bereft. She has been suddenly stripped of the convenient cloak of schizophrenia that functioned as a sheltering cocoon—a medically constructed identity bordering on the poetic, valorizing her difference, and confirming her *in*difference to social conformity. Henceforth, the newly released survivor will have to search unaided for her "Is-Land," a peaceful sanctuary in a private, self-created microcosm. "I asked myself that old question, . . . why *was* the world? And where was my place?" (*A* 131).

This aspiring artist begins to find her unique location in the world of literature when she is finally "placed" as an author in someone else's esteem and shares, for the first time, a place at the table of a person who respects her—the writer Frank Sargeson, her mentor and guardian angel. A spiritual father, teacher, guru, and friend, Sargeson is the first man with whom Frame openly shares not only physical nourishment but a fertile space for conversation, care, advice, admiration, and mutual solicitude. With his gifts of a dilapidated army hut and endless concern, Sargeson dares to name Janet as a talented writer and, in offering her the confidence that the name bestows, serves as an initiator who bolsters her professional confidence.

Beginning a literary apprenticeship that forces her to sit at her typewriter and pound out repetitive, mantra-like phrases, Janet succeeds in completing and publishing her first novel, *Owls Do Cry*. Sargeson functions as beneficent patriarch, a representative of the symbolic order initially associated with the hermetic textual space of crossword puzzles and detective stories so jealously guarded by Janet's father. Frank proves to be an invaluable ally who loves the young girl's spirit and causes it to soar toward horizons of the aesthetic imagination. Janet detects, however, in his homosexual conversation, a misogyny that threatens her fragile sense of sexual self-esteem. "Frank talked kindly of men and of lesbian women, and I was neither" (*A* 250).

Suffering the lingering effects of post-traumatic stress disorder, Janet fails to cathect with her own body, which she dismisses as a bewildering "nothingness" (*A* 250). By her social marginality and idiosyncratic behavior, she dwells in a domain of abjection that her manic mind can envisage and her depressive moods embrace like a dream. Haunted by the memory of unbearable loss, and gifted with keen poetic sensibilities, Janet cannot identify with her corporeal presence in the world, the "nagging and perpetual 'withness' of [female] flesh" (*FW* 41). She defensively takes refuge in the in-between—in those interstitial psychic spaces between discourse and silence, dream and hallucination, madness and genius. Gender is a cultural performance that she is unable to master and, indeed, refuses to practice in reiterative gestures of normative behavior.

Her very real female body is, however, *not* nothing, as she discovers on her round-the-world odyssey through London and Paris to the paradisal island of Ibiza. This Spanish haven initially resembles a fairy-tale kingdom, with its "tideless ocean . . . creating a mirror city" (*A* 329). In Ibiza, Janet senses herself uncannily at home, as she enthusiastically contemplates the magical landscape of her future vocation: "I knew that whatever the outward phenomenon of light, city, and sea, the real mirror city lay within as the city of the imagination" (*A* 336); "as if, like the shadows in Plato's cave, our lives and the world contain mirror cities revealed to us by our imagination, the Envoy" (*A* 300).[12]

For Frame, the mirror proves to be a highly suggestive trope, with its long history of psychological and mythic symbolism. As Jenijoy La Belle reminds us, the "mirror image represents an otherness—an other-ing or splitting of the self—that can become a form of insanity called, loosely speaking, schizophrenia" (122). The Mirror City of Frame's imagination is constructed, in contrast, as a magical realm that reflects an artistic subject inscribed in romantic myths of wholeness and plenitude—an authorial self whose traumatic losses have been sutured by the act of autobiographical testimony that serves to integrate an alienated and fragmented consciousness doubly disempowered by grief and social ostracism. If the psychological trope for schizophrenia has always been the metaphorical representation of a cracked mirror, Janet embraces a mirror image of the shattered mirror in order to redefine and resubjectivize the shattered self damaged by institutional abuse.

Corporality remains a troubling source of undefined longing and sublimation, as the "tideless ocean" of her body begins to ripple with unacknowledged drives long repressed and swelling beneath the surface calm of the expatriate *escritora* who feels "as sexless as a block of wood" (*A* 343).[13] Her malaise suddenly gives way to amorous experimentation when she encounters Bernard, a narcissistic American poet eager to take advantage of the island's romantic ambiance. Though unprepared for the urgency of male libidinal desire, Janet struggles to realize clichéd fantasies of seduction drawn from *True Romance* magazines and makes a valiant effort to conceal her embarrassing inexperience. "Sexually but not technically a virgin" (*A* 347), she somehow manages convincingly to play the role of postcolonial femme fatale. Enacting an idealized scenario of erotic surrender, she couches her defloration in lyrical hyperbole, then revels in the sensations of lovemaking and flaunts her newly acquired reputation as a she-devil (*la diable*). Janet succeeds in satisfying a multitude of hungers, as she and Bernard decadently feast on French bread and tins of corned beef shipped to Spain by her solicitous Irish suitor, Patrick Reilly.

These adventures in Ibiza expand Frame's experience, but the price of sexual knowledge proves higher than anticipated. Like Anaïs Nin, this unwitting ingenue begins dimly to discern the perplexing mélange of pleasure and danger that haunts the subject-position of female corporality. Her feckless lover is free to return to "Spring in Ohio" (*A* 348), leaving Janet framed by the consequences of their impulsive encounter. Self-exiled to Andorra, she endures Bernard's absence as an emotional lacuna filtered through a naive awareness of unplanned pregnancy and ominous inklings of the social stigma attached to single parenthood at mid-century. Terrified and conflicted, the snowbound *escritora* knits booties, cavorts suicidally on precipitous mountain slopes, and wistfully swills a folkloric abortifacient, "increasingly fearful and pleased at [her] condition" (*A* 358).

Like Ursula Brangwen at the end of D. H. Lawrence's *The Rainbow*, Janet suffers a painful, but convenient miscarriage. While standing on a chair to change a lightbulb, she experiences a minor shock and dizzily collapses in a pool of uterine blood: "The blood was bulky. I collected it in a towel and flushed it down the lavatory, pulling the chain several times before it shredded (a quick horror-filled glance told me) and vanished" (*A* 358). It seems eerily symbolic that pregnancy-loss is precipitated by an electric shock—now an ostensible agent of mercy, in contrast to the 200 applications of electroconvulsive therapy administered by New Zealand medical officers. Janet reacts to her spontaneous abortion with profound emotional ambiguity. Though mourning the "lost path" of maternity, she welcomes an exhilarating sense of freedom at the "prospect of living a new life in Mirror City" (*A* 358).

Frame's brief sojourn in Andorra would seem picaresque in a novel, if not digressive. In the more fragmented context of autobiographical narrative, her Andorran adventure reiterates the problematic consequences of excruciating shyness and emotional malleability. Utterly passive, Janet tacitly condones the courtship of an Italian suitor, El Vici Mario, only to find herself swept up in a flurry of marriage plans—an impossible alliance fueled by the fires of poetic fantasy, as well as by the emotional anesthesia characteristic of post-traumatic stress disorder. "I felt myself under the spell of the Spanish and Italian faces . . . that belonged in the paintings of the masters who 'about suffering were never wrong'" (*A* 362). Though not in love with her Mediterranean suitor, Janet risks being trapped in a lyrical vision of agrarian domesticity, a picture of peasant life framed by the "old masters" celebrated in W. H. Auden's poem, *"Musée des Beaux Arts."* Never wrong in their portraits of human suffering, Auden's Renaissance maestros depict the stark isolation of individual tragedy. While Icarus drowns in the Hellespont, a tranquil farm laborer, oblivious of the young man's disaster, quietly perseveres in his tillage of the soil. Quotidian responsibility overshadows the horror of a failed artificer's legendary hubris.

Like Joyce's Stephen Dedalus, Janet eventually refuses the doomed role of the mythic Icarian aviator who flew too close to the sun. As she contemplates the seductive agrarian world of Auden's Tuscan painters, she knows that, realistically, marriage to El Vici Mario would thrust her into an alienating domestic environment "where the cherubs cried and wet their nappies" (*A* 362). Fortified by a redemptive egotism, she determines to flee the continent and return to the more familiar landscape of London. How, the young woman wonders, could she ever have considered marriage to a man who commits the unforgivable sin of wearing two-toned shoes—not to mention the couple's shocking misalliance of class, language, nationality, values, intelligence, and education? She determines, as a writer, to bear "triple witness, in silence, flames and immobility" (*A* 363). This idealistic pledge, which she attributes to Albert Camus, clearly echoes, but metaphorically modifies, the vows of "silence, exile, and cunning" sworn by Joyce's artist-hero in *A Portrait of the Artist as a Young Man* (247).

The future sought in Ibiza and Andorra is finally realized in London through Janet's accession to a newly valorized subject-position as artist and bona fide writer. Psychiatrists at the Maudsley Institute, after extensive tests and observation, reassure her that she has "never suffered from schizophrenia" and "should never have been admitted to a mental hospital." She is startled to realize that any "problems I now experienced were mostly a direct result of my stay in hospital" (*A* 375). When Janet is counseled by her therapist, Dr. R. H. Cawley, to write out the story of her traumatic incarceration in graphic detail, scriptotherapy finally releases her from persistent symptoms of post-traumatic stress disorder. Like Anaïs Nin before her, she realizes that the alternative to writing is the threat of madness—the abyss of "infantile" silence imposed by tongue-tying doubts that vitiate personal testimony. Only by bearing literary witness to a coherent and compelling life narrative can she resuscitate traumatic memories "to try to help [her] unearth [her]self" and inaugurate a cathartic ritual of healing: "I arrived at the point of knowing the agony of the luxury of trying to tell my story, of demanding and accepting the luxury of 'the truth'" (*A* 383).

Frame eventually finds an enabling discourse that allows her to reconstruct the trauma and to compensate for the "wastage of being other than [her]self" (*A* 383) by composing *Faces in the Water* in the exaggerated persona of Istina Mavet. This thinly veiled autofiction reiterates the psychic torment precipitated by years of institutional abuse. It seems ironic that the inaugural reviewers of Frame's compelling novel skeptically conflated author with protagonist. Stubbornly denying the book's authenticity, they insisted that a "woman who has been what this woman has been would never be able to remember and write about it in this way" (*A* 392).[14]

In exorcising the stigma associated with purportedly psychotic behavior, Frame dares to expose in her autofiction the cruelty and torture vividly recalled from her eight-year incarceration. *Faces in the Water* clearly participates in the genre that Doris Sommer defines as *testimonio*, with "an implied and often explicit 'plural subject.'" The author's "singularity achieves its identity as an extension of the collective" (107-8). Recalling the "memorable family" of fellow inmates portrayed in *Faces*, Frame testifies: "It was their sadness and courage and my desire to 'speak' for them that enabled me to survive" (*A* 221). Imbricating her novel in the "general text of struggle" against society's dehumanization of mental patients, Frame positions her fictional alter ego so that she "represents her group as a participant" (Sommer 129). "What I have described in Istina Mavet," Frame tells us, "is my sense of hopelessness as the months passed, my fear of having to endure that constant state of physical capture" (*A* 221). "The fiction of the book lies in the portrayal of the central character, based on my life but given largely fictional thoughts and feelings, to create a picture of the sickness I saw around me" (*A* 194).[15]

This semiautobiographical text is both testimonial and cathartic, though cautiously restrained as a "subdued rather than a sensational record" (*A* 387). In the interest of mimetic authenticity, Frame apparently felt obliged to dilute her rhetorical exposé in order to avoid the appearance of melodrama. And yet, *Faces in the Water* stands as a powerful and convincing testimonial to nightmarish medical practices in understaffed New Zealand mental hospitals at mid-century. According to Frame's report, patients were routinely neglected or forced to undergo horrific electroshock treatments administered as punishment for unacceptable behavior. *Faces in the Water* describes much of the degradation in shocking detail—the endless aural bombardment of screaming voices, the pain of sleep deprivation, the loss of physical privacy when bathing or using the toilet, the endurance of untreated wounds and festering sores, weekly hair-washings with kerosene, infestations of lice, and sadistic gladiatorial contests among patients forced to compete for sweets and treats. The list goes on and on, relentless in its assault on the reader's sensibilities.

Worst of all, perhaps, is Frame's heartrending description, based on her own experience, of solitary confinement in a bare, prison-like cell, where the character Istina is denied books, magazines, or writing paper, and resorts to scratching fragments of recollected poetry on the wall with a pencil stub, only to be supplied with a bucket of water and ordered to wash away these poignant spiritual inscriptions. "Deprived of my pencil, . . . I recited poems to myself or sang or, silent, remembered and feared" (*FW* 206-7). *Faces in the Water* is, indeed, a consciousness-raising text in the genre of *testimonio*.[16] At the end of the novel, Istina Mavet, in the persona of a narrator ostensibly whole, sane, and healed, recalls sardonically the warning formulated by a solicitous nurse: "[W]hen you leave hospital you must forget all you have ever seen, put it out of your mind completely as if it never happened." Istina challenges the naive admonition when she directly addresses the reader, whom she brashly implicates in the social apparatus of medical apathy: "And by what I have written in this document you will see, won't you, that I have obeyed her?" (*FW* 254).

After an eight-year detour in those bastions of mental conformity known as asylums for rebellious, fractious, or deviant elements of society, Janet Frame could at last envisage an imaginary Mirror City to ground her aesthetic location—a utopian mental geography inhabited by transformed specters of memory and dream. The experience of writing *Faces in the Water* proved a cathartic exercise in scriptotherapy that allowed her to defuse the power of haunting traumatic memories. "The only graveyard in Mirror City," Frame tells us, "is the graveyard of memories that are resurrected, reclothed with reflection and change, their essence untouched. (A truthful autobiography tries to record the essence. The renewal and change are part of the material of fiction)" (*A* 416).

At the end of Frame's *Autobiography*, the nascent fiction-writer sails back to New Zealand feeling released from the psychic fragmentation of post-traumatic stress disorder. She has completed a seven-year odyssey, each year of which symbolically compensates for one of those years of life lost to a mental institution. Like Odysseus, Janet returns nostalgically to her place of psychic origin, Willowglen. For this female artist-hero, however, no Penelope awaits—only the memories of a tragic antipodean childhood and the promise of new literary frontiers. Having come to terms with the trauma of sororal loss, as well as with the debilitating effects of prolonged incarceration, Frame describes herself as "a mapmaker for those who will follow nourished by this generation's layers of the dead" (*A* 415). Like Dante returning from the Inferno, she speculates that those who endure the hell of captivity in a mental asylum and manage to "return living to the world bring inevitably a unique point of view that is a nightmare, a treasure, and a lifelong possession" (*A* 213-14).

The ending of Frame's *Autobiography* is visionary and utopian, as Janet wistfully contemplates Dunedin transmogrified into a fantasmatic Mirror City. In adopting the metaphor of doubleness and reflection evoked by this magical urban landscape, she appropriates the image of schizophrenia as a trope for artistic creation.[17] Through the process of constructing her own crystal palace, she has established a *place* of embarkation for future aesthetic voyages: "It is Mirror City before my own eyes. And the Envoy waits" (*A* 435).[18]

In writing her autobiography, Frame sets out to reconstruct the authorial self as a speaking subject reintegrated through a narrative of trauma and healing that virtually deconstructs and reinterprets the schizophrenic identity earlier imposed by medical authorities. By adapting to her own use the romantic trope of an aesthetic mirror, she is able to reflect in her impassioned life narrative the diagnosis of schizophrenia as a site of resistance rather than of victimization. If Julia Kristeva is correct in suggesting in *Revolution in Poetic Language* that the schizophrenic subject is a failed poet overwhelmed by the semiotic and incapable of the thetic break necessary for instantiation into the symbolic register, then Frame takes refuge in the mirror image of schizophrenia as a reflection of the metaphorical mind capable of translating pain and suffering into poetic triumph. The trope of the mirror is no longer the cracked mirror emblematic of schizoid consciousness, but the mirror of an artistic imagination capable of restoring the necessary illusion of presence and plenitude to the fragmented historical subject. "Nothing was without its use," Frame testifies. "I had learned to be a citizen of the Mirror City" (*A* 405). By reconfiguring her clinical persona in the mode of empowered creativity, the author successfully refracts and rehumanizes the schizophrenic subject objectivized by the ideological state apparatus of modern medicine.[19]

Janet Frame's autobiography concludes on a note of promise and exultation. Has this riveting tale of "rememory" unfolded as fact or fabulation, a vision or a waking dream? Only the *magister ludi*, Janet Frame, knows for sure. "Writing an autobiography," she tells us, "usually thought of as a looking back, can just as well be a looking *across* or *through*, with the passing of time giving an X-ray quality to the eye" (*A* 191). The process of scriptotherapy successfully liberates the author/narrator from her tormented past, as she self-consciously escapes the prison of trauma through testimonial acts of narrative recovery. "I repeat that my writing saved me," Frame tells us, in a voice that reiterates the conviction that life-writing can function as a valuable defense against madness and despair (*A* 222). "If I could not live within the world of writing books, then where could I survive?" (*A* 217). And indeed, writing *did* rescue Janet Frame, in many senses of the word, and in more ways than either autobiography or autofiction can fully reveal.

FIVE

Audre Lorde's African-American Testimony

Within . . . the war we are all waging with the forces of death, . . . I am not only a casualty, I am also a warrior. (*SO* 41)

I. BIOMYTHOGRAPHY: *ZAMI: A NEW SPELLING OF MY NAME*

Audre Lorde describes her personal testimony *Zami: A New Spelling of My Name* as a "biomythography"—a deliberate amalgamation of autobiographical fact and mythically resonant fiction that locates her racial identity and self-identity in the context of a battle against racism, sexism, classism, and homophobia in America. The story of her own triumphant journey through this particular political, sexual, and cultural minefield is framed by the ideology of U.S. individualism thoroughly reenvisioned through a rich cultural heritage of African-American myth and oral history. "You might call Zami a novel," Lorde remarks in an interview with Claudia Tate, but then corrects this kind of reader response and relocates her hybrid text in the context of scriptotherapy: "I don't like to call it that. Writing *Zami* was a lifeline through the cancer experience. As I said in *The Cancer Journals*, I couldn't believe that what I was fighting I would fight alone and only for myself" (115-16).[1]

In Grenada, in Carriacou, "it is said that the desire to lie with other women is a drive from the mother's blood" (Z 256). In Lorde's biomythography, the plural lesbian identification "Zami" emerges as a sacred epithet, "*a Carriacou name for women who work together as friends and lovers*" (Z 255).[2] The author's picaresque journey through Harlem and Morningside Heights leads her back to Grenada and Carriacou to all those matriarchal figures of strength and empowerment who constitute a long bloodline of female wisdom. Her roots go back to the Caribbean and, ultimately, to Mother Africa, Afrekete, whose signifier is the lesbian body of Kitty, the last in a succession of lovers who emblazon emotional tattoos on the mind/body/heart of a half-blind Black lesbian poet searching for home in the sensuous bodies of women and the utopian spaces of a supportive female community. Audre Lorde insists that woman's rite of passage into adulthood is fraught with perils unknown to the masculine heart or body. She rebels against a phallocentric society, while turning her back on male-dominated and white-dominated culture, and refuses the lure of male identification. Proudly, she invokes puns and erotic metaphors to proclaim allegiance to a maternal/lesbian genealogy: "Images of women flaming like torches adorn and define the borders of my journey, stand like dykes between me and the chaos" (Z 3).

Squatting as a child enveloped by the flesh of her mother's voluptuous brown thighs, the young Audre learns to associate warmth and security with the nurturant pleasures of maternal corporality. In her childhood, "between your legs" is a euphemism for the female genitalia, the unmentionable nexus of that mysterious lower region (*l'oregion*) whose proper name the mother tongue cannot directly utter. Although woman's womb and vagina are both veiled in secrecy, the daughter reenters the sacred space of that lost maternal territory when she crouches between her mother's legs "inside of the anxiety/pain like a nutmeg nestled inside its covering of mace" (Z 33).

Returning to the womb of warmth, Audre imbibes her mother's secret language of feminine difference, a world of words that ushers her into a hidden realm of Caribbean mystery far removed from the blazing white sidewalks of our nation's capital, where phallic monuments celebrate those forefathers implicated in the making of a white America. Beneath a fatherland enveloped in Communist-hunting hysteria lies a subterranean memory of the motherland, the island of Grenada, with its geographical appendage Carriacou evoking a tribal memory of female Dahomey warriors brandishing militant spears. *L'oregion* reaches back and down and under to Ma Liz's older sister Anni who, remembering the "root-truths taught her by their mother, Ma-Mariah," acted as midwife for each of her sister Ma-Liz's seven daughters. "My mother Linda," says the narrator, "was born between the waiting palms of her loving hands" (Z 13) in a tropical land of palm trees and gynocentric spaces.[3]

In a chapter entitled "How I Became a Poet," the author describes herself as a child imbibing from Linda Belmar Lorde a metaphoric mother tongue couched in mysterious utterances like "next kin to nothing," "from Hog to Kick 'em Jenny," "smack on the backass," "bamsy," "bam-bam," "zandalee" and "cro-bo-so" (Z 32).[4] *"I am a reflection of my mother's secret poetry,"* she confesses, *"as well as of her hidden angers"* (Z 32). The Caribbean emigrant mother unwittingly invokes the semiotic language of female utterance—the lilting rhythms of lyrical echolalias resonating across oceans and over centuries of Afro-Caribbean tradition. "My mother had a special and secret relationship with words," Audre declares in *Zami* (31). It is a dialogic relationship with Kristeva's semiotic *chora* that "precedes and underlies figuration and thus specularization, and is analogous only to vocal and kinetic rhythm" (*KR* 93-94).[5]

"Sight is very important to me," Lorde explains to Karla Hammond in a 1981 interview. "I was born almost blind" (24). "I did not speak until I was four" (Z 31). And when she did begin to master linguistic utterance, the young Audre would respond to questions by reciting poems that seemed to encapsulate the feelings she wanted to express. "I had this long fund of poetry in my head," she recalls. "I really do believe I learned this from my mother" (*SO* 82-83). "I used to get stoned on poetry when I was a kid. When life got just too difficult for me, I could always retreat into those words. . . . So poetry is very important to me in terms of survival" (Hammond 1981, 19).

In *Zami*, Linda Lorde introduces her nearsighted daughter to the magical world of lyrical language, an auditory mode of perception that cracks open the prison of shadowy confusion entrapping the myopic child. Linda's maternal body proves to be a sensuous storehouse of palpable pleasure, a narcissistic territory of exotic/erotic free play and delight. A prepubescent Audre sinks into the sheltering protuberance of her mother's "large soft breasts," breathes the perfume of a "glycerine-flannel smell," and tumbles toward the "rounded swell of her stomach, silent and inviting" (Z 33). The maternal body provides a rich cornucopia of nurturance and satisfaction reverberating with rhythmic reassurance and sweet, milky odors. Infantile desire is displaced onto the amniotic sac(k) symbolized by a "liquid-filled water bottle" that extends the "firm giving softness" of her mother's fleshy folds (Z 33). Audre nuzzles against Linda's comforting physical presence in a preoedipal moment of peace, protection, and utter tranquility.[6]

The imaginary pleasures of this mother-daughter liaison offer a brief respite from pain and oppression, but filial bliss proves rare and fleeting indeed. Slow to speak, the observant Audre carefully weighs the power of words and becomes keenly aware of linguistic nuance. She feels perplexed by her light-skinned mother's conspiratorial silences and apparent adaptation to white racism. Linda Lorde simply ignores the crude aggression of New York pedestrians spitting at her daughter and complains of their insouciant spitting into the wind, just as she pretends to remain oblivious of a white woman's cringing disdain in a crowded subway car. "So of course as a child," says Lorde, "I decided there must be something terribly wrong with me that inspired such contempt" (*SO* 146). Linda refuses ever to discuss the political ramifications of integumental differences among African-Americans in general and her own family members in particular. Confused about U.S. constructions of racial identity on an arbitrary continuum of skin color and negroid features, Audre fiercely rebels against her mother's self-effacing strategies, as well as the presumption that the dark-skinned daughter would "eventually be forged into some pain-resistant replica of herself" (*Z* 101).[7]

Lorde summarizes her ambivalent relationship with her mother in the essay "Eye to Eye": "My light-skinned mother kept me alive within an environment where my life was not a high priority. She used whatever methods she had at hand. . . . She never talked about color. . . . And she disarmed me with her silences. . . . Her silences also taught me isolation, fury, mistrust, self-rejection, and sadness" (*SO* 149). Though acknowledging Linda's circumspect survival strategies as possibly the "greatest gift of love," Audre continues to mourn the disastrous consequences of racial self-effacement: "[M]y mother taught me to survive at the same time as she taught me to fear my own Blackness" (*SO* 165).

Lorde's powerful poem "From the House of Yemanjá," published in *The Black Unicorn*, is a lyrical protest directed against a pale and inscrutable maternal figure, whose socially inscribed hunger forces her to cook her daughters in a cultural melting pot until they scream with pain from the tortures of assimilation. Such ambiguous mentoring in the face of racial bigotry molds the helpless girls into amorphous pseudo-American subjects doomed to demeaning scripts of ethnic self-hatred. In "Story Books on a Kitchen Table," Lorde angrily indicts her mother's pragmatic deceits. But in "Black Mother Woman," she adopts a more compassionate stance and begins to chart her own self-definition filtered through parental denials. Torn asunder by rebellious fury, the daughter nonetheless develops as a dark sanctuary for her mother's repressed but restless spirit. Describing her mother's love as "terrible" and "blind" in the *Black Unicorn* poem "Outside," Lorde explains to Karla Hammond in a 1980 interview: "Certainly I didn't recognize it as love for many, many years. . . . But it was that distorted love that kept me alive" (18). In fierce defiance of cultural accommodation, an adolescent Audre rejects Black bourgeois dissimulations that "flow into rainbows and nooses" (*Z* 58). In defiance of her mother's counsel, Lorde tells us, "I grew Black as my need for life, . . . Black as *Seboulisa*" (*Z* 58).[8]

If Afrocentric integrity and appreciation of her dark-skinned identity is the teleological end of Lorde's bildungsroman, her journey toward political agency requires a long initiation. The author recalls endlessly "scrubbing with lemon juice in the cracks and crevices of [her] ripening, darkening, body" in humiliating beauty rituals aimed at integumental bleaching. At school, Audre is assaulted by wily black "hands, punching, rubbing, pinching, pulling at [her] dress" and degrading epithets that brand her an "ugly yaller bitch" (*SO* 149). But sexual harassment is not limited to infuriating pinches and juvenile catcalls. At the age of ten, Audre is raped by a bully who threatens to smash her glasses if she refuses to cooperate with his sexual experiment. Penetration of her developing genitalia by the boy's pencil-thin penis seems an inexplicable annoyance to the bewildered girl. The disturbing incident gives rise to obscure but overwhelming anxieties associated with surreptitious coition: "I knew only that being pregnant had something to do with sex, and sex . . . was in general nasty" (*Z* 75).

Aware of the mechanics of copulation, but ignorant of the fertility cycles that regulate female physiology, Audre tries to puzzle out the inscrutable "relationship between penises and getting pregnant" by fervid research in the library's closed stacks. For four years, she suffers unnecessary dread of conception and feels convinced that her menarche has been delayed by the forced sexual encounter she never dared report. Until the onset of menstruation, she tries to sort out fragmentary shards of knowledge about sex and the body and agonizes all the while over the possibility of incipient gestation. When her first menstrual period finally occurs, the event is cause for both relief and celebration. As she sensuously pounds garlic for West Indian *souse*, the menstruating girl feels a profound connection with "the molten core of [her] body whose source emanated from a new ripe fullness" allied with a "tiding ocean of blood" proffering "strength and information" (*Z* 78). Audre's menarche releases a flood of newfound knowledge and forges a semimystical bond with a maternal genealogy that leads back to rites of empowerment associated with African *Orisha* transported to the new world.[9]

In stark contrast to the exhilaration of implicit maturity, Audre is helplessly forced to witness the degradation of her girlfriend Gennie, an alter ego whose psychic pain and domestic misery only rise to the surface, half-recognized, when couched in threats of suicide. Gennie loves, plays, and constructs her gender identity through carnivalesque masquerades on the expansive stage of New York City. One day a prostitute and a big city hotshot, the next day a worker singing union songs in the back of a crowded urban bus, she experiments with a variety of female identities until all her fantasized roles have been exhausted. The one role that she cannot find strength to play is that of a battered and abused daughter, with an alcoholic father who is guilty of unmentionable atrocities that drive her to homelessness and a "final solution" in gelatin capsules of rat poison. Woman's body, tortured and exploited, is symbolically articulated to the carcass of vermin haunting the tenements of a Harlem housing division.

Without sanctuary, Gennie roams the streets and sleeps on the subway. Thoroughly depleted of energy and resources, she finally seeks respite in a desperate act of self-destruction.

Gennie emerges in this text as a scapegoat who dwells in the "exclusionary matrix" of abjection described by Judith Butler in *Bodies That Matter* as the unlivable, uninhabitable boundary that constitutes "the defining limit of the subject's domain," the "site of dreaded identification against which—and by virtue of which—the domain of the subject will circumscribe its own claim to autonomy and to life" (3). Without a social network of familial support, Gennie is consigned to the corrosive category of homeless renegade. She is perceived as an unwelcome alien whose presence in society is so uncanny as to be unthinkable. Like the sewer rats who scavenge human waste products in a decaying urban environment, she herself is a de-sexed body cast off from the communal security of a protective oedipal matrix (Daddy, Mommy, Me). Locked in the frustrations of adolescent impotence, Audre cannot offer her friend refuge or even provide shelter for the night. Gennie is forced to seek comfort in the darkest shelter of all—the Earth Mother awaiting a troubled teenaged daughter. Like a Black Ophelia, whose tortured filial love signals her demise, the abused daughter is denied Catholic burial in sanctified ground: "*No hallowed ground for suicides. The sound of weeping women*" (*Z* 103).

The tragic loss of the first woman that she has ever loved has a shattering impact on Audre's developing consciousness. Gennie's death is the occasion for the first poem the author records in *Zami*—an elegy mourning the senseless annihilation of this victimized alter ego drowned in a whirlpool of societal indifference. Like Janet Frame after the death of her sister Myrtle, the bereft Audre retreats into a self-protective shell of emotional isolation and vows to eschew the risk of future abandonment. She resolves "*never [to] love anybody else again for the rest of [her] life*" (*Z* 141).

During an anxious adolescence, Audre precariously constructs a marginal subject-position on the boundaries of a sex-gender system that refuses to acknowledge the place of lesbianism or bisexuality in a conservative heterosexual economy. She swings tentatively between the fragile positions of subject and ab-ject, eschewing subjection by others despite powerful pressures toward conformity. "I moved in a fen of unexplained anger that encircled me and spilled out against whomever was closest that shared those hated selves" (*SO* 150). Forced to endure a situation of embattled domestic turbulence punctuated by nightmares and nosebleeds, the young girl finally terminates her prolonged emotional misery by a rebellious flight from home and family. "I made an adolescent's wild and powerful commitment to battling in my own full eye" (*Z* 104), she tells us. Luckily, she comes from a long line of survivors: *"Their shapes join Linda and Gran'Ma Liz and Gran'Aunt Anni in my dreaming, where they dance with swords in their hands"* (Z 104)

At seventeen, Audre defiantly takes a white male lover, only to find heterosexual intercourse wildly disappointing: "Sex seemed pretty dismal and frightening and a little demeaning" (Z 104). Abandoned and pregnant on the eve of her eighteenth birthday, the isolated Black teenager seeks a "homemade abortion" that threatens both life and sanity. Her graphic description of a miscarriage induced by Foley catheter relates a stoic narrative of excruciating pain and the shocking loss of bodily integrity, as a hard rubber tube is forcibly introduced into the young woman's uterus, without benefit of anesthetic. The catheter, a "cruel benefactor," lies coiled like a serpent in the womb of a guilty Eve, ready to spring and release her from unwanted pregnancy by its invidious and potentially fatal bite. Audre impassively describes how the tube's "angular turns ruptured the bloody lining and began the uterine contractions" (Z 109). Hemorrhaging her way through severe psychological shock, she survives the initial trauma of this makeshift surgery, then tries to heal spiritually through exercises in scriptotherapy that result in "strange poems of death, destruction, and deep despair." Dysphoria is virtually displaced onto lyrical personae that shelter the fragmented subject. Emotionally anesthetized by her frightening ordeal, Lorde confesses: "Writing was the only thing that made me feel like I was alive" (Z 118). As a Black lesbian ex-Catholic, numbed and disoriented, the nascent poet composes anguished, melodramatic verses in which she identifies with the crucified and resurrected Christ.

Through a long series of trying initiations, Audre does indeed rise as both warrior and survivor. She endures every kind of racial, sexual, and class oppression, including mind-deadening and soul-destroying labor on an assembly line in Stamford, Connecticut, where the unprotected use of an X-ray machine possibly contributes to the cancers of breast and liver that would eventually kill her. "Nobody mentioned that carbon tet destroys the liver and causes cancer of the kidneys" (Z 126). As always, Lorde's greatest enemy is the infamous "nobody" of American political life, the absent phantom of a white hegemony whose purity is never questioned and whose capitalistic irresponsibility is rarely challenged.

Audre feels rejuvenated by the experience of coming out gay with a woman lover whose body is gorgeously fat, *"like the Venus of Willendorf"* (Z 136). An adorable art object, scrumptiously seductive, the spicy Ginger resurrects the crucified Christ in a mythic epiphany of lesbian pleasure. Describing her erotic baptism, Audre declares: "Uncertainty and doubt rolled away from the mouth of my wanting like a great stone" (Z 139). This exuberant sexual conversion is paradoxically couched in Eurocentric Christian symbolism.

The displaced stone evokes resonances of Easter, and the "rich myrrh-taste" of the lover's body suggests the Oriental gifts offered to a newborn Christ child. This religious experience of mutual exploration and sensual discovery bears an aura of spiritual beatitude: "Loving Ginger that night was like coming home to a joy I was meant for" (Z 139). The lesbian lover is an erotic replication of the lost maternal territory nostalgically grieved for and forever sought in the inaccessible imaginary. Lovemaking proves a paradisal return to infantile spaces of bodily pleasure, the realm of longing and lost satiety that haunts the sexual and textual unconscious of *Zami*.[10] The erotic, Lorde passionately proclaims in *Sister Outsider*, "is the nurturer or nursemaid of all our deepest knowledge" (56). It "is a measure between the beginnings of our sense of self and the chaos of our strongest feelings. It is an internal sense to which, once we have experienced it, we know we can aspire" (54).

After her affair with Ginger has come to an end, Audre sets out on a picaresque journey in search of the mysterious erotic knowledge that will enlighten and empower her. She travels south to Mexico where, in the figure of the tough, enigmatic Eudora, a middle-aged Amazonian alcoholic, she encounters a woman who makes love in a way that introduces her, for the first time, to the orgasmic delight of reciprocal sexual pleasure. The single-breasted survivor of a radical mastectomy, Eudora will serve as a role model far beyond her ken, as this tale of adolescent affiliation is recounted by an adult Lorde battling for courage after a life-threatening bout with breast cancer. From Eudora she learns an invaluable lesson: "*Waste nothing, . . . not even pain*" (Z 236). The author of *Zami* is clearly in dialogue with her younger self, as well as with the capitalist patriarchy responsible for her physical and psychological wounds.[11]

In the gay girl community of Greenwich Village in the 1950s, Audre can find "no mothers, no sisters, no heroes. We had to do it alone, like our sister Amazons" (Z 176). In Muriel, an Italian schizophrenic poet who has apparently bounced back from mental breakdown, Audre sees a figure of the repressed poet-self she would like to be—an alter ego and sister/outsider whose symbolic triumph over adversity evinces Lorde's own sense of maternal solicitude. Once again, the author employs dialogic, myth-making strategies when she uses Christian imagery to depict lovemaking with Muriel as a pentecostal event, "from which she rose to me like a flame" (Z 194). Muriel, however, complains that electroshock therapy has violently extinguished the warmth and luminosity of her "own little flame" (Z 200), and she has been left alone to combat the circumambient dark.

Despite the exhilaration involved in love, commitment, and the joys of a year's cohabitation, Audre knows that she cannot indefinitely try to rescue her beloved from the jaws of chaos and a lapse into asphyxiating psychosis. When Muriel flaunts her sexual infidelity, it is Audre who reacts with gestures of masochistic self-mutilation, turning rage inward and releasing poisonous feelings of jealousy by scalding her hand with a torrent of boiling water—a grotesque baptism mimicking devastations by fire and flood. The adult author seems to allude to the seven plagues suffered by Pharoah in a Mosaic act of messianic vengeance when she describes her doomed relationship with Muriel in terms of "venom and recriminations" metaphorically vomited "like wild frogs" (Z 235).

In an extraordinary epiphanic moment, Audre realizes that it is truly time to leave, to embark on a new spelling of her name to the tune of a Negro spiritual that invokes a glorified and transcendent Christ in the lyrical reiteration, "ain't gonna die no more!" (Z 239). As AnaLouise Keating suggests, it is at this point that Audre "strips away the false labels and acquires a sense of agency," and "an important part of this process is the protagonist's 'new naming'" (162). Chaos, after all, can give birth to a flood of creative energy, and Audre now feels ready to confront the maelstrom of her own psychological turbulence. As Lorde observes in *Sister Outsider*, "The very word *erotic* comes from the Greek word *eros*, the personification of love in all its aspects—born of Chaos, and personifying creative power and harmony" (55).

It is, finally, the semimythic figure of Kitty/Afrekete who teaches Audre/Zami the empowering mythos of African and Caribbean roots, puts her in touch with the androgynous goddess MawuLisa, and brings her back to those sacred maternal spaces first recognized in the warm, strong body of Linda, a Caribbean exile stranded in the perplexing environment of a new and unfamiliar world.[12] Like Audre's mother, Kitty shops for tropical fruits under the bridge in Harlem and introduces the author to the sumptuous delights of a feminine/feminist lesbian feast that both nurtures and empowers. Anointing the body of the beloved with the juice of a ripe avocado, Audre rhythmically massages the thighs and breasts of Afrekete and slowly licks the oil from her lover's body in a ritual of amorous delight.

Virtually eating the Mother/Nature-Goddess, Audre/Zami breaks down the barriers that separate mother and daughter, humankind and nature, Demeter and Persephone, child and MawuLisa, male and female, East and West, body and spirit. In this erotic initiation, Audre bursts forth like a ripe fruit burgeoning with a seed kernel that will take root and flower in the glory of creative communion with a partner who exudes hermaphroditic energies reminiscent of the African *Orisha*.[13] A "goddess pear" releases its nourishing juices in a ritualistic ex-semination of symbolic "cum" on the coconut-brown body of the androgynous lover/beloved. "A woman celebrating the eucharist with her mother," observes Luce Irigaray, "sharing with her the fruits of the earth she/they have blessed, could be delivered of all hatred or ingratitude towards her maternal genealogy, could be consecrated in her identity" (*IR* 46).

This moment of cum/munal feasting revises and reverses the text's earlier horrific tale of vicious infanticide and familial cannibalism, voiced by Gennie's downtrodden stepmother Ella: "Momma kilt me/ Poppa et me/ Po' lil' brudder/ suck ma bones" (Z 251).[14] Ella's lugubrious ballad, a distorted version of "The Almond Tree" story in *Grimms' Fairy Tales*, is creatively transformed by the lesbian role-reversal implicit in Audre's tonguework on the apotheosized body of Kitty/Afrekete.[15] Taking strength and nourishment from the transubstantiated body of Mother Africa, Audre plays "Poppa" to her prostrate lover and celebrates a paradoxically sanctified Black Mass on the altar of a newly deified Mother/Goddess who simultaneously nurtures and enables the daughter of her dreams. "And now I think the goddess was speaking through Ella also" (Z 251). In a final orison, she prays: "*Afrekete ride me to the crossroads where we shall sleep, coated in the woman's power*" (Z 252).

Throughout Lorde's biomythography, the body of the mother has been hypostasized and reified as an object of filial cathexis. At the conclusion of *Zami*, Audre speaks a new lyrical language reiterated through the sexualized body of Mother Africa engendered female and fetishistically available for worshipful adoration, in contrast to and in sacrilegious replacement of the body of Christ transubstantiated in the Eucharist. This poetic sacrament of lesbian *jouissance* mimetically reenacts and subverts the Catholic sacrifice of the Mass, as Audre's lifelong search for mystical union with a (m)other/ lover explodes in semiotic rapture. More than a seductive object of sexual pleasure, Kitty is mythically transformed into the transcendent Afrekete, the expansive maternal territory that nurtures a hungry daughter and initiates her into a genealogy of female heroes stretching back to the Dahomey warriors of Africa. Lorde invokes a love between lesbian sisters/daughters/ mothers whose lips, both vocative and vulval, speak together in a feminine chorus of exultation. This reconfiguration of lesbian Eros "binds the remotest past to the most distant future, and this is why the semi-mythical Afrekete is so important as self-projection. Myth is the fictional construct that frames past, present, and future selves in *Zami*" (Chinosole 384).

If the Grimm brothers have inscribed the myth of female sadomasochism into the Eurocentric imagination, the liberated lesbian poet can defy white male hegemonic discourse by mimicking and revising the tragic fairytale script imprinted on western consciousness. Although the ideological state apparatuses of the family dictate a patriarchal drama that murders the female subject and abjects her skeletal remains to be cannibalized by the father and brother who survive her, Lorde will defiantly parody this lugubrious scenario and offer a carnivalized version of the oedipal tale. Refusing any longer to be a victim of racism or homophobia, she reconstructs the subject-position of her autobiographical persona by ignoring phallocratic social organization and re-creating a gynocentric and Afrocentric space of survival in the heart of white heterosexist society. Heroically re-membering the contradictory "*pieces of myself*" dispersed through traumatic fragmentation, Audre/Zami emerges from her narrative of personal and artistic development "blackened and whole," triumphantly "*Becoming/ Afrekete*" (*Z* 5). In "Eye to Eye," she declares: "We are African women and we know, in our blood's telling, the tenderness with which our foremothers held each other. It is that connection which we are seeking" (*SO* 152).

Lorde's own biographical experiences of marriage and motherhood have been symbolically erased from this therapeutic tale, though later essays in *Sister Outsider* and *A Burst of Light* will specifically address issues of lesbian parenting that she and her partner Frances confronted in the rearing of Lorde's son and daughter. In *Zami*, the author self-consciously narrows her focus to the story of revitalized lesbian subjectivity and to her racial, social, and psychological empowerment through the aegis of passionate women "pushing [her] into the merciless sun" (*Z* 5). The oedipal family romance proves irrelevant to Lorde's dream of feminist sisterhood, as she boldly challenges the phallic Same and dismantles its homologies.[16] Lorde designs her discourse of desire in terms of an erotic replication of preoedipal bonding in loving relationships with other women. The Grimm script of female sadomasochism and homicide will not apply to her—not, at least, in the utopian spaces of *Zami*.[17]

II. AUTOPATHOGRAPHY: *THE CANCER JOURNALS* AND *A BURST OF LIGHT*

Perhaps the aporia, the substratum of Lorde's poignant biomythography, is the shadow of a "prequel" written in a different genre—*The Cancer Journals*, a confessional text of autopathography that confronts capitalism and its perpetrators, along with the destructive ideologies purveyed by the corporate beauty complex, to dismantle the master's house with none but the poet's tools—honesty, compassion, and clarity of vision. Here the Grimm prophecy of Ella's chant materializes in a ghastly illness that *Zami* traces back to the nightmare of alienated labor. Lorde's naive adolescent narrator, assaulted by carbon tetrachloride and X-rays, remains oblivious of the perils that would eventually lead to cancer and mastectomy. The diary/memoir published as *The Cancer Journals* provides, in contrast, a stark confrontation with illness, physical mutilation, and the specter of mortality. Lorde insists that even a "life-threatening cancer and the trauma of mastectomy can be integrated into the life-force as knowledge and eventual strength" (*CJ* 63).[18]

In response to the terrible ordeal precipitated by breast cancer, Lorde composes two concurrent but entirely different autobiographical texts: *The Cancer Journals*, which function as an immediate chronicle of the pain, humiliation, rage, and horror erupting from a severe and life-threatening illness; and *Zami*, a retrospective narrative that recounts the struggles of childhood and adolescence refracted through a mature vision of trauma and bodily injury. *"I must let this pain flow through me and pass on,"* Lorde proclaims. *"If I resist or try to stop it, it will detonate inside me, shatter me. . . . There must be some way to integrate death into living"* (*CJ* 12-13).

The vehicle of integration and narrative recovery turns out to be *Zami*, an autobiographical text framed by the poignant revelations of Lorde's *Cancer Journals*. The journals constitute a docudrama of destabilizing illness, a photographic reproduction of searing physical and psychological pain orchestrated by a deadly serious philosophical inquiry into issues of race, class, gender, and bodily integrity. *The Cancer Journals* bear passionate witness to Lorde's fierce battle against disease and its societal construction. As Thomas Couser explains in *Recovering Bodies*, authors "who narrate their illness . . . share their bodies with others in a kind of secular healing ritual" (293).

In contrast to *The Cancer Journals*, *Zami* paints a wry portrait of childhood and adolescence in a bildungsroman shaped by the teleology of self-invention. "Growing up Fat Black Female and almost blind in america," Lorde declares, "requires so much surviving that you have to learn from it or die. Gennie, rest in peace. I carry tattooed upon my heart a list of names of women who did not survive" (*CJ* 40). Both *Zami* and *The Cancer Journals* are powerful inscriptions in the genre of *testimonio*. Lorde graphically records in *The Cancer Journals* the agonizing pain of mastectomy, as well as the inevitable intimations of mortality evinced by breast cancer. "Sometimes fear stalks me like another malignancy," she confesses. "I am learning to live beyond fear by living through it" (*CJ* 15). In contrast to the "European view . . . of living in terms of crisis," Lorde embraces what she interprets as an "African view which is one of saying 'This is a situation to experience. What can I learn?' So change becomes something that is integral" (Hammond 1980, 20).[19]

"The pain of separation from my breast," Lorde testifies, "was at least as sharp as the pain of separating from my mother" (*CJ* 25-26). Yet her first reaction to physical mutilation is characterized by traumatic constriction, a psychic numbing that mitigates the shock of symbolic castration: "I had no real emotional contact yet with the reality of the loss; it was as if I had been emotionally anesthetized" (*CJ* 37). This trancelike indifference, prolonged by the machinations of an infantilizing medical establishment, leaves the trauma victim swirling in a miasma of "psychic mush" (*CJ* 46). The challenging alternative, Lorde realizes, is "to begin feeling, dealing, not only with the results of the amputation, . . . but also with . . . the demands and changes inside of me and my life" (*CJ* 46).

Lorde brashly refuses to wear a prosthesis because such a false simulacrum reduces mastectomy to a cosmetic deficit. She feels that the social mask of prosthetic compensation prevents women from directly confronting the pain of loss, as well as from tapping into their own hidden resources. Social programming and consumer brainwashing contribute to a debilitating conspiracy of silence: "We are surrounded by media images portraying women as essentially decorative machines of consumer function, constantly doing battle with rampant decay" (*CJ* 64). Lorde determines to take a bolder, more dignified and creative stance: *"In some way I must aerate this grief . . . to lend it some proportion"* (*CJ* 52). "Declining to wear a prosthesis and . . . refusing to closet her postsurgical body," she "performs elective reconstructive surgery on her self—not her body—using her pen" (Couser 53).

The bereft poet, feeling like a pariah suffering the "very unreal and lonely" liminality of an "untouchable" (*CJ* 49), takes refuge from overwhelming loss by embarking on a calculated exercise in scriptotherapy—a graphic and detailed reiteration of earlier traumatic experiences that threatened to kill her but strengthened her instead. If the protagonist of *Zami* could successfully triumph over childhood rape and an abortionist's butchery, then the adult author can surely draw on a lifetime of lessons in survival to conquer a life-threatening disease. Lorde declares: "I had felt so utterly stripped at other times within my life for very different reasons, and survived, so much more alone than I was now" (*CJ* 40). She recalls, once again, her emotional desolation the summer after her friend Genevieve committed suicide.

In *Zami*, Lorde re-invents herself as a Black feminist hero, valiantly transcending the cultural vicissitudes of poverty, racial alienation, and sexual confusion. A younger Audre emerges as the Amazonian protagonist of a therapeutic narrative that empowers its author even in its making. As Lorde testifies, writing *Zami* proved to be a source of spiritual sustenance in the wake of her struggle with cancer—a way to work through and work out the traumatic events of her youth in order to cultivate an irrepressible energy and a will to live, create, love, and teach. By delineating her adolescent self as a developing subject strengthened by a growing Afrocentric consciousness and the discovery of lesbian sisterhood, Lorde could further enable her mature self to rage against the extinction of vitality and to challenge the physical, sexual, and personal devaluation imposed by a racist and homophobic culture. Scriptotherapy, she implies, "is an important function of the telling of experience. I am also writing to sort out for myself who I was" (*CJ* 53). In her journal entry of January 20, 1980, Lorde celebrates the completion of *Zami* and proclaims its value as a lifeline through the cancer experience: *"The novel is finished at last. . . . . My work kept me alive this past year, my work and the love of women. . . . In the recognition of the existence of love lies the answer to despair"* (*CJ* 13).

In *The Cancer Journals*, an African-American poet/survivor joins hands with her suffering sisters in defiance of the greed and lies purveyed by corporate America. She insists that "women with breast cancer are warriors, also. I have been to war, and still am" (*CJ* 60). As Couser observes, "Lorde embraces the trope of war; she takes pride in identifying her one-breasted self as an Amazon warrior, and she chooses to define her scar as a badge of honor" (52).[20] Having given literary birth to a younger Audre as Zami/Afrekete, this single-breasted warrior emerges from physiological trauma emotionally euphoric and spiritually whole. At the end of her extraordinary memoir, Lorde stands like an Afro-Amazonian chieftain, showing us her wounds with the pride of a Dahomey soldier after an arduous battle, the outcome of which must necessarily remain indeterminate. For the time being, however, she feels exultant, *"like another woman, de-chrysalised"* (*CJ* 14). Vowing that "either I would love my body one-breasted now, or remain forever alien to myself" (*CJ* 44), Lorde reiterates the paradoxical truth that "in the process of losing a breast I had become a more whole person" (*CJ* 55). She emerges heroic in the ongoing "war against the tyrannies of silence" and the ubiquitous "forces of death" (*CJ* 20-21).[21]

As Anne Hunsaker Hawkins explains, the "myth of rebirth, which is central to autobiographies about conversion, is also the organizing construct for a good many pathographies" that "focus on extraordinary or traumatic experience" (33).

> The subject of these books is a kind of experience that is so painful, destructive, and disorienting that it results in a counterimpulse toward creation and order, . . . a reparative process that deals with trauma by imagination and interpretation. . . .
>
> Pathography can be seen as *re*-formulation of the experience of illness: . . . it gathers together the separate meanings, the moments of illumination and understanding, the cycles of hope and despair, and weaves them into a whole fabric. (24-25)

If *Zami* is a text that celebrates the recovery of Audre Lorde's childhood and adolescent selves, and *The Cancer Journals* delineate her self-conscious battle with breast cancer and recovery from mastectomy, *A Burst of Light*, her last published prose work, embarks on an entirely different experiment in autopathography. Having worked through the fear, terror, pain and humiliation of surgical mastectomy, Lorde now faces a more powerful enemy in the form of metastasized liver cancer. She testifies: *"On February 1st, two weeks before my fiftieth birthday, I was told by my doctor that I had liver cancer, metastasized from the breast cancer for which I had had a mastectomy six years before. . . . The struggle with cancer now informs all my days, but it is only another face of that continuing battle for self-determination and survival that Black women fight daily, often in triumph"* (*BL* 49).

If earlier traumatic experiences were articulated as wounds that cried out for healing, the ravages of liver cancer evoke an ongoing trauma—a physiological and psychic wound that cannot be healed, but whose assault must perpetually be contested. In contrast to earlier examples of scriptotherapy, *A Burst of Light* is a text whose very production constitutes the provisional triumph of a woman warrior whose spirit refuses to be quelled. The act of journal-writing enriches its author with "a sense of outrageous beauty and strength of purpose." Lorde tells us: "One reason I watch the death process so acutely is to rob it of some of its power" (*BL* 121). By consciously anatomizing the trauma that attends terminal illness, she can assert authorial control over physiological catastrophe. Meticulously describing her suffering, as well as her heightened consciousness, Lorde constructs an empowered subject-position and asserts its agency against the threat of imminent breakdown. Autobiographical writing in the face of impending disintegration reintegrates the various selves dispersed and beleaguered by illness and focuses personal creativity on the artistic management of depersonalization. If cancer threatens to rob the subject of its unique individuality, then scriptotherapy can create a temporary bulwark against the onslaught of debilitating disease.[22]

The trauma victim cannot, in this case, establish a position of safety in the interest of self-recuperation. Instead, she must continue writing as a way of fighting for her life, binding up wounds to body and spirit even as they invade the territory of consciousness and threaten to consume her sense of self. Lorde observes that "living fully means living with maximum access to my experience and power, loving, and doing work in which I believe" (*BL* 130). *"I work, I love, I rest, I see and learn. And I report"* (*BL* 134). And in the act of reporting, she valiantly challenges *"a physiologically engendered despair"* (*BL* 131).[23]

Lorde's "burst of light" metaphorically alludes to a meteoric intensity of the spirit, a sudden brilliant explosion of creativity that insists on celebrating the experience of living in the face of dying, on cherishing each moment of love and creativity that can somehow be rescued from the jaws of inevitable mortality. Lorde constantly articulates her position as a Black lesbian feminist in the context of all the various struggles, both personal and political, that demand her attention and focus her energies. Conquering her fear, she launches an ambitious battle against disease, political injustice, racism, class privilege, and homophobia. The strategies she masters in this fight for life provide "important prototypes for doing battle in all other arenas," she explains. "Battling racism and battling heterosexism and battling apartheid share the same urgency inside me as battling cancer" (*BL* 116). "Dear goddess!" she prays. "Do not let me die a coward, mother. Nor forget how to sing" (*BL* 55).

Lorde's ongoing theme is "Sisterhood and Survival" (*BL* 73); and the healing effort to establish community, the third stage of trauma recovery, proves, in this case, a necessary tool for both physical and spiritual sustenance. After her mastectomy, she recalls, "the love of women healed me." It was the "tangible floods of energy rolling off these women" that gave her the "power to heal" (*CJ* 39). The women who attended her were "macro members in the life dance" (*CJ* 47). Lorde's project demands a feminist sisterhood not only of friends and family gathered around a single Black lesbian poet, but of women struggling against apartheid in South Africa, of Aboriginal voices singing in Australia, of Maori women speaking up in the *marae* of New Zealand, and of single mothers in New York City fighting to save the lives of children imperiled by poverty, racism, and economic vicissitudes.

"I'm going to go out like a fucking meteor!" Lorde proclaims valiantly, even as she insists that the ongoing reclamation of whatever life she can salvage will involve a shattering confrontation with traumatic experience in an effort to master its soul-destroying resonances. "I am going to write fire until it comes out my ears, my eyes, my noseholes—everywhere. Until it's every breath I breathe" (*BL* 76-77). Defiantly, Lorde challenges the medicalized impotence and demeaning infantilization so often associated with the treatment of terminal illness. She refuses to submit to a liver biopsy, just as she had contemptuously rejected a mammary prosthesis. Metaphors of heat and light imbue her feisty prose, as she determines to enjoy each brilliant moment allotted her and to use her suffering as a lamp to illumine a hitherto repressed and hidden territory. In the act of dying, she will bequeath to her sisters "the vision of a living woman's poetry as a force for social change" (*BL* 77).[24]

All "the stories we tell," Lorde declares, "are about healing in some form" (*BL* 93). Lorde's own scriptotherapy will offer a healing narrative for those who come after her and for all women engaged in political, economic, psychological, or physiological struggles. The poet's determination demands a strenuous amalgamation of her multiplicitous selves—the self that is beleaguered by illness, as well as the self that triumphs with each new day of survival. "It takes all of my selves, working together," she confesses, "to fight this death inside me. Every one of these battles generates energies useful in the others" (*BL* 99).

Indeed, Lorde's *Burst of Light* constitutes an invaluable gift to all those who read it and survives as an inspiring legacy from the mouth of the dying poet. The intense prose of this impassioned *testimonio* reminds all of us who are "temporarily abled" and enjoying an illusory reprieve from the specter of mortality that the cancer patient's pathography configures a paradigm for the trajectory of every human life. The book's epilogue might, in fact, serve as a manifesto of hope and survival for each of Lorde's readers, as she voices the visionary wisdom of poet, prophet, philosopher, and seer:

> *This is my life. Each hour is a possibility not to be banked. These days are not a preparation for living. . . . It is the consciousness of this that gives a marvelous breadth to everything I do.* (*BL* 132)
>
> *Once I accept the existence of dying, as a life process, who can ever have power over me again?* (*CJ* 25)

S I X

Sylvia Fraser's My Father's House: *A Canadian Memoir of Sexual Trauma and Narrative Recovery*

My daddy and I share secrets. (MFH 6)

In *Trauma and Recovery*, Judith Lewis Herman suggests a diagnosis for "Complex Post-Traumatic Stress Disorder" that focuses on victims of war, terrorism, and sexual abuse. All three categories of survivors manifest symptoms that include dysphoria, psychic numbing, traumatic flashbacks, and emotional anesthesia. Janet Liebman Jacobs further explains that, in the case of incest survivors, a common psychic defense entails the construction of an alternative personality or "divided consciousness . . . wherein the victimized daughter internalizes both the identity of the powerful father as well as a representation of self as powerless victim" (12). The effects of post-traumatic stress disorder elide, in many cases, with even more serious symptoms of multiple personality or "dissociative identity" disorder—a condition in which the victim literally enacts the metaphorical figure of a shattered subject, psychologically fragmented and emotionally "in pieces." Such was the case for Sylvia Fraser, whose autobiography *My Father's House: A Memoir of Incest and of Healing* offers poignant testimony to the traumatic repercussions of father-daughter incest. Fraser's life narrative claims documentary status, though names have been altered to protect both the innocent and the guilty.

Sylvia Fraser's early accounts of infantile violation are particularly graphic, though she warns the reader in an inaugural note that italicized passages denote "thoughts, feelings and experiences pieced together from recently recovered memories," as well as reconstructed dream material. A creative writer and a university lecturer, Fraser carefully circumnavigates the highly contested territory of recovered memory by typographically distinguishing between autobiographical discourse and imaginary projections (or reconstructions) that occupy a liminal space between fantasy and reality. She thus protects herself, at least theoretically, from accusations of "false memory syndrome."[1] By attributing recovered data to the realm of the imaginary, Fraser feels free to explore the fertile terrain of dream and childhood recollection without subjecting herself to the kind of skeptical scrutiny that currently surrounds adult confessions of repressed trauma. "Whether you believe me or not," she seems to be saying, "I know what I experienced." Her narrative proves so vivid and convincing that we, as readers, do indeed believe her.[2] The author has spent a lifetime recovering from the effects of post-traumatic stress disorder, and the clear and coherent articulation of her tale of childhood abuse proves to be the most effective healing strategy in her repertoire of therapies. Fraser turns to self-analysis for relief from the tormenting flashbacks associated with trauma, and it is precisely this self-conscious engagement in both fictive and autobiographical reconstruction that offers her the best hope of narrative recovery.

Liberated by the liminal spaces between imagination and reverie, Fraser boldly explores the prediscursive memories of her infantile self: "*Something hard pushes up against me. . . . It bursts all over me in a sticky stream*" (*MFH* 8). "*I'm afraid to complain because daddy won't love me*" (*MFH* 10). As Jessica Benjamin points out in *The Bonds of Love*, a young girl's "early love of the father is an 'ideal love': the child idealizes the father because the father is the magical mirror that reflects the self as it wants to be" (100). Ironically, this idealized love of the father is emotionally strengthened in cases of childhood sexual abuse where the young girl "perceives her only ally to be the abuser with whom she empathizes" (Jacobs 66). Bound in a viselike filial/erotic relationship with the man who exploits her, the abused daughter becomes entirely dependent on her violator for emotional validation and psychic mirroring. The echo effect of maternal reinforcement, described by Heinz Kohut as essential to healthy development, attenuates as the confused child looks to the most powerful man in her life for nurture and for praise. As Jane Gallop observes in *Feminism and Psychoanalysis*, "The daughter's desire for her father is desperate. . . . If the phallus is the standard of value, then the Father, possessor of the phallus, must desire the daughter in order to give her value" (70).

Why does the body of a beautiful daughter, golden-haired, like a magical sprite from the fairyland of the adult imagination, suddenly become the victim of her father/lover/protector/God? "Daddy won't love me" is a perpetual refrain reiterated throughout Fraser's heartrending tale. The father/God/rapist emerges as an implacable authority, an insatiable antagonist demanding a love that dare not speak its name. Emotional valorization intermittently bequeathed by the father refuses to be unconditional: his favor comes at the high price of sexual innocence, bodily integrity, and psychological wholeness.[3]

Daddy and his baby daughter have secrets. They share a tableau that is ineffable and inarticulate, a scenario of shameful incestuous practices that inscribe paternal desire on the vulnerable body of the infant daughter who cannot comprehend her violation.[4] Hence the confusion that "surrounds an act of aggression for which the young victim has no name" (Jacobs 61), "where the young girl has no margin of safety, no room to withstand the father's desiring body, and especially no space to speak her desire" (De Lauretis *Love* 152). Like the tongueless Philomela, the awestruck child searches for words to express her pain, but language invariably fails her because her rudimentary vocabulary is a compendium of physical need and inchoate desire. The demands of the body elide with the maleficent world of the *interdit*. Sexual spaces are consigned to the realm of the unspeakable that borders on the unknowable, and can only be delineated euphemistically in the infantile imaginary by fecal analogies that conflate vaginal spaces with anal apertures. Young Sylvia complains of feeling inexplicably soiled and fears telling Mommy *"because I am dirty"* (*MFH* 14).[5]

Sylvia and Daddy share secrets—the secrets of intimacy framed on all sides by dread and disdain, ugliness and disgust, fear and helplessness. The law and the word of the Father take precedence in defining the parameters of this exploited daughter's imaginary life-world. Little more than a baby, the toddler who succumbs to Daddy's imprecations has no choice at all, no power to resist the authority that engulfs her, despite her playful mimicry of adult refusal when she publicly mouths the words of a song popular during World War II: "No, no, a thousand times no" (*MFH* 5).[6]

The Father's forbidden phallus is revealed to his uncomprehending daughter through a yawning chasm of ignorance and evil, satanic spaces of viscosity and disgust. When the veiled Lacanian symbol of paternal potency transmogrifies into Daddy's erect and exposed penis, this serpentine appendage slides for Sylvia into the uncanny world of excremental anxiety, the translinguistic spoor of psychological abjection. Like the menstrual blood and tissue cast off as detritus by the clean and proper maternal body, excrescences of the paternal phallus seem utterly uncanny. Daddy's erect penis is brandished as an aggressive weapon that stiffens against his daughter's body, then explodes with an ejaculate that the child interprets as excremental residue. An infantile neologism crudely represents the object of horror as "Daddy's wet-ums," metonymically analogous to the urinal simulacrum of a Betsy-Wetsy doll. "I hate Wet-ums Dolls," protests Fraser's protagonist in the novel *Pandora*. "They're so . . . *'fil-thee!'*" (*P* 24).

When the little girl is incontinent, she wets the bed and spoils the sheets: "Liquid scalds Pandora's thighs. It gushes through flannel ditches; . . . *oh you, filthy, naughty, filthy*; . . . then grows cold" (*P* 13). To be wet and to wet is a source of shame for a child being socialized into cultural practices of strict bodily control. Hence the confusion wrought by the father's licentious liberties. When Daddy wets Sylvia's body and ejaculates semen between her legs or against her buttocks, the daughter cannot protest. She is left to wallow in the muck, to feel her skin tingling uncomfortably with a strange viscosity. To the horrified toddler, the ejaculate manifests itself as a clear and gluey urine that emits a fishy stench like the smell of chicken guts. Her father's penis seems to expel a mysterious excremental fluid that drowns his daughter in a world of ignorance and shame.[7]

Suddenly overwhelmed by a recovered memory of forced fellatio, an adult Sylvia gags, sobs, and literally relives the "convulsions of a child being raped through the mouth" (*MFH* 220). No italics indicate the textual register of imaginary representation. This violent epiphany, depicted through vivid historical reenactment, constitutes the psychological epicenter of Fraser's incest trauma. The moment of "rememory" in which the author/narrator abreacts unthinkable aggression explodes like a bomb in the penultimate section of her confessional text. Imagination has given way to historical testimony, dream and self-analysis to recovered memory. Fraser's entire autobiographical reconstruction of infantile sexual abuse culminates in a cathartic dramatization of her father's brutal assault. Hence the young girl's experience of prolific night terrors and inexplicable eruptions of anxiety over repressed memories of oral rape. Fear of ingesting the father's phallus elides in her infantile imagination with a fetishistic terror of hermaphroditic transformation, whereby she fantasizes developing "crinkly hair and a slimy wet-ums" (*MFH* 12).

From the beginning of Fraser's autobiographical narrative, the body of the daughter is a tabula rasa—a clear slate to be inscribed with the father's illicit desire. Infinitely alluring in her beauty and fragility, the untouchable virgin can be violated through symbolic forays into every hole, aperture, and crevice in her tantalizing figure. Fetishistic substitutes for adult female sexuality appeal to the father intent on appropriating his daughter's body through incestuous mimesis—a scenario of love and desire that mocks the mutuality of adult Eros by disfiguring the integrity of the idealized fairy princess, a golden-haired Rapunzel imprisoned in a tower of her father's making. If "love" be the word universally applied to childhood affection and mature sexual activity, how can an infant who enjoys kissing and cuddling, who longs for physical warmth and bodily contact, understand the crucial difference between normal intimacy and sexual perversion? Where does affection end and incest begin?[8]

On the cover of the 1989 Harper edition of *My Father's House* stands a blond child, two or three years old, cuddling a doll and broadly smiling, with all the openness of infantile trust in an adult world that nurtures and protects her. In the far right corner of the picture stands, half-hidden, a box that once contained a toilet, labeled "Vitro Closet Tank." Does the alluring photograph implicitly evoke an ironic association between this young girl's impressionable visage and its unthinkable violation by a male parent who treated his daughter's body as little more than a wastebin for his excess sperm, a human toilet tank for seminal ejaculations? What does it mean that the fictive Pandora is swaddled, "struggling, wheezing, spewing, in the ragbox" (*P* 9), and treated like garbage from the day of her birth?

The price of life is, of course, love—that miraculous monosyllable that evinces a thousand different meanings with every iteration. A deviant and egotistical patriarch fantasizes seduction by his tempting daughter, who unwittingly longs to please a lover she can never fully satisfy. When she naively exhibits her virginal body before his specular gaze, the aroused father delights in her tantalizing presence and savors the paradox of inadvertent flirtation. Innocent of sexual knowledge, the young girl offers her body as a gift to the man she adores, ingenuously exposing her genitals to his probing hand or eye. When Daddy, in turn, feels the urgency of libidinal desire, he capitulates to powerful incestuous drives, then demands that the child connive in their secret sin. The father's unspeakable acts must never be revealed in any social context.[9]

Fraser's shockingly self-indulgent perpetrator is armed with a battery of fantastic threats. The daughter who "tells," he warns, will be disowned and sent to an orphanage, where she will be starved, tortured, and neglected.[10] Unless she agrees to play the ignominious role of sexual plaything, the toy-girl of a lascivious elder, her own toys will be incinerated in the family furnace. "*Everything in this house belongs to me*" (*MFH* 11), her father insists—including, of course, the body of his victimized daughter and the life of her precious pet Smoky. Sadistic threats of feline murder finally crush Sylvia's resistance: "*Smoky's life is in my hands,*" she believes. "*Our bargain is sealed in blood*" (*MFH* 12). The cat's survival is symbolically contingent on Sylvia's speechless complicity. If she breaks the pact of secrecy, her cat will be sent to the pound for gassing, and she herself will die of grief. The authoritarian bully has chosen, on a microcosmic scale, tactics similar to those of the Nazi leader contemporaneously threatening a larger global populace.

Totally intimidated by her irascible father/lover, Sylvia finds sanctuary in the only refuge available—the schizoid subject-position of multiple personality disorder. Both Judith Herman (*Incest* 103) and Janet Liebman Jacobs have examined the strategic adaptation of a "double self" in response to childhood sexual abuse and conclude that impotent victims often "describe the presence of a shadow self whose identification with the abuser is manifested in unconscious strivings toward sexual dominance and control that reverse the power dynamic of traumatic sexualization" (Jacobs 95-96).

> Through the trauma of incest, the victimized daughter learns that her body represents danger and vulnerability. Unable to protect herself from the sexual and physical assaults of her father, her only recourse from victimization may be found in her ability to dissociate from the traumatic situation. With dissociation, normal awareness is transformed through an alteration in consciousness whereby the child "leaves her body" during the act of sexual violence. (Jacobs 129)

Sylvia Fraser's description of her "blanking out" offers a clinical case history of the survivor's schizoid deployment of an alter ego to embody the temptress constructed by Daddy's lascivious gaze.[11] The daughter's poignant desire for love and affection is perverted into a licentious persona that the victim can substitute when her father's authority engulfs and overwhelms her personal will. This alternate personality provides sanctuary for the self-identified subject entirely obliterated by the denial of agency in the experience of physical abuse. Sylvia confesses: "I created a secret accomplice for my daddy by splitting my personality in two. . . . My loss of memory was retroactive" (*MFH* 15).

Both physical and psychological integrity are appallingly compromised by the exercise of paternal authority over a girl-child who is far too young to comprehend the pleasure or danger of adult sexual relations. Her body becomes an instrument of perversion, a faceless and featureless automaton whose consciousness and memory are repressed at the moment of violation. Traumatized by each sexual assault, Sylvia buries her "good" personality beneath a cloak of enforced complicity that obviates her social (and conscious) self. She takes refuge in the construction of a precocious alter ego, a surrogate self who "loved my father, freeing me to hate him" (*MFH* 15).

And if the daughter should refuse to comply with Daddy's demands? But how *can* Sylvia refuse? That option is simply unthinkable, because "Daddy won't love [her]" and Smoky will perish. The father's love generates a sustaining faith in life, providence, authority, safety, affection, nurturance, and survival. In the child's eye, "I am loved" is tantamount to the Cartesian *cogito*. Without parental protection, the daughter fears virtual annihilation. Her only recourse is to cultivate anonymity when Daddy assaults the "other self" whom Sylvia refuses to be. If she cannot succeed in defying her father's incestuous demands, she must nonetheless repress her humiliating victimization. Sylvia and her father descend together into the underworld of the unspeakable: in the hidden spaces between words that cannot be uttered, they enact a drama prohibited to waking consciousness. Henceforth, this secret scenario will be accessible to Sylvia only through the Jungian collective consciousness embodied in folklore or through the symbolic topography of nightmare and dream.[12]

Before words can name the object of her incestuous violation, the young girl closes her eyes and refuses to see the terrifying "wet-ums" that explodes against her body. She turns a deaf ear to the curious groans of a breathless male panting in orgasmic release. She blots out the fishy stench of semen and thinks of the prizes awaiting her—candy and cookies, dolls and toys, and most important of all, Daddy's love. His affection is a treasure beyond purchase, though the payment schedule be inexorable, the emotional installment plan thoroughly enervating. This particular transaction in the economy of desire is especially invidious, since it necessarily precludes the possibility of final payment.

If the gaze of the mother valorizes the infant at the mirror stage of ego identification, it is the gift of paternal approval that inscribes the child into the infinitely desirable, but dangerous symbolic system identified with the law and the word of the Father. Only acquiescence in a series of unspeakable demands can elicit the words of paternal valorization that subjectivize Sylvia in her tenuous role as developing daughter. The impossible challenge of pleasing an implacable authority breeds overwhelming anxiety, as well as irrational hostility. When the victim of sexual abuse finds herself unable "to express her anger for fear of losing the father, her development is characterized by ambivalence and an association of love with suffering and sacrifice" (Jacobs 67-68). A furious defiance lies buried in the unconscious, and impotent rage erupts unexpectedly in personal relationships. The young Sylvia suffers "fits" and "tantrums" that defy domestic explanation. Similarly, the fictional Pandora is isolated from her family by screaming bouts and infantile panic attacks provoked by a terrifying loss of her Lacanian mirror image: "Pandora tries to see her face in her mother's upturned eyes: She cannot. . . . She screams. She feels her name fly up from her body. . . . Pandora awakes. . . . Pandora knows: *I am bad*" (*P* 11-12).

As early as 1932, Sandor Ferenczi, the renegade Freudian who continued to support Freud's early association of adult hysteria with childhood sexual trauma, insisted in an essay on the "Confusion of Tongues Between Adults and Children" that survivors of abuse tend, paradoxically, to identify emotionally with incestuous perpetrators: "One would expect the first impulse to be that of reaction, hatred, disgust, and energetic refusal. . . . [But] the real and undeveloped personality reacts to sudden unpleasure not by defense, but by anxiety-ridden identification and by introjection of the menacing aggressor" (quoted in Jacobs, 75-76).

More recent studies indicate that it is fairly common for female incest victims to "engage in a variety of self damaging behaviors, including self-neglect and self-sabotage, addictive and compulsive behaviors, self-mutilation, and suicidal tendencies" (Jacobs 90). Such survivors, Jacobs explains, frequently go through a vicious cycle of behaviors that put them at risk for revictimization through "rape, attempted rape, unwanted sexual advances, and physical violence in intimate relationships" (101). As Louise DeSalvo observes, "women who have been incestuously abused are more likely than other women to disfigure themselves; to suffer severe substance abuse; to enter into relationships in which they are repeatedly physically or sexually assaulted; to be raped; . . . to make suicide attempts; to commit suicide" (*Woolf* 11).

Sylvia Fraser's own revictimization began very early indeed, in the form of nightmarish sexual assaults by the seedy and licentious boarder Mr. Brown. Sylvia the narrator describes herself as a victim in the third person, since her alter-ego bears the brunt of Brown's sadistic advances. After abusing Sylvia sexually and beating her with his belt, Brown warns: "*You tell anyone, kid, and I'll kill you!*" (*MFH* 33). Not surprisingly, Sylvia's father and Mr. Brown meld in her imagination and are unconsciously amalgamated with newsreel images of German assailants. Because the narrative plays itself out in a Canadian community raising victory gardens on the home front during World War II, it seems inevitable that Sylvia should disguise her own sexual victimization in symbols of Nazi aggression. As Janet Jacobs points out, it is fairly common for incest survivors to relegate their terror to phantasmic projections of nocturnal visitors: "the feared intruder may be an alien being or a Nazi soldier. These imaginary perpetrators emerge in response to the overwhelming reality of the father's violence and his sexual assault" (36).

Was Sylvia's encounter with the monstrous Mr. Brown real or imaginary? We do not know. Nor does it matter. Was Brown's attack further evidence of the deliberate blindness of a timorous mother, or did the young girl transfer her memories of paternal aggression onto a particularly unsavory male reeking of alcohol and abuse—a figure of the demonized Hun who enacts, on a smaller scale, Hitler's sadistic aggression? Identifying her own suffering with that of victims of the Holocaust, Sylvia can repress the knowledge of her father's treacherous behavior and transfer her anger to a world stage where the Nazis would eventually be defeated and the downtrodden gloriously liberated. In the young girl's fantasies, an imperious Daddy has been articulated to the image of an imperial dictator whom all the world loves to hate.[13] Fraser further elaborates infantile impressions of demonic World War II rhetoric in her novel *Pandora*, where the protagonist fears that "*if the Nazis catch me they will cut off my curls and make whips of them like they did to Rapunzel. . . . If the NAZIS catch you they hang you, naked, on a hook, and they shave off your hair, and they whip you*" (*P* 14-15).

One thinks, inevitably, of another Sylvia, whose poetic indictment of Daddy identified her father, Otto Plath, with the Panzer-man who shared his Austro-Germanic origins. In the poem "Daddy," Sylvia Plath conflates metaphorically her masochistic devotion to a prematurely dead father with the sufferings of Jewish Holocaust victims. As extravagant and hyperbolic as Plath's language seems to be, her attempt to exorcise the haunting specter of an idealized father who abandoned her by dying offers a trenchant poetic analogy for Sylvia Fraser's own experience of anxiety and rage against a spectral patriarch who is everywhere and nowhere—whose nefarious deeds are hidden in the shadows of the unconscious, and whose authoritarian presence his daughter can never fully escape. Even as she formulates her narrative of childhood trauma, Fraser empathizes implicitly with the paternal imago she has unconsciously introjected. No one, not even the scurrilous Mr. Brown, can exorcise the specter of her daddy/lover/persecutor. In high school, Sylvia's personality fragments into still another surrogate self, a glamour girl that she whimsically calls "Appearances"—"an alter ego I created to hide my shadow-twin" (*MFH* 65). Despite Appearances, Sylvia remains haunted by dreams of terror, as she hallucinates naked bodies in the dome of the family bathroom and "*a trail of bloody footprints*" (*MFH* 71).

Unconsciously identifying with her father, the incest victim often feels especially threatened by the physical changes that accompany puberty. At the time of menarche, her "body becomes the symbol of her victimization and thus the focus of her desire for control" (Jacobs 88). Anorexia and bulimia are frequent symptoms of the survivor's desperate struggle to discipline a pubescent body that seems to be veering toward a bloated sexual maturity. The adolescent girl becomes obsessed with the need to maintain a thin, boyish figure that symbolizes the triumph of will and androgynous ego over unwelcome physiological development. The onset of menses is particularly repulsive, with its sanguinary reminders of feminine vulnerability and the concomitant possibility of pregnancy. "*I am drowning in blood,*" screams a frantic Sylvia (*MFH* 89). Even the slightest tremor of sexual arousal immediately produces hysterical symptoms, as the teenaged girl watches her alter ego "*withdrawing all sensation*" (*MFH* 80). Her ability to feel has been totally obliterated by post-traumatic dysphoria.

Adolescent terrors proliferate. To the sense of violation is added an overwhelming fear of insanity. To nervousness about sexual defloration, the threat of accidental pregnancy. Sylvia dreams of the body of a mummified pregnant teenager, murdered by Daddy and buried in the family's back garden. With mounting anxiety, she chooses a common masochistic defense and begins to starve herself on a crash diet that reduces her weight to 98 pounds. Finally, she engages in ritual self-mutilation and boasts: "I can burn my arm with a cigarette and not feel it" (*MFH* 101). Like Audre Lorde, she pours scalding water over her forearm, then diffidently takes pleasure in torturing a detached alter ego.[14]

When her high school boyfriend Daniel Hobson assures Sylvia that she need not "put out for the guys," she feels her false self-system suddenly dissolving into a million fragments: "I shatter like a reflection shot through with a bullet" (*MFH* 106). Miraculously, Danny seems to offer the kind of emotional shelter that can facilitate the reintegration of Sylvia's dissociated personality: "He holds me, binding the pieces of myself together" (*MFH* 109). Sylvia identifies her handsome suitor as a fairy-tale Prince Charming, but not without a tinge of cynicism.

Although love may strike like a bolt of lightning, trust takes longer to cultivate. The repressed "*other self is still wary, bitter, case-hardened, vengeful, jealous, frightened, furious, egocentric, inventive and sly*" (*MFH* 113). Perpetually tormented by the long-term effects of incest trauma, Sylvia continues to display the erratic behavior of a borderline personality. Amid temper tantrums and night terrors, she swerves unpredictably between an obsessive need for approval and infantile expressions of senseless rage. She demands constant emotional reassurance in the face of irascible outbursts that reek of childish impulsivity but suggest, at the same time, an insatiable demand for love rooted in hysterical insecurity. In contrast to her exploitative father, Danny offers Sylvia a matric and nurturant love, free of performative demands. The two share a simple, almost sibling affection characteristic of fraternal/sororal partnership. They revel in the joys of adolescent attachment and the heady openness of first love. Such unconditional affection creates for Fraser's protagonist self, at least temporarily, an emotionally safe space conducive to psychic healing.

But how free can an incest survivor actually be, when the trauma of childhood sexual abuse is repressed like a specter haunting both dreams and waking imagination? The shadow of another self hovers on the margins of Sylvia's mind and attends her wedding to Daniel Hobson like an uninvited guest in a dark fairy tale, obliterating all memory of the union's consummation. The marriage, she insists, must be childless. As she tries to explain her intense fear of pregnancy, Sylvia teeters dangerously on the brink of the unspeakable: "'I have to admit . . . the idea of pregnancy itself is . . . pretty horrendous to me. It's so . . . parasitic' . . . . *like having daddy's wet-ums inside me for nine months*" (*MFH* 132).[15]

With the text's changing typography signaling hysterical logorrhea, Sylvia equates the experience of pregnancy with that of insanity. Her "severed head" persona has taken command of her emotional life, and simply imagining the invasion of her body by a parasitic embryo evokes incipient panic. She cannot allow herself to become the physical property of another, a vehicle for the biological colonization of her body by the species. No wonder that when Sylvia studies philosophy at a university in the 1950s, she believes that she must split head from body, logocentric thought from emotional sensation. Pregnancy would involve an unacceptable loss of physical control, a violation of integrity that her fragmented personality could never tolerate. She must remain ever vigilant against the unwelcome transformation of self into split female/maternal subject, lest her dissociated subject-position be shattered into a mass of atomized particles beyond psychological recuperation.[16]

In states of unrelieved depression, Sylvia is haunted by the hangman's noose that once uncannily decorated the childhood drawings that she now disinters from an attic collection of domestic memorabilia. Her absurdly pregnant teddy bear, Teddy Umcline, parturiates a horned devil; then the bear's "jaunty tie eventually transmogrifies into a hangman's noose" (*MFH* 148). Incapable of interpreting the cryptic and violent symbols of her infantile art, Sylvia attempts to tap the censored material of repressed memory through a self-conscious exercise in scriptotherapy. She begins to write a bildungsroman with clear autobiographical resonances. Naming her protagonist Pandora, Sylvia cracks the lid of a teeming Pandora's box: "*My other self has learned to type, . . . throwing up masses of defiant memories. . . . My other self leads me to the edge of her secret world*" (*MFH* 149-50)

Narrative recovery nudges Sylvia in the direction of psychological revelation, as she boldly explores a lost childhood landscape while remaining oblivious of the abyss below. Her two-thousand-page manuscript has been composed "in the first person hysterical. It's like a gush of primordial pain" (*MFH* 151). This experimental autofiction dredges up buried memories screened carefully by an unconscious censor. Sylvia remains entranced, like the Lady of Shalott, "weaving her endless tapestries from shadows in mirrors" (*MFH* 151). Lost in another world, she finds herself enveloped in penumbrous psychological symbolism that evinces analysis without synthesis. The pieces of the puzzle are scattered in a rebus around her authorial (un)conscious, tantalizing the author to crack the code of repressed memory, but stubbornly refusing direct communication.

Through her protagonist Pandora, Sylvia's alter ego conjures a voice that speaks in muffled, disguised iterations. She articulates the oedipal struggle in dreamlike hieroglyphs that deliberately obfuscate their dangerous treasure-trove of metaphorical meaning. Why, wonders Sylvia, does she portray her fictional father as a World War I amputee with a hooked arm? Why has she darkened her family history with shadows of incest and suicide? Only her alter ego knows for sure.

Fraser's novel *Pandora* suggests a daring aesthetic experiment—a hybridized fable/bildungsroman amalgamating William Blake's poetic exposure of the corruption of childhood innocence with James Joyce's lexical ingenuity in *A Portrait of the Artist as a Young Man*. Neither man nor artist, Fraser's semiautobiographical protagonist, Pandora Gothic, experiences extreme personal and familial alienation from infancy to the age of eight, when the novel ends. Fraser captures the young girl's ingenuous imagination, imbued as it is with fairy-tale stories and parental prohibitions, religious rhetoric, and coded community mores. This is, quite literally, a Gothic tale of a dysfunctional family haunted by inexplicable patriarchal rage, maternal timidity, and sibling brutality.

Clearly set in the genre of fabulation, the unusual bildungsroman simulates the infantile vision of a child tormented by what she believes to be an evil spell cast by a "Wicked Witch who cursed her out in her cradle" (*P* 16). The Christian ritual of baptism is apparently ineffectual against this primordial curse. Baptism cannot rid Pandora of the "carrrrnal affections [*sic*]" that plague her infancy, nor can it empower her "to triumph against the Devil, the worrrld, and the flesh [*sic*]" (*P* 10). Though it promises to exorcise the culpabilities of Mother Eve from the child's potentially corrupt female body, the church merely instills a legacy of guilt and shame for an unknown crime that will haunt the young girl's developing consciousness. Pandora's mother Adelaide is, it would seem, perversely enamored of the crucified Christ. She humbly allows herself to "lick up His carmine wounds" in an act that renders the impotent Gothic father "*[c]uckold of a deadman*" (*P* 10). "Pandora's father is tall and fleshy with a bald head and glistering steel-rimmed eyes: Pandora's father smells of blood and rage" (*P* 11). "Pandora's mother doesn't hear. . . . Pandora's mother doesn't see. . . . She hurls her passion to '. . . E-TER-NITY!'" (*P* 11).[17]

Like a princess confined in a tower prison, the young Pandora is exiled to a gloomy attic room, where she sleeps on "the fever-cradle of Aunt Cora who died in this bed of diphtheria" (*P* 12). The child learns a painful lesson of physical humiliation when she dares touch the forbidden genital crevice of her body: "She opens her legs . . . *Crack!* Adelaide's palm stings Pandora's cheek. Pandora gapes, her now-guilty hand between her now-guilty legs. . . . Adelaide panics: *Crack!* She strikes Pandora's other cheek. *"Don't ever let me catch you do such a filthy thing again!"*" (*P* 13). The same scene will be repeated, almost verbatim, in *My Father's House*.

In both novel and autobiography, the family is clearly organized around service to a demanding patriarch, who sits in his "sagging fetch-me chair" (*MFH* 206) like a king on his throne and issues imperial orders for King Cola with lemon, homebaked cookies, pencils and writing implements, newspapers and knives. The entire household connives in placating the irascible father, a World War I amputee with a prosthetic left armhook symbolically poised in a menacing "Captain Hook" gesture.[18] Pandora, like Peter Pan, must try to guard her childhood innocence in the face of an ominous adult enemy who can, at any moment, slash her to pieces, and who savors the pleasure of issuing intimidating death threats whenever his unruly daughter disobeys him. A butcher by trade, Lyle Gothic emerges as a fascistic figure, larger-than-life and demonic in his behavior. Inflated in the eyes of his vulnerable progeny, he seems like a towering giant, "a big man, over six feet. His lightly-haired flesh . . . fits him like a poorly-tailored suit" (*P* 65). In a fit of rage, the father snatches up his truculent daughter and thrusts her into a basement storage-room, where she feels suffocated by heat and the stench of mothballs. She "vomits into a pair of cleat-boots" (*P* 22), entertains fantasies of Nazi torture, and tries to strangle herself with a coathanger. Lyle Gothic's rhetorical warnings almost materialize when a panic-stricken Pandora hysterically attempts suicide.

One of the most threatening scenes in the novel occurs when Pandora visits her father's butcher shop and discovers the corpse of a slaughtered rabbit hanging from a hook in his freezer: "Pandora gropes inside. . . . Her hand touches it: a white bunny, pierced through one eye with a meathook. . . . His belly is scooped out. His puff-tail hangs by a tendon. . . . Pandora bows her head: *My father has killed the Easter bunny, . . . and one day he will kill Charlie-puss. . . . Then he will kill me. He will . . . scoop out my belly, and he will hang me on a hook*" (*P* 53-54).

After Pandora discovers that her parents have had her beloved Charlie-puss euthanized at the local pound, she hurls furious accusations at her father: "*You killed puss!* You *gassed* him the way you always said!" (*P* 132). An affronted Lyle Gothic forces his daughter to perform a humiliating striptease before the entire family. When Pandora huddles trembling in her underpants, mother and sisters connive in her victimization and forcibly remove the last protective garment from her seven-year-old body. Bellowing "in a rage gone cockeyed," the triumphant patriarch "scoops up Pandora with hand and hook, and drags her . . . into the hall. He hangs her, full-length, in front of the mirror" (*P* 134). Thrust, once again, into the basement storage-vault, Pandora hallucinates her own asphyxiation in a Nazi (or animal) gas chamber.

> Her lungs sear, expand, explode. She claws the gas chamber with the bloody stumps of her paws. . . . "Strip! Go naked to the orphanage! Go eat dust!" . . .

> *Pandora lies naked, on the pound floor. . . . The cleat-boot slices her into serving-size pieces to be hung on silverhooks.* (*P* 135)

Is it any wonder that Sylvia/Pandora portrays her menacing father in the image of a domestic Hitler? And yet, to the reader's astonishment, the dominant theme that Sylvia culls from the composition of this logorrheic and cathartic novel is an obsessive nostalgia for Daddy, a repressed desire to "rescue her daddy-king from mommy so they could live happily ever after" (*MFH* 153). Such an ambitious emotional project requires both a father substitute and a mother rival.

Oedipal longing has set the stage for a threatening scenario of revictimization. Compelled to reenact the incest trauma with an adult paternal surrogate, Sylvia recklessly embarks on a love affair with Paul Lawson, the father of her childhood friend Lulu and a war hero once worshipped as a Clark Gable look-alike. This illicit relationship is doomed from the start, since commitment to a married man guarantees Sylvia endless pain and rejection—precisely the kind of betrayal unconsciously associated with her father's earlier cruelty. Falling in love with a partner twice her age, Sylvia sacrifices herself on the altar of oedipal desire in order to seduce the fantasized father of personal prehistory. Betrayed at the moment of *Spaltung* or splitting, the victimized daughter must continue to search for a patriarchal figure to valorize her feminine identity. By compulsively re-living emotional patterns frozen at an earlier stage of arrested development, she desperately tries to rescue her princess self by seducing an archetypal Daddy/King caught in the clutches of a witchlike Mommy/Queen. If she can emerge victorious in this contest for masculine favor, Sylvia will (in fantasy) reintegrate her shattered self. Her imagination knows more than does her waking mind about the Freudian family romance she so perilously reenacts: "*My other self, disguised as a princess, enters a maze of mirrors,*" where a weeping "*king sits on his throne, holding his bleeding heart*" (*MFH* 163).

The love affair unfolds on a schizoid psychological stage where Paul Lawson takes on the persona of a demanding and abusive patriarch, and Sylvia obsessively struggles to play her prescribed role as Daddy's good little girl. Sensual memories of her father's sexual advances mingle in scenes of seduction played out by Sylvia's repressed alter ego in deeply entrenched patterns of filial docility. A confused autobiographical narrator describes her initial erotic encounter with Paul filtered through screen memories of incestuous abuse. Paul's moist, talcum-scented flesh evokes shadowy reminiscences of her freshly bathed father's naked thighs squeezing his infant daughter's bare legs in a viselike grip.

In this dangerous game of oedipal entanglement, Sylvia has chosen to reenact the sadomasochistic scenario of her father's emotional exploitation in the hope that this time the traumatic situation might magically come out right: *this time* she will successfully play the role of beloved princess; *this time* she will win her father's affection and triumph over the wicked witch who colludes in her humiliation. Mommy will be defeated and Daddy will be won by/one with his darling daughter. The princess will be released from the tower of her dreams, and King Daddy will save her from emotional perdition.[19]

Such a fantasy of oedipal triumph over a domineering father is, by definition, necessarily self-defeating. Paul Lawson represents the imago of an unattainable paternal surrogate, ever receding into the future and never available to the needy lover who appeals to him for psychological support. Paul is clearly a sybaritic roué, absurdly self-indulgent and unconscionably manipulative. The price of his elusive affection proves very high indeed. He requires that his adulterous paramour be perpetually malleable and responsive to his every whim. Without rights and devoid of power, Sylvia agrees to play the role of cooperative mistress, never complaining or asserting a will of her own. She knows that if she should misbehave, "Daddy won't love [her]," and life will lose its emotional grounding. Defined by the incriminating gaze of patriarchal judgment, Sylvia's alienated self capitulates to Paul's egotistical demands, despite her second-class status as the other woman in the façade of his respectable married life.[20]

Not surprisingly, the stress of this exploitative arrangement leads to the kind of frustration and instability that propels Sylvia into melodramatic self-destruction. Initially traumatized by her father's incestuous assaults, she unconsciously repeats a similar power dynamic in a troubled relationship that precludes the possibility of emotional reciprocity. Having felt "naughty" and "dirty" when complying with her father's erotic overtures, a mature Sylvia continues to punish herself through futile forays into oedipal seduction. She confesses: "Like a sleepwalker I watched askance while someone who looked like me cast aside everything I valued" (*MFH* 154).

When her marriage to Daniel Hobson disintegrates, Sylvia attempts to embark on an independent life. But like the princess Rapunzel, she is now imprisoned in a tower constructed by a long psychohistory of sexual abuse. Driven to the brink of suicide by feelings of impotence and self-abasement, Sylvia identifies with the phantasmic figure of a dying princess and vows hysterically to kill herself on the evening of October 31. A Halloween party hosted by Paul Lawson allows her to dress in a cat costume, with startling accoutrements of feline boldness. Fortified by numerous glasses of champagne, she publicly challenges the (doubled) father figures that have held her in thrall by physically attacking the enemy who masquerades, in this incarnation, as the King of Hearts. *"At last I say the won't-love-me words"* (*MFH* 195). Furiously striking Paul's impassive torso with clenched fists, she breaks a champagne glass against his chest and symbolically wounds the bully who, to her amazement, fails to defend himself. Astonished by the temerity of her outburst, she gloats over this temporary triumph and blithely remarks: *"I leave my king with a bleeding heart"* (*MFH* 195).

Although Sylvia's gutsy defiance of Daddy/lover and father/betrayer is momentarily cathartic, her rebellious behavior suddenly forfeits the centering subject-position defined by her victimized and complicitous role. Dramatically abreacting the original trauma of incestuous abuse, she must now confront the chaos of ineffable bereavement: "Lost husband, lost lover, lost cat—everything is mixed together" (*MFH* 199). The inebriated cat lady, raving and desperate, hikes along a frozen highway in search of a fantasmatic hanging-tree. Her father's belt provides the symbolic rope that will strangle her, just as the red ribbon around her cat Ting-Ling's neck suggests ownership and appropriation, gloomily forecasting death by strangulation. In this schematic tale of trauma and recovery, Ting-Ling becomes the scapegoat who enables Sylvia to survive. The cat dies so that the cat lady might live. Fearing feline murder, an obedient Sylvia had once remained silent in an effort to hide her unspeakable pain even from herself. Now the worst has happened. Her cat has died, and Sylvia finally has permission to speak, since there is little else left to lose.

Fraser's autobiographical testimony is particularly powerful insofar as it delineates two separate stages of narrative recovery: the initial process of writing *Pandora*, a work of fiction that taps into the unconscious through a process of free association; and the subsequent psychoanalytic unraveling of traumatic sexual abuse through dream analysis, hypnosis, and cathartic abreaction. The autobiographical narrative we are reading valorizes the "birth of knowledge through the testimonial process" by transforming the unconscious into a "conscious testimony that itself can only be grasped in the movement of its own production" (Felman "Education" 25).

Throughout her memoir, Sylvia as autobiographical narrator/protagonist exhibits protracted symptoms of post-traumatic stress disorder, including "recurrent distressing dreams," "psychic numbing," "emotional anesthesia," a "markedly reduced ability to feel emotions," "self-destructive and impulsive behavior," "dissociative symptoms," and "feelings of ineffectiveness, shame, despair, [and] hopelessness" (APA 425). Fraser's double(d) exercises in scriptotherapy offer her reader a fictional elaboration of psychic pain in a coherent narrative of childhood survival, followed by the autobiographical reconstruction of subjectivity through a testimony that attempts to "reassemble an organized, detailed, verbal account, oriented in time and historical context" out of "fragmented components of frozen imagery and sensation" (Herman *Trauma* 177). Childhood trauma initially generates material for autofiction, deftly transmuted in Fraser's memoir into a publicly accessible historical testimony—a "ritual of healing" that inscribes the survivor into a sympathetic discourse community. Hypnosis and dream analysis both contribute to Sylvia's gradual rediscovery of the haunting emotional crisis that shattered her infant self. It is, however, the process of narrative reconstruction through autobiography that so poignantly illumines the dark recesses of repressed memory and liberates the emotional wellsprings of anger originating in incestuous abuse.

Fiction-writing initially offers Sylvia a therapeutic strategy that she fails entirely to understand. In creating a fictitious alter ego named Pandora, she opens a Pandora's box of family secrets. The protagonist of her novel is portrayed as a young girl who successfully fends off sexual molestation by a lascivious breadman with a Hitleresque mustache—a figure psychologically substituted for the paternal "breadwinner" who earlier molested Sylvia as a child. In *My Father's House*, Fraser describes a hostile television interview conducted by her friend Gerald (Joker) Nash. Emcee and author discuss a controversial scene of child abuse in *Pandora*—a fictional incident reported almost verbatim in *My Father's House*, with one notable difference between the novel and Fraser's reproduction of this portion of the text in her memoir.

Ironically, the moment of graphic sexual assault in *Pandora* is omitted from Nash's reading of the text for the benefit of his Canadian television audience. Perhaps he bowdlerizes Sylvia's representation of child abuse when he omits the episode's climactic paragraph: "The breadman . . . coaxes her hand into his pocket. It is a big pocket. It is ripped. . . . It is a while before Pandora realizes how cruelly she has been tricked. She tries to pull out her hand. The breadman holds it tight. 'What's the matter? Don't you like the nice puppy? Pat the nice puppy. Play with the nice puppy'" (*P* 70-71) "I didn't allow the breadman to succeed with his attack," Sylvia explains to Nash. "I wouldn't know how to write about a kid as emotionally damaged as that" (*MFH* 158). Fifteen years later, she would. The truculent Nash, exposed in Fraser's autobiography as a pedophile himself, insists on blaming the victim when he argues that some "little girls can be seductive at an early age" and dismisses *Pandora* as a book typical of extravagant feminist "imaginings" (*MFH* 158).[21]

Fraser's first novel *Pandora* articulates the unspeakable, but simultaneously veils its horrific revelations in the guise of aesthetic transformation. The fabulations of a novelist cannot, after all, be scrutinized in the light of historical accuracy. Fraser's fictional protagonist Pandora is free to explore intriguing emotional puzzles that are never fully unraveled. Deliberately re-creating her troubled childhood in the guise of autobiographical fiction, the circumspect author can tell the truth aslant. She reconfigures her emotional history of alienation and betrayal in such a way that even she fails to comprehend the fury erupting from her volatile prose. Yet the semi-autobiographical character Pandora, in an impulsive outburst, clearly accuses her father of sexual abuse: "*I thought it was the breadman, but it was YOU!*" (*P* 134).

Pandora unfolds in hieroglyphic language filled with pregnant symbols erupting from the unconscious. It functions as a waking dream, a frame for the reconstruction of a trauma narrative so dangerous that it can only be expressed in the veiled discourse of a fictional persona. Fraser's alter ego Pandora, curiously constructed by her dissociated "other self," reiterates repressed memories split from conscious recollection and buried in the secret chambers of a tormented psyche. A censored truth seeps out in fictional form, disguising and distorting the incest trauma that Sylvia is not yet ready to acknowledge. Her early novels, Fraser tells us, were rife with intimations of sexual violence that she herself found puzzling. Unable to mourn her invalid father's death, Sylvia experiences a sense of relief and exaltation when she buries this "man stuffed full of rage" (*MFH* 208).

Over the next decade, the other self of Fraser's fiction metamorphoses into a symbolic self of dream—a fairy princess trapped in a phallic tower without apparent exit. It is, finally, the fertile terrain of a horrific nightmare sequence (ironically released when Sylvia loses her uterus to a hysterectomy for fibroid tumors) that liberates the narrator/protagonist from a lifetime of emotional repression. The lost womb gives birth to uncanny memories couched in grotesque and monstrous symbolism suggestive of oral rape and demonic possession, as well as the feeling of having "aborted Satan's child" (*MFH* 217). "*A blond child is curled like a cat around her swollen belly. A demon-monster raped her many years ago. . . . Inside the blond girl's womb the priest finds a fetus, half-human, half-animal. . . . 'See Satan's child'*" (*MFH* 212-13). In her dream, Sylvia hears the prophecy: "THE PRINCESS WHO IS A PISCES IS TO BE KILLED" (*MFH* 215).

When Sylvia learns about Gerald (Joker) Nash's history of child molestation, she finds herself suddenly confronted with the climactic revelation of her own incest trauma and admits, with shock and incredulity, "I think my father raped me. . . . Spasms pass through me, powerful, involuntary. . . . I start to gag and sob, unable to close my mouth—lockjaw in reverse. These spasms do not feel random. They are the convulsions of a child being raped through the mouth" (*MFH* 220).

Both reader and author/protagonist come full circle in this circumlocutory narrative. Knowing and not knowing, throughout the text, the history of Sylvia's repressed sexual secrets, the reader shares her horror in facing a violent explosion of recovered memory reenacted through her senses in graphic detail. This autobiographical testimony reconstructs the subject-position and lost agency of the abused daughter, now empowered to effect the "de-siring" of amorous desire. It is only by demythologizing the Father/God and deposing his figure from the position of patriarchal judge and king that the victimized daughter/princess can free herself from Daddy's death-dealing gaze. "I forgive my father so I can forgive myself," she tells us. "[B]ecause I love him. That is the biggest shock of all" (*MFH* 241).[22]

"Daddy won't love me" is no longer a viable threat for the woman who has reclaimed a sense of agency by successfully coming to terms with the father of personal prehistory. The newly enabled subject of utterance, recuperated from traumatic amnesia, is free to write and to create, to articulate the narrative of incestuous abuse and emerge from its telling as a speaking survivor. With powers of language denied her from infancy, the rebellious daughter finally "tells" on her deceased father and, in a gesture of impassioned testimony, reveals his diabolical behavior to an incredulous but sympathetic mother.

Relieved that her repressed family secrets can at last be valorized by both mother and sister, a long-suffering Sylvia feels released from the debilitating effects of four decades of post-traumatic stress disorder. The construction of a coherent narrative—first as fiction, then as autobiography—frees her to transfer filial affection from a treacherous but seductive father back to the altruistic and victimized mother who warmly embraces her daughter and offers unqualified emotional support. Having murdered the specter of a fascistic Daddy figure, Fraser is liberated to reinvent herself as woman and author, creative writer and historical witness to the sufferings of abused children everywhere struggling to find a meaningful voice in contemporary society.[23]

> Now I close my father's coffin. . . . Now I am flying, . . . a seabird on its way to the ocean. . . .
>
> My other self is dead. My father is dead. The king is dead. The princess is dead. . . . Now I close the coffin, truly close it. (*MFH* 242)

Conclusion

The pain of trauma is like physical pain. (Nin *WS* 169)

Stories are the only enchantment possible, for when we begin to see our suffering as a story, we are saved. (Nin *D* 3:296)

This study began by asking questions about the relationship between autobiographical writing and the psychoanalytic process of "working through" traumatic experience. There is a great deal of evidence to suggest that translating confessional speech into written language may profoundly expand the healing potential embedded in testimonial discourse. Several of the authors discussed in *Shattered Subjects*—H. D., Anaïs Nin, and Janet Frame—relied on both psychoanalysis and scriptotherapy for significant periods in their adult lives. Although Otto Rank initially feared that Nin's compulsive journal-writing might be tantamount to an addictive behavior, Anaïs convinced him artfully that her diary functioned as a different kind of therapeutic tool. Logorrhea, free association, and diary-writing all complemented one another by exposing layers of the unconscious that could facilitate abreaction and the reconstruction of a fragmented analytic subject.

Evidence of childhood, adolescent, or early adult trauma emerges in each of the case histories examined in *Shattered Subjects*. In chapter 1, I have deliberately suppressed the chronology of Colette's life-writing in order to focus on the traumatic repercussions of her troubled conjugal history. Emotionally, psychologically, and physically battered by an insensitive and egotistical partner, Colette needed to write through the loss of her preoedipal attachment to Sido in order to reclaim matrifocal mythology, as well as a mother tongue that would eventually empower her to speak and bear witness in self/life-writing. Obsessed with the memory of Willy's brutality, Colette was compelled to reconstruct the narrative of her conjugal misery and to reenact traumatic experience in the masterful mode of ironic comedy.

Only after Willy's death did she begin to anatomize the painful period of apprenticeship that shaped her feminine and artistic sensibilities. Scriptotherapy allowed Colette to reinvent herself as willing partner in a ten-year initiation rite that eventually gave her the right to claim an autonomous subject-position as master of herself, her heart, and her artistic production. Only the historical trauma of Nazi aggression proved too powerful an enemy. But who could withstand such barbaric atrocities without succumbing to permanent emotional scars?

For Hilda Doolittle, the childhood trauma that would resonate throughout an emotionally fraught maturity was the experience of witnessing, at the age of ten, a mysterious accident that rendered her father figuratively blind, castrated, and unresponsive to his daughter's need for paternal valorization. Helpless in the face of Charles Doolittle's sightless gaze, the young girl repressed both the memory of her father's concussion and her grandmother's hysterical revelation of the Moravian cult of *Wunden Eiland*. Hilda refused to acknowledge either wounded father or wounded Savior—figures that were buried in the recesses of her unconscious for more than 30 years. It was Freud himself who recommended that H. D. supplement her psychoanalytic sessions with a serious effort to write out and write through the traumas of World War I that continued to haunt her in the 1930s. Professor Freud ordered his patient to recover the trauma narrative by writing the story straight, without fictional embellishment. Paradoxically, the shock of German bombings during the London blitz of World War II disinterred the long-buried emotional substratum of childhood bereavement recorded in *The Gift*. In *Bid Me to Live,* H. D. assembled a bricolage of thinly veiled autofictions that contributed to an astonishing therapeutic catharsis and released her from three decades of mental torment.

Was Anaïs Nin eventually cured of the obsessions provoked by her father's early betrayal and by her sexual revictimization two decades later? If one is to believe Nin's self-report, her devotion to life-writing, sustained for more than 50 years and productive of 150 journal volumes, saved her from mental breakdown. Scriptotherapy, she testified, allowed her to live at peace with herself, integrated and emotionally centered in the last decade of her life. In an essay included in *Recollections of Anaïs Nin*, I have described my own meeting with Nin in 1972 and our later correspondence in 1975-76. Without question, this vibrant sexagenarian impressed me as a charismatic and emotionally centered speaker, a convincing orator, and a sensitive interlocutor. But I suspect that the relative tranquility Anaïs enjoyed in her final years was attributable to a combination of factors. She felt invigorated by her enormous success with a literary public that responded enthusiastically to the serial release of her edited *Diary*. From 1947 until her death in

1977, Anaïs managed to contrive a relatively stable, though bifurcated private life, divided between her husband Hugh Guiler in New York and her devoted companion Rupert Pole in California. When, in December 1982, Rupert Pole invited me to a concert of chamber music at the house he had shared with Anaïs in Los Angeles, I gleaned from his impassioned recollections of this beloved companion the kind of admiration and respect that must have strengthened Nin in her maturity. Did the process of scriptotherapy save her from neurosis, traumatic obsession, madness, and despair—as she herself so frequently testified? There can be little question that the diary rescued her from psychic fragmentation and provided the gift of absolution—the diary, along with psychoanalysis, the solicitude of Hugh Guiler, the love of Rupert Pole, and the tributes offered by an adoring audience of captivated readers.

For Janet Frame, both autobiography and autofiction comprised exercises in scriptotherapy that fashioned an enabling counternarrative in the wake of her unspeakable *saison en enfer* in New Zealand mental hospitals. Frame achieved healing catharsis by describing the horrors of institutional incarceration in the voice of her fictional alter ego, Istina Mavet. The cracked mirror of ostensible schizophrenia gave way to the illuminating Mirror City of Frame's fertile artistic imagination, as the erstwhile mental patient "unburied" herself through joint ventures of writing and psychotherapy. After nearly a decade of mind wastage, she employed both talking cure and writing cure in the context of narrative recovery.

All the writers discussed in *Shattered Subjects* lived through a major world war that proved to be a powerful and politically defining moment. Colette, H. D., and Anaïs Nin endured two world wars. Janet Frame, Audre Lorde, and Sylvia Fraser integrated war-consciousness into their autobiographical accounts of youth and adolescent development. Haunted, at some point, by the specter of Nazi aggression, all six authors coped simultaneously with personal crises and the challenge of historical trauma. Their experiences of post-traumatic stress disorder were inevitably affected and often overshadowed by the ominous threat of global disaster.

Frame, Lorde, and Fraser consciously fashioned their autobiographical texts in the genre of *testimonio*. For Audre Lorde, traumatic experience acted as a spur to urgent political activity in the service of a disintegrating society very much in need of advocates for healing. Adopting the existential premise that no one can truly be happy so long as a single human being suffers poverty or persecution, Lorde gave voice to individual pain in the context of a larger struggle for racial equality and social justice. A poet warrior, she led a metaphorical army of avid disciples on a passionate crusade to do nothing less than transform the world. On the one occasion when I heard

Lorde address a feminist audience, she seemed almost larger than life—very much the figure of the Amazonian hero I had always imagined her to be.

Testimonio is one of the primary motives implicitly operative in Sylvia Fraser's memoir of incest and healing. A classic victim of incest trauma, Fraser drew on the resources of psychotherapy, dream analysis, and life-writing to recuperate the shattered subject-position so chaotically dissociated by childhood sexual abuse. By telling her unspeakable story in graphic detail, she worked toward a personal catharsis that could, simultaneously, offer validation and hope to other incest survivors trapped in the miasma of traumatic amnesia or haunted by recovered memories too terrible to acknowledge.

The authors I have chosen to examine in *Shattered Subjects* were literally writing for their lives in articulating their poignant stories of trauma and narrative recovery. There are, perhaps, as many literary and therapeutic strategies to exorcise the demons of personal history as there are individuals haunted by ghosts of psychic fragmentation. For each of the writers discussed in this study, autobiographical testimony proved to be a powerful tool in the process of reconstructing the beleaguered subject and remembering the self shattered by traumatic experience.

Notes

INTRODUCTION

1. See Evelyne Ender, *Sexing the Mind*; Sander L. Gilman, et al., *Hysteria Beyond Freud*; Phillip R. Slavney, *Perspectives on "Hysteria"*; Ilza Veith, *Hysteria*; Elaine Showalter, *The Female Malady*, "Hysteria, Feminism, and Gender," and *Hystories*; and Claire Kahane, *Passions of the Voice*.
2. Robert Folkenflik notes that "Freud's 'talking cure' would seem to provide an obvious model for the writing cure that autobiography offers" (11). In *Telling Lies*, Timothy Dow Adams concedes that autobiography "could be thought of as a written form of self-therapy" (12). Throughout *Being in the Text*, Paul Jay draws parallels between autobiographical practice and "the psychoanalytic process of Freud's 'talking cure'" (23). For a fascinating analysis of autobiography as confession see Leigh Gilmore, "Policing Truth." For a summary of the case against autoanalysis, see Eakin's *Touching the World*, pp. 83-87, and Paul Smith's *Discerning the Subject*, chapter 5. See also van der Kolk et al., *Traumatic Stress*.
3. In a section entitled "The Combat Neurosis of the Sex War," Herman notes that "[n]ot until the women's liberation movement of the 1970's was it recognized that the most common post-traumatic disorders are those not of men in war but of women in civilian life" (*Trauma* 28). Herman has continued to argue for the professional recognition of "complex PTSD" by the psychiatric establishment. See also Richard B. Ulman and Doris Brothers, *The Shattered Self*, especially chapters 1 through 3; Bessel A. van der Kolk, "The Psychological Consequences of Overwhelming Life Experiences"; and van der Kolk and Greenberg, "The Psychobiology of Trauma Response."
4. Janice Haaken has, in fact, raised serious ethical questions about "the implications of combining survivors of child abuse, war, political terrorism, religious cults, and the Holocaust under a single psychiatric category"—a tendency that she attributes to a "search for the unifying basis to human suffering and for parallels between male dominance in the family and those forms of domination that govern public life" (1079). See also Dominick LaCapra, *Representing the Holocaust*.

5. Benstock makes a convincing case for the genre of "life-writing" in her essay "Authorizing the Autobiographical." For an illuminating discussion of life-writing as a genre, see Marlene Kadar's introduction "Coming to Terms" in *Essays on Life Writing*. Kadar observes that the "Anglo-Saxon rooted phrase 'life-writing'" has a long history as "a more inclusive term, and as such may be considered to have certain critical advantages" (4). Evelyn Hinz notes similarities between life-writing and both drama and the romance (*Data and Acta* vii). See also Leigh Gilmore's *Autobiographics*.
6. For further discussion of the intersection of autobiography and autofiction, see Suzanne Nalbantian's *Aesthetic Autobiography* and Paul Jay's *Being in the Text*. For analyses of the genre of autobiography, see Adams, Andrews, Butterfield, de Man, Eakin, Folkenflik, Gunn, Gusdorf, Lejeune, Loesberg, Mandel, Neuman, Olney, Pascal, Spengemann, Sprinker, Stanton, Stone, Sturrock, and Weintraub.
7. Robert Folkenflik summarizes the paradox when he asks: "Is autobiography to be found in referentiality, textuality, or social construction? Is there a self in this text? The subject is radically in question" (12). Eakin, in *Touching the World*, challenges Barthes' assertion by claiming that "autobiography is nothing if not a referential art, and the self or subject its principal referent" (3). He complains that poststructuralist critique has invariably, and mistakenly, assumed "that an autobiographer's allegiance to referential truth necessarily entails a series of traditional beliefs about self, language, and literary form" (30). In "Autobiography as De-facement," Paul de Man launches a powerful attack on autobiographical referentiality, arguing that autobiography is not a genre at all, but rather, a figure of reading generated by rhetorical tropes of prosopopoeia.
8. Similarly, Shirley Neuman proposes a tentative resolution to the ongoing "debate between humanists and poststructuralists as to whether the 'subject' is individuated and universal or whether the subject is discursively produced" by advocating a poetics of autobiography that would acknowledge both "that subjects are constructed by discourse" and "that subjects construct discourse" by virtue of individual agency ("Autobiography" 223). Timothy Dow Adams, in analyzing the "autobiographical paradox," concludes that autobiography "possesses a peculiar kind of truth through a narrative composed of the author's metaphors of self that attempt to reconcile the individual events of a lifetime by using a combination of memory and imagination—all performed in a unique act that partakes of therapeutic fiction making" (3).
9. This is not to ignore some exciting experiments in the genres of autobiography and autofiction, including texts by Paul Valéry, André Malraux, Roland Barthes, Michel Leiris, and Monique Wittig. See Eakin, *Touching the World*; Jay, *Being in the Text*; and *Autobiography and Postmodernism*, eds. Kathleen Ashley, Leigh Gilmore, and Gerald Peterson. Gilmore provocatively notes that "to so many

others located on the culturally constructed margins of power, the postmodernist glee associated with the dissolution of notions of the self is hardly a welcome prospect for those already too familiar with the social reality of selflessness" ("Mark" 15n).

10. On the impossibility of "origins," see Laplanche, *Life and Death in Psychoanalysis*. The "central contradiction that plagues any autobiographical text," argues Paul Jay, is "the ever-present ontological gap between the self who is writing and the self-reflexive protagonist of the work" (29). Leigh Gilmore proposes that the "mark of autobiography . . . can be located provisionally in the always problematical deployment of the I. . . . To the extent that definitions of autobiography derive from the reference between the person who says I and the I that is not a person but a function of language, these definitions can always be destabilized" ("Mark" 6).

11. "Autobiography," note Brodzki and Schenck, "localizes the very program of much feminist theory—the reclaiming of the female subject—even as it foregrounds the central issue of contemporary critical thought—the problematic status of the self" (1-2). For analyses of female subjectivity, see Allen and Young, *The Thinking Muse*; Judith Butler, *Bodies That Matter* and *Gender Trouble*; Teresa de Lauretis, *Technologies of Gender*; Jane Gallop, *Feminism and Psychoanalysis*; Elizabeth Grosz, *Volatile Bodies*; Luce Irigaray, *This Sex Which Is Not One* and *Speculum*; bell hooks, *Feminist Theory*; Julia Kristeva, *Desire in Language*; Diana Tietjens Meyers, *Subjection and Subjectivity*; Denise Riley, *"Am I That Name?"*; Sidonie Smith, *Subjectivity, Identity, and the Body*; and Domna Stanton, *The Female Autograph*. For theoretical discussions of women's life-writing, see Bell and Yalom, *Revealing Lives*; Shari Benstock, *The Private Self*; Jeanne Braham, *Crucial Conversations*; Brodzki and Schenck, *Life/Lines*; Margo Culley, *American Women's Autobiography*; Rita Felski, *Beyond Feminist Aesthetics*; Leigh Gilmore, *Autobiographics*; Carolyn Heilbrun, *Writing a Woman's Life*; Estelle Jelinek, *The Tradition of Women's Autobiography*; Marlene Kadar, *Essays on Life Writing*; Françoise Lionnet, *Autobiographical Voices*; Morgan and Hall, *Redefining Autobiography in Twentieth-Century Women's Fiction*; Jeanne Perrault, *Writing Selves*; Personal Narratives Group, *Interpreting Women's Lives*; Sidonie Smith, *A Poetics of Women's Autobiography*; and Smith and Watson, *De/Colonizing the Subject*.

12. In *Male Subjectivity at the Margins*, Kaja Silverman remarks that the Lacanian *je* "not only occupies a different psychic register than the *moi*, but it reveals the latter to be a veritable 'mirage,' . . . the result of a series of misrecognitions. The irreality of the ego, however, in no way diminishes its effectivity. . . . The self . . . fills the void at the center of subjectivity with an illusory plenitude" (4-5).

13. Paul Smith explains that the "imaginary . . . operates to construe for the 'subject' the sense of plenitude or lack-of-lack which is a necessity for the ego

and its functioning" (76). "The imaginary is that set of representations and identifications which supports an illusory plenitude of the ego, or acts as the ego's broker" (20). "For Lacan," says Paul Jay, "recovery in analysis depends on the subject's creation of a self-reflexive discourse that can historicize conscious memory into an eventually 'perfected' narrative. The process of perfecting this narrative becomes the vehicle for the subject's cure" (26).

14. Caruth further observes that anyone dealing with trauma must confront a "peculiar paradox: that in trauma the greatest confrontation with reality may also occur as an absolute numbing to it, that immediacy . . . may take the form of belatedness" (*Trauma* 6).

15. Bessel van der Kolk explains: "The intrusive responses are hyperactivity, explosive aggressive outbursts, startle responses, intrusive recollections in the form of nightmares and flashbacks, and reeactment of situations reminiscent of the trauma. . . . The numbing response consists of emotional constriction, social isolation, retreat from family obligations, anhedonia, and a sense of estrangement" ("Overwhelming Life Experiences" 3).

16. For further information about the role of the amygdala in traumatic memory, see Daniel Schacter, *Searching for Memory*, pp. 212-17. In "The Body Keeps Score," van der Kolk emphasizes the crucial function of the amygdala, that "is thought to integrate internal representations of the external world in the form of memory images with emotional experiences associated with those memories," and that "guides emotional behavior by projections to the hypothalamus, hippocampus, and basal forebrain" (230). See also Freyd, chapter 5, "Ways of Forgetting."

17. Throughout this study, I have used the hybrid term "author/narrator" to designate the split between the historical subject and the autobiographical persona that she or he constructs in the life-writing text; and "narrator/protagonist" to suggest the split between the "I now" who tells the story and the "I then" textually constructed as the narrative unfolds. I generally refer to the author/narrator by surname and to the autobiographical protagonist by first name, though there are some exceptions to this convention, especially in chapter 3.

18. Many of the essays in Benstock's collection *The Private Self* validate such a thesis. See, in particular, contributions by Shari Benstock, Susan Stanford Friedman, and Jane Marcus. Sidonie Smith notes that "autobiography has continued to provide occasions for the entry into language and self-narrative of culturally marginalized peoples, of peoples who are assigned inauthentic voices by the dominant culture" (*Subjectivity* 61).

19. Anne Hunsaker Hawkins analyzes the genre of *pathography* in *Reconstructing Illness*. G. Thomas Couser discusses Lorde's *Cancer Journals* as *autopathography* in *Recovering Bodies*.

CHAPTER ONE

1. In elevating Sido to an exalted status, Colette recuperates both psychic and archetypal resonances of female potency. She resuscitates what Adrienne Rich describes as "images of the prepatriarchal goddess-cults" that "told women that power, awesomeness, and centrality was theirs by nature" (*Of Woman Born* 81). Rich notes that the "cathexis between mother and daughter . . . is the great unwritten story" (226). Jane Lilienfeld offers a more shadowy interpretation of Sido as "a charming woman of great privacy and unavailability," whose uncanny matriarchal power made her resemble a sorceress or a witch ("The Magic Spinning Wheel" 165, 167).
2. In *Colette and the Fantom Subject of Autobiography*, Jerry Aline Flieger situates Sido in the realm of the Lacanian imaginary, "a domain of *illusory* harmony and plenitude, which veils a mutual hostility bred in part by the threat of stultification; the Imaginary relation requires the mediation of a third term in order to escape from mutual fascination, seductive and suffocating" (39). Mary Kathleen Benet remarks that "Sido's voice and personality seem to have had the 'penetrating omnipresence' that Erikson identifies as characteristic of the possessive mother" (190).
3. Michèle Sarde describes this dream of abduction as a primal fantasy that would haunt Colette's mature imagination: "the lure of abduction (rape, sexuality, marriage), an hallucinatory and actual return to the home (the womb, affection, the arms) of the mother" (57). The incorrigible Sido "was to provide her daughter with the model of a woman . . . who loved others because she had begun by loving herself" (20). Colette's half-sister, Juliette, was less fortunate: "when her marriage turned out badly, she made an unsuccessful attempt at suicide and succeeded in hanging herself in 1906, at forty-seven" (53).
4. Flieger indicts Sido at this juncture in the text: "*This* Sido is not the site of infantile pleasure, but is rather the agent for its denial, its rechanneling into the adult functions of communication governed by Law" (53).
5. Analyzing the Captain's melancholy, Flieger invokes the Lacanian analogy of Poe's purloined letter, a secret "that has always been out in the open, in plain sight. The daughter/detective now claims to dig up the secret that was always there in full view, too obvious to be noticed: Captain Colette suffers 'the sadness' of his physical wound" (81).
6. Mary Katherine Benet remarks that Colette "seems to have felt the pathos of the situation more keenly than the betrayal, and to have taken it to heart by assuming the task of writing her father's unrealized works" (190).
7. In *The Bonds of Love*, Jessica Benjamin describes the sadomasochistic dynamic reflected in Colette's marriage and operative, it would seem, in ostensibly normal love relationships: "one gives, the other refuses to accept; one pursues,

the other loses interest; one criticizes, the other feels annihilated" (65). "We suspect," says Jennifer Freyd, "that psychological torment . . . or gross emotional neglect may be as destructive as other forms of abuse" (133).

8. For further commentary on Colette's use of the imagery of disgust, see Henke, "Toward a Feminist Semiotics of Revulsion."
9. Consult Sarde (122-24) for a description of this somewhat farcical melodrama, which left Willy stupefied and Colette stunned and disillusioned. "Lotte Kinceler," Colette remarks, "taught me a great deal. With her came my first doubts of the man I had given myself to so trustfully" (*MA* 31). The pitiable Lotte eventually directed emotional violence against herself. "One afternoon of stifling summer rain she went into her backshop parlour and shot herself through the mouth. She was twenty-six years old" (*MA* 33).
10. "Is it not possible," asks Anne Duhamel Ketchum, "that the mysterious sickness of Colette . . . may well have been some Satrean nausea, a brutal awakening of consciousness at finding in Paris, institutionalized on a large scale, the relations of power, of master and slave, the exploitation from which she suffered so much in her private life?" (24). Another explanation of Colette's mysterious illness might be found in symptoms of constriction associated with interpersonal stress disorders (APA 425).
11. See, for instance, the various accounts of the Colette/Willy collaboration offered by Michèle Sarde and by Joan Hinde Stewart. According to Mary Kathleen Benet, the majority of "Willy's interpolations concern Maugis, the music critic, who was in part a caricature of Willy himself. . . . He also corrects Colette's exuberant style. . . . He crosses out repeated words . . . and adds notes about literary soirées, foreign writers, and English and German terms" (207). When the first of the Claudine novels appeared in 1900 under Willy's name, he protested in a preface "that he had received the manuscript from an anonymous donor. . . . Willy was telling the truth with the confidence that no one would believe it" (Sarde 146).
12. Some readers have been surprised to discover that Sido's inaugural letter in *Break of Day* is partially fabulated and that, in her actual response, Colette's mother happily acceded to Jouvenel's invitation. Here is the historical document of Sido to Sidi: "Your invitation . . . is so gracious that for many reasons I've decided to accept it. Among these reasons there is one which I never resist: the sight of my daughter's dear face, and the sound of her voice. And then I want to meet you, and to judge as far as I can why she has been so eager to kick over the traces for you" (quoted in Richardson 49). Jane Lilienfeld comments that Colette's reconstruction of the text is "a direct reversal of the truth. . . . Colette chose not to see Sido, and she reversed in fiction what happened in life. For her own reasons she transformed denial of the mother into denial of the daughter" (175).

13. Nancy Miller observes: "Much of Colette's work unfolds as a meditation on solitude, on the possibility—for a woman—of living alone beyond despair" (*Subject to Change* 231). Such an independent life entails the construction of a female subject-position beyond the authority of the male gaze. According to Miller, "Colette's texts . . . constitute a discourse *on woman*. . . . *'écriture féminine' avant la lettre*. . . . Colette offers feminist fables of resistance and self-preservation" (240). The "theme of emergence from love into something more sane, something healthier, is one of Colette's founding fables; indeed this leitmotif has the status of an obsessional myth" (Flieger 20).
14. Jerry Aline Flieger believes that "Colette's autofictions are less *Bildungsromans* than *Bildsromans*, picture-novels, which give access to overdetermined images, with the help of a vertical metaphoric memory sifting down through layers of accrued experience" (185). The "'I' of her works is situated somewhere between the fictional status of the *Bildungsroman* protagonist and the 'real' status of the conventional autobiographical subject. . . . And the identity of the narrating 'I' is plural, shifting, overdetermined with multiple ages and perspectives" (184). Catherine Slawy-Sutton describes Colette as "a *brouilleuse de piste*—one who chose to deliberately confuse/provoke her readers" (24-25). Invoking the genre of *Mentir-Vrai* or *True-Lying*, she concludes that Colette's "strategies are defined by a play between revelation through fiction and disguise through autoportrait" (34).
15. Marianne Hirsch offers an excellent analysis of the "duple logic" Colette embraces at the end of *Break of Day*. "It is multiple, containing the voices of 'Sido' and 'Colette,' signaled by a mixture of italic and roman print. . . . The novel hovers indefinably between fiction and autobiography. . . . In the novel, the love plot, proceeding forward chronologically, rivals the mother/daughter plot, which proceeds associatively and retrospectively. These indeterminacies demand of the reader an acceptance and an acting out of contradiction, an oscillating reading. . . . They chart the plot of mother-daughter love within the heterosexual institution of narrative which both silences and articulates it" (107-8).
16. I have adopted the notion of matric masculinity from Angela Moorjani's provocative article on "Fetishism, Gender Masquerade, and the Mother-Father Fantasy." In delineating a "matric fetishism (fetish surrogates for the father's matrix) as compared to phallic fetishism (the stand-ins for the maternal phallus)," Moorjani uses the "word *matrix*, 'womb,' which is derived from the Latin *mater*, to indicate the fantasized nature of the father's childbearing capacities. . . . In line with recent usage, the terms *phallic* and *matric* also include the power, both generative and social/symbolic, that accrues to the father and the mother and with which the child identifies and/or which it envies" (25).

CHAPTER TWO

1. In the typescript of *The Gift*, H. D. describes the Fascist menace as an invidious tarantula and testifies that "this host of Devils flies to incarcerate us or incinerate us, from Germany." She compares her own traumatic memories to a "Time-bomb" set off by the "possibility, at any given second, of complete physical annihilation" (*G Ts* Box 40/Folder 1036/p. 2). In describing the effects of trauma, H. D. explains: "Shock can also, like an earth-quake or an avalanche uncover buried treasure, . . . the *camera obscura* where our living inheritance is stored" (*G Ts* Box 40/Folder 1035/p. 26). For an excellent discussion of the wartime pressures surrounding H. D.'s composition of *The Gift*, see Fuchs.
2. Deborah Kelly Kloepfer in *The Unspeakable Mother* calls our attention to H. D.'s early imaginary identification with Orestes and to a "fantasy of matricide" embedded in *Paint It Today* (48-49). For an analysis of H. D.'s historical relationship with her mother, and of her recrudescence of the maternal images of Demeter and the Great Mother, see S. Friedman, *Psyche Reborn*, pp. 137-54. Despite adolescent conflicts with Helen Wolle Doolittle, H. D. eventually came to believe "that the mother holds a prior, even primal position in the unconscious of the individual" (145).
3. See Joan Jacobs Brumberg, *Fasting Girls*, and Leslie Heywood, *Dedication to Hunger*, for the history of anorexia. Kloepfer suggests that the H. D. figure in *Hermione* "borders on anorexia throughout the novel" (86).
4. Susan Friedman cites, among H. D.'s dream records, a nightmare "in which she sees her mother lying passive, about to be raped. Another presents that favored brother trying to strangle her with a length of braided cord from a box of candy they are sharing" (*Psyche* 48). Identifying Gilbert Doolittle as H. D.'s "psychological double," Friedman tells us that his death in battle contributed to two of H. D.'s psychological breakdowns, in 1919 and 1934, respectively. For a discussion of editorial changes to the manuscript of *The Gift* prior to its publication by New Directions in abridged form, see DuPlessis, "A Note on the State of H. D.'s *The Gift*."
5. In *H. D. and Freud*, Buck offers a complex and insightful reading of the Madonna lily as a "symbol of the phallus obtained from the father," but whose significance is "defined by the mother" (108). "The fantasy can however also be read as female penis envy" (110). Susan Friedman interprets this "Easter-lily or Madonna-lily" in both *Advent* and *The Gift* as a symbol of the castrated phallic mother. "As flower of the Annunciation and the Resurrection, as representation of female genitalia in the town of Mary (the Mother), the Madonna-lily cut by the Father signifies both the Mother's power and castration" (*PW* 316).

6. Freud explains, "Among the store of unconscious phantasies of all neurotics, and probably of all human beings, there is one which is seldom absent and which can be disclosed by analysis: this the phantasy of watching sexual intercourse between the parents" (*SE* 14: 269). Susan Friedman also believes that "this dream can be read as a representation of the primal scene" (*PW* 338).
7. In relation to the snake imagery dominant in this section of *The Gift*, one should consider H. D.'s pronouncement in *Notes on Thought and Vision*: "The world of vision has been symbolised in all ages by various priestly cults in all countries by the serpent," which the poet herself associates with both the jelly-fish and the "over-conscious mind" (40). See also Robinson, "Psychoanalytic Concept," pp. 243-44. In the typescript of *The Gift*, H. D. recalls a Moravian narrative describing two snakes who brought good luck to the historical figure Martin Mack: "The serpents passed over the paper and his hand held steady" (*G Ts* Box 39/Folder 1029/p. 30). The Native Americans interpreted this event as a sign of the Great Spirit's protection of the Moravians.
8. According to Susan Friedman, the Aladdin story represents the "parable of 'castration.' . . . The second snake rears erect to accomplish what the story has predicted—the wound which leaves an ugly scar that can never be healed. Female genitals and mouth conflate in a scene of 'castration'—the theft of both erotic pleasure and speech—which is the destiny of both mother and daughter in the primal scene and its repetition" (*PW* 338). As Sidonie Smith notes, the "surrender of woman's reason to embodiment also contaminates her relationship to the word. Allying her speech with the seductive Eve and the serpent, . . . gender ideologies of the early nineteenth century reaffirmed the association of the hole in woman's face with the contaminations of sex" (*Subjectivity* 15-16).
9. Those familiar with Mary Daly's *Pure Lust* and *Gyn/Ecology* might recall that the snake is an ancient, pre-Hellenic symbol of the Mother Goddess and of female empowerment through menstruation and change. As the snake sloughs off its skin, it becomes a symbol of renewal and resurrection. In *The Glory of Hera*, Philip Slater describes the ancient Greek "symbolic equation between the serpent and the umbilicus, so that the snake is seen as a bridge to the mother, to the womb, and hence of non-life, the unconscious, and the supernatural realm" (95). See also Donna Hollenberg's analysis of the snake as a bisexual, "oral-narcissistic" symbol and an "age-old symbol of fertility and chthonic power" (26-28). It is fascinating to recall that the Greek physician Asklepios inaugurated the analytic practice of dream interpretation in his Asklepion in Pergamon (now Bergama, Turkey).
10. One of the figures that H. D. envisages in her famous vision of "Writing on the Wall" in Corfu is "the tripod of classic Delphi, . . . this venerated object of the cult of the sun god, symbol of poetry and prophecy" (*TF* 46). Bryher,

she tells us, "had the detachment and the integrity of the Pythoness of Delphi" during this extraordinary experience (*TF* 48). "Delphi . . . was the shrine of the Prophet and Musician, the inspiration of artists and the patron of physicians" (*TF* 50). For further discussion of Apollo and the Python in Greek myth, see Philip Slater, *The Glory of Hera*, especially pp. 94-118; and Hollenberg, *H. D.*, pp. 26-30.

11. In *Penelope's Web*, Susan Friedman reminds us that H. D. herself alluded to the Eleusinian mysteries in *Notes on Thought and Vision*, where the rites celebrating the dyad of Demeter and Persephone are "held up as the model for fully integrated creativity" (9). In the Eleusinian mysteries, "the initiate passed through three rooms representing the dimensions that must be experienced and integrated: the passion of the body; the detachment of the intellect; and the mystery of the spirit" (10). See also Donna Hollenberg's analysis of the Eleusinian rites in chapter 1 of *H. D.: The Poetics of Childbirth and Creativity*.

12. Barbara Guest observes that Charles Doolittle's accident "came to have a disproportionate meaning in H. D.'s life. . . . It seems that one evening her father had returned home, incoherent and fainting from a wound in his head. . . . For years she was traumatized by this event. She spoke of it to her various analysts, including Freud and Havelock Ellis, and the episode returned in her dreams" (18). It was not until 1933 that H. D. "was able to describe more literally what had happened" and to acknowledge that her father "had been struck by the streetcar that passed their house in Upper Darby" (18-19). Her breakthrough, she felt, was a result of analysis with Dr. Hanns Sachs. In that same year, she confided to Havelock Ellis that she had had "terrible phobias after [her] father's death" (19).

13. As Cathy Caruth notes, "what returns to haunt the trauma victim in Freud's primary example of trauma . . . is, . . . significantly, the shocking and unexpected occurrence of an accident. . . . Paul de Man's notion of referentiality . . . associates reference with an impact, and specifically the impact of a fall" (*Unclaimed Experience* 6). See Caruth's intriguing analysis of trauma and falling in chapter 4 of *Unclaimed Experience*. According to Susan Friedman, the "wounded Father/Freud occupies the position of woman" (*PW* 296). "*The Gift* works through the transferential construction of the Father Who Terrifies by (re)constructing an ideal father who redeems. Like Christ, the power of this re-visioned father figure depends upon his wounds" (*PW* 340).

14. H. D. seems to have been somewhat stunned by Freud's emphasis on her "mother fixation." She confesses, rather excitedly, in a letter to Bryher that "F[reud] says mine is the absolutely FIRST layer, I got stuck at the earliest pre-OE[dipal] stage, and 'back to the womb' seems to be my only solution. Hence islands, sea, Greek primitives and so on" (quoted by S. Friedman in *PW* 319). H. D. appears to have been grateful to Freud for pointing out the uniqueness

of her "perfect bisexuality" and for refusing to condemn her love of women outright, despite various hints that she would never be emotionally satisfied with lesbian attachment. Friedman suggests that it was precisely this working through of the maternal transference that enabled H. D.'s "development of a gynopoetic empowered by the Mother/Muse" (*PW* 322). See also Claire Buck, *H. D. and Freud*, and Angela Moorjani, *The Aesthetics of Loss and Lessness*.

15. In *The Practice of Love*, Teresa de Lauretis elaborates on "Laplanche and Pontalis's notion of fantasy as narrative scenario" or "structuring scene of desire" (123) and observes that these theorists "make a convincing case for the metapsychological status of fantasy and for its structural, constitutive role in subject processes. They reject the formal separation between conscious and unconscious fantasies—between daydreams, for instance, and memory traces or fantasies recovered in analysis—and instead see a 'profound continuity between the various fantasy scenarios—the stage-setting of desire' in the history of the subject" (82).

16. For perspicacious readings of H. D.'s reinterpretation of Freud's psychosexual theories, see chapter 5 of S. Friedman's *Psyche Reborn*; Claire Buck, *H. D. and Freud*; Janice Robinson, "What's in a Box?"; DuPlessis and Friedman, "Woman is Perfect"; and Angela Moorjani, "Fetishism, Gender Masquerade, and the Mother-Father Fantasy." Buck, in particular, notes that the "central insight which H. D. takes from psychoanalysis is that the split self is a text to be read" (99). Relying on Freud's notions of the family romance, H. D. predicates a split subject whose condition of radical lack is contingent on the practical impossibility of ever realizing the sufficiency implied by an originary mother-father fantasmatic dyad. The Freudian premise of bisexuality nonetheless proves "central to H. D.'s writing. Bisexuality stands for the possibility of a new sexual identity, bringing together masculinity and femininity into a new unity which is also a transcendence of difference" (Buck 11).

17. For a more positive interpretation of Charles Doolittle's feminization in *The Gift*, see *Penelope's Web*. Susan Friedman identifies the wounded father with the "pacifist Moravian Jesus" and places him "within the context of the daughter's recovery of the primal Mother. . . . *The Gift* repeats H. D.'s maternal transference with Freud and extends it into a healing gynopoetic that opposes the Law of the Father embodied in the Nazi attacks" (341-42).

18. Cassandra Laity, in her introduction to *Paint It Today*, also cites this quotation and notes that the "terrible" aspect of her love for Frances Gregg "continued to fuel H. D.'s imagination long after the relationship had ended," indeed, until the poet was "nearly fifty years of age" (xxxiii). Susan Friedman analyzes the complex intertextual relationship among *Paint It Today*, *Asphodel*, and *Bid Me to Live* in *Penelope's Web*. For an intriguing hypothesis concerning H. D.'s

composition of *Asphodel*, see Robert Spoo, "H. D.'s Dating of *Asphodel*: A Reassessment."

19. Susan Friedman elaborates on H. D.'s Freudian strategy by comparing her autobiographical writing to the scene of psychoanalysis: "As analyst, the 'I now' who narrates eyes the 'I then.' As analysand, the narrated self is positioned in the part of resisting analysand whose unfolding story works through the tangle of repression into the clearing of recovered memories" (*PW* 83). H. D. apparently emulated in her autobiographical prose the kind of autoanalysis practiced by Freud in his *Interpretation of Dreams*. "H. D.'s self-analysis in the scene of writing boldly asserts that she can split the subject so as to reconstitute it—not as a unitary subject, but as a self with unconscious as well as conscious manifestations" (*PW* 83). Janice Robinson declares that, for H. D., "the techniques of psychoanalysis had become a technique of writing as well as a way of coping" ("What's In a Box?" 244). See also Buck, chapter 4, for an interesting discussion of the way in which "H. D.'s writing method corresponds . . . to the analytic method" (114).

20. In May 1915, Richard Aldington described the couple's loss in a letter to Amy Lowell: "Hilda was delivered of a little girl still-born, about 2. am. this morning. . . . Poor Hilda is very distressed, but is recovering physically" (Zilboorg 1:20). In *Tribute to Freud*, H. D. ascribes the stillbirth to "shock and repercussions of war news broken to me in a rather brutal fashion" (40). As Trudi Tate explains, H. D. "had been shocked by the news that the passenger ship *Lusitania* had been sunk with 1200 civilian casualties" (10). See Tate's discussion of H. D.'s war fiction in *Modernism, History, and the First World War*.

21. Hermione recalls the trauma of giving birth in a cellar during an air raid—a fictional construction that departs emblematically from H. D.'s own biographical experience. H. D. clearly intends to heighten the association between her own pregnancy-loss and the war wounds endured by soldiers during World War I. The analogy might be metaphorically strengthened if one compares Hermione's mourning over stillbirth to Weir Mitchell's observations of a "phantom limb" lingering in the psychic economy of soldiers and accident victims who have suffered amputation. In *Volatile Bodies*, Elizabeth Grosz offers an extended philosophical discussion of the "phantom limb" syndrome—a phenomenon that seems closely to coincide with the traumatic resonances of pregnancy-loss as described by H. D. in *Asphodel* and *Bid Me to Live*. Both texts imply a startling analogy between war-wounds and interrupted gestation—to such an extent that the specter of her stillborn daughter haunts H. D.'s autobiographical imagination as if it were a phantom limb. Might the loss of a symbiotic presence psychologically embedded in maternal consciousness during pregnancy continue to haunt the female subject like the ghost of an amputated limb? To extend Freud's analogy between the gestating infant and

the phallus, might pregnancy-loss be interpreted intrapsychically as a symbolic castration?

22. In his foreword to Abraham and Torok's study, *The Wolf Man's Magic Word: A Cryptonymy*, Jacques Derrida suggests that in cases of melancholia, the imago of the lost one is psychologically "encrypted" or "incorporated." "The Self tries to identify with the object it has 'incorporated.' . . . Sealing the loss of the object, but also marking the refusal to mourn, such a maneuver is foreign to and actually opposed to the process of introjection. I pretend to keep the dead alive, intact, *safe (save) inside me*. . . . With the real loss of the object having been rejected, . . . incorporation is a kind of theft to reappropriate the pleasure object. . . . The crypt is the vault of desire" (xvi-xvii).

23. Despite his wartime love affairs with Flo Fallas and Dorothy "Arabella" Yorke, Richard Aldington continued to write passionate love letters to Hilda from France throughout the spring and into the summer of 1918. His mood was sentimental and nostalgic, as he reminisced about their romantic travels in Italy and elevated H. D. to the status of soulmate and poetic muse. On July 7, 1918, he proclaims: "I am tenderly and passionately in love with you as always" (Zilboorg 1:95). On July 24: "My dear, dear beautiful child-wife, you don't think that our love could end?" (113-14). On July 28: "Faun and Dryad will always live & always love each other" (115). These communications are especially poignant in light of the Aldingtons' impending separation, though it is interesting that both Richard and Hilda continued to celebrate their premarital honeymoon in Italy as a nostalgic idyll throughout their lifelong correspondence. See Zilboorg 2, *passim*.

24. Barbara Guest comments that H. D. "had developed an almost pathological fear of pregnancy and would not have sexual relations with him [Richard Aldington]" (78). Considering the trauma of H. D.'s stillbirth, however, her reaction hardly seems pathological. In *Asphodel*, Hermione acerbically comments that, despite promises on the part of her husband Darrington and her lover Cyril Vane to "be careful," she twice found herself accidentally pregnant. A woman as cerebral as H. D. must have felt enormous vulnerability in the face of nature's relentless determination to reproduce the species. She undoubtedly experienced a sense of alienation and helplessness, as if the species had parasitically colonized her unwilling somatic self. Hence H. D.'s heroism in choosing to continue her second pregnancy, despite the emotional and legal complications of illegitimacy. Evidently, the birth of her daughter Perdita proved to be a powerful psychological compensation for the earlier stillbirth. When H. D. found herself pregnant again in 1929 with Kenneth Macpherson's child, she agreed, with remarkable docility, to seek an abortion in Berlin. Barbara Guest reports that H. D. made a "miraculous, guiltless

recovery from what could have been a rotten scene" and concluded that "it was ALL FOR THE GOOD" (195).

25. In a number of letters to Hilda during the summer of 1918, Richard Aldington complains about Dorothy Yorke's overweening possessiveness: "Arabella is trying hard . . . to enslave me completely. . . . I am appalled . . . at the degree of subjugation she intends for me" (Zilboorg 1:100). In contrast, H. D. feels that she has managed to exorcise the powerful ghost of D. H. Lawrence through the completion of *Madrigal*. "I got a sort of Hail and Farewell into my last chapter," she explains in a letter to Aldington. "I felt that I did not have to worry any more to 'place' old Lorenzo, having 'placed' him in time and space and eternity, at last, to my own satisfaction" (Zilboorg 2:140). By the time she finished the first draft of *Bid Me to Live [Madrigal]* in 1939, H. D. had overcome her writer's block and was writing prolific prose and poetry. For an analysis of H. D.'s clever intertextual "embedding" of D. H. Lawrence's fictional themes into her own exposition of their aborted relationship, see S. Friedman, *Penelope's Web*, 151-70.

26. I am grateful to Bonnie Kime Scott for initially calling my attention to the association between *Notes* and the concept of *gloire*. Susan Friedman makes a similar connection in *Penelope's Web*, as does DuPlessis in "Romantic Thralldom." For a discussion of H. D.'s *Notes* in relation to her poetics of childbirth and creativity, see Donna Hollenberg's *H. D.*, chapter 1, "Serpent and Thistle." As Hollenberg explains, H. D. in *Notes* "gives the physical experience of childbirth metaphysical dimensions: she claims 'womb vision' and focuses on the mother-child dyad as the psychic structure underlying creativity" (19). In relation to the *gloire*, Joseph Milicia writes: "Julia gives the word a variety of meanings, but chiefly it is the vitality, the animation of a thing—the instress, the life within, as in the 'charged' paintings of Van Gogh" (295). As Deborah Kelly Kloepfer explains, the elusive *gloire* may be translated as both "child-consciousness" and the "unborn story." A "woman writing creates/becomes a great mother who thrusts herself both around the story and into it; inside the mother is child/writer; within her is the unborn text, and within that story, herself again, both mother and daughter, parthenogenic, birthing the word, born of the word, born of the *gloire*" (92).

27. Susan Friedman identifies the discourse of pregnancy in *Asphodel* as "consistently lyric and rhythmic, repetitious and hypnotic, an eruption of the Kristevan Semiotic into the Symbolic—in H. D.'s text, not only inscribing the daughter's longing for the maternal body, but also representing the mother speaking. . . . The conventions of dominant discourse provide no language in which to speak as pregnant subject. But Hermione's interior monologues about pregnancy create an alternative discourse, one characterized by a linguistic

and rhythmic experimentation that deconstructs the opposition of subject and object and anticipates contemporary theories of *écriture féminine*" (*PW* 187).

28. Richard Aldington seems also to have been suffering from post-traumatic stress disorder as a result of combat experience during the war. He writes in January 1919 that he is "on the verge of a complete mental collapse" and complains of "extraordinary head-aches," as well as difficulty concentrating (Zilboorg 1:183-84). In a letter to Ezra Pound, H. D. reports that in April 1919 "it was madness in London . . . to see him look out at me through a strange great hulk of strange passion and disintegration" (1:207). She confides to George Plank that Richard "was, I am quite certain, all but 'certifiable' [as insane] that season just before I finally left him" (1:208). Despite the claim that she herself had initiated their separation, H. D. was thunderstruck in 1937 when she received Richard's request for a legal divorce: "My mind is cold like ice but my heart thumps when I even think of it" (Zilboorg 2:61). And yet, remarkably, this resuscitation of postwar feelings of conjugal betrayal helped H. D. "break through the writer's block which had led to her psychoanalysis in the early thirties" (Zilboorg 2:64). Confronting Richard again in 1938 was, she felt, "much better for the UNK [unconscious] . . . better to get him in perspective." She describes the awkward reunion in a letter to George Plank: "RA turned up here. . . . He is very fat. I never knew anyone make such a muddle of anything" (2:66). Like Colette, H. D. has chosen to caricature her ex-husband rather than to demonize him.

29. In her article on "Fetishism, Gender Masquerade, and the Mother-Father Fantasy," Angela Moorjani delineates a psychologically composite male-female figure in the context of a "matric fetishism" predicated on the imaginary father's "childbearing capacities" (25). H. D., she contends, "counters phallic fetishism's fixation on female lack and the phallic woman with matric fetishism's emphasis on male lack and the matric man fantasy. If women need the phallus to be complete, then men need the matrix to be whole again" (33). "Although her tendency was to make of Freud the mother in transference," Moorjani observes, "in consonance with the fantasy of mother-father integrity, she preferred to make of him a matric male" (34)—and to use this androgynous mother/father phantasm as the ground for her aesthetic theories of spiritual *gloire*. Susan Edmunds remarks that "H. D. also has two bodies. One occupies the [maternal] space of epiphany: it is hale, whole, holy. The other occupies the [paternal] space of narrative or history, a body containing pain and contained by plot" (1). One might recall Freud's allusion to female bisexuality in his essay on "Femininity": "Regressions to the fixations of the pre-Oedipal phases very frequently occur; in the course of some women's lives there is a repeated alternation between periods in which masculinity or femininity gains the upper hand. Some portion of what we men call 'the

enigma of woman' may perhaps be derived from this expression of bisexuality in women's lives" (*SE* 22: 131).

CHAPTER THREE

1. Elyce Wakerman writes in *Father Loss* that if a daughter feels somehow responsible for her father's desertion of the family, "she must also accept that she wasn't good enough, wasn't worth his staying around" (109). "An internal battleground of contradictions, . . . the girl whose father left home is sure of only one thing: the first man she ever loved walked out on her" (110). "I lost my first beauty contest," Nin laments. "To lose one's first beauty contest means you lose them all" (*D* 6:98).
2. Deirdre Bair speculates that the story of the journal's inauguration as a letter to her father seems to have been invented by Anaïs around the age of eighteen and has remained something of a moot issue, though it seems clear that, from its initiation in 1914, the diary reflected its adolescent author's emotional obsession with Daddy and her "fixation on wooing and winning her father back into the family" (Bair 29). Throughout this chapter, I refer to any of the seven volumes published as *The Diary of Anaïs Nin* (1966-1980) in italics as *Diary* and volume number; and to the original 150-volume journal, as well as recently published early diaries and the unexpurgated *Journal of Love*, in the larger category of "journal" or "diary" (lowercase, roman type).
3. According to Joan Bobbitt McLaughlin, "the world of the diaries is a carefully contrived and beautifully synchronized artistic creation, a world fashioned and executed by Anaïs Nin" (191). "The pages of a diary," observes Kim Krizan, "cannot contain the true self in any real sense, but only a self which is an interpretation, an arrangement of facts and fictions, a construction" (23). As Duane Schneider notes, Nin's expurgated diaries must be approached as "carefully wrought works of literature" that constitute "something of a new art form—the journal-novel" (10). Nin declares in *The Novel of the Future*: "I have often said that it was the fiction writer who edited the diary" (85). On the persona in the *Diary*, see Wendy DuBow and Duane Schneider. For further discussion of journal-writing as therapy, see Ira Progroff, *At a Journal Workshop*; and articles by Niemeyer, Begos, Rainer, Finlayson, Hoy, Moffat, and Margaret Miller. For an analysis of the diary genre, see Rebecca Hogan.
4. Elyce Wakerman confirms that a young girl, "suddenly deprived of the first man she ever loved," will inevitably "carry that rejection with her for the rest of her life" (55). The resultant complex of "father hunger" can engender symptoms of "unhealthy narcissism," as the abandoned daughter obsessively searches for "self-esteem through the admiration of others" (63). Many of Nin's

future relationships would be dominated by a need to seduce the absent father through the conquest of paternal surrogates like Edmund Wilson, who embodied for Anaïs the "full tyranny of the father" (*D* 4:89). "In Edmund Wilson I sought reconciliation with the father," she admits. "Or was I seeking to conquer the father?" (*D* 4:97).

5. When Nin's psychotherapist Dr. Clement Staff identified Joaquin's "violent spankings" as her "first humiliation at the hands of man," Anaïs was able to understand the pre-trauma that had precipitated her own sadomasochistic compulsions. "Staff asked her to consider the possibility that because of her father's abuse, she had somehow linked humiliation with pleasure. She said it was true, that from the first spanking, she had accepted a kind of 'slavery' even as she went on to abandon, punish, and hurt all those who had hurt her" (Bair 319). In the third volume of her *Diary*, Nin rewrites as "erotica" the story of these childhood spankings and the adult epiphany that made her aware of the short circuit between pleasure and pain dominating her emotional life: "It was as if the spankings came too near to regions usually devoted to sensuous pleasure. Both pain and pleasure suddenly revealed to be in proximity to each other, physically and emotionally" (*D* 3:171). A number of the stories in *Delta of Venus* and *Little Birds* focus on incidents of childhood sexual abuse. For further discussion of *Seduction of the Minotaur*, see Henke, "Lillian Beye's Labyrinth."

6. As Ellen G. Friedman observes in "Escaping from the House of Incest," the offense is voyeuristic, insofar as "the father's naked eye does not confront the actual daughter. Rather, through the two lenses he transforms the daughter he had called 'ugly' into an object shaped to his desire" (40). At the 1994 Anaïs Nin Conference held at Long Island University, Joaquin Nin-Culmell protested in his keynote address that the practice of taking nude pictures of young children was common in Europe at the turn of the century and had innocuous, sexually neutral implications. It is clear from her diary entries, however, that Anaïs subjectively experienced her father's photographic intrusions as sexually demeaning. My attributions of sexual abuse refer to Joaquin Nin's scopophilic practices, as well as to his ritual spankings. I am not intimating that his abusive behavior went beyond the lascivious gaze and equally ambiguous backside beatings that made such a powerful impression on Anaïs. As Diane Richard-Allerdyce observes, "Nin's work resonates with her unsayable response to early paternal abuse (whether sexual or otherwise psychological and physical) and the 'earth-shattering' effects of that violation" (*Anaïs Nin* 7). "We do not know whether Nin was sexually abused by her father as a child. . . . What we do know is that Nin's lifelong writings show the effects of severe traumatization around the issue of the paternal" (42).

7. In the erotic tale "Mandra," the narrator titillates her audience with a description of Mary, a woman who "has never known a real orgasm, at thirty-four, after a

sexual life that only an expert accountant could keep track of" (*LB* 140). In *Fire*, Nin complains of a nonorgasmic liaison with Gonzalo Moré: "I cannot feel the orgasm with him" (329). "This force in me . . . I now carry like unexploded dynamite" (331). See also *Fire* 352, 371, and 411. Later, her celebration of erotic *jouissance* will explode in a triumphant catalogue of physical ecstasies enhanced by electric "flesh-arrows" and a "foam of music" (*D* 2:264).

8. Many of Nin's stories in *Delta of Venus* and *Little Birds* offer disconcerting scenarios of sadomasochistic sexual violence. Edmund Miller, in "Erato Throws a Curve," questions Nin's pervasive assumption that "women only come to appreciate sex through force" and allies her erotic writing with the "central rape fantasy" of male-authored pornography (176). For a different judgment, see Smaro Kamboureli's eloquent defense of Nin's "fusion of discourse and intercourse" through lyrical pornography (96): "As her own aphrodisiac is poetry, so her stories are exciting . . . because their sexual content is enriched by her poetic sensibility" (102). When later questioned by interviewers about her "secret erotic desire" for violation, Nin conjectured that such feelings might be socially constructed and that these "dreams may disappear when woman is freed of guilt for her sexual desires" (*WS* 61). By the time Nin wrote "In Favor of the Sensitive Man" for *Playgirl* in 1974, she decried the "purely macho type" and exposed loutish behavior as "false masculinity" (*SM* 46). She insisted that no new woman would tolerate, in this Age of Aquarius, the sadistic strategies of a man who humiliates, dominates, or subjugates his partner.

9. "The hostility seething in abandoned daughters is only barely muted," writes Wakerman. "Ignited by the rejection of childhood, . . . the anger frequently surfaces as determination. She *will* succeed; she *will* be safe; she will not need" (114). According to Nancy Scholar, Anaïs "wished to emulate her mother during adolescence, referring to her in the second early Diary . . . as 'the woman nearest perfection in the world,'" but later rebelled against the mother she perceived as a "domestic tyrant" (2-3).

10. Wakerman further elucidates this mentality: "We are angry with mother for a number of reasons. The feeling of helplessness that accompanies grief . . . is assuaged to some extent by anger. . . . [M]other has proved herself to be powerless. She could neither prevent father's departure, nor soothe our pain or her own. She is at least as powerless as we" (130). For an interesting interpretation of Nin's conquest of the internalized, self-destructive, and devouring mother, see Stephanie A. Demetrakopoulos Gauper, "Anaïs Nin and the Feminine Quest for Consciousness." For more on the phenomenon of mother blame in paternally abusive households, see Herman, *Incest*, as well as Armstrong, Jacobs, Rush, and Russell.

11. For an intriguing discussion of Otto Rank's influence on Nin's own analysis of her Don Juan syndrome, see Philip K. Jason, "Doubles/Don Juans." Rank hypothesized in *The Don Juan Legend* that the male obsessed with sexual conquest might suffer from an insatiable need to compensate for maternal rejection. The female Don Juan, Jason concludes, must be driven by a similar compulsion: "the unattainability of the *father* and the compensatory substitute for *him*" (92).
12. Fitch declares that Nin's "final and greatest work will be her diary, which she has learned to rewrite, condense, and edit. She . . . will remove all wrinkles and scandal. . . . But by selecting, eliminating, and hiding she is working on a new genre" (360). "This is indeed a fictionalized, some will say deceptive, autobiography in diary form" (368). Anna Balakian warns that the "diary and the creative work are like two communicating vessels, and the division is an imaginary one: they feed each other constantly" ("Poetic Reality" 115-16). Nin's life, insists Diane Wakoski, "is lived and written so fully as to seem fictional" (148). "Nin's ability to present the abstract in concrete form," says Richard Centing, "and her use of novelistic techniques transforms autobiography into universal truth" (170).
13. "And if I resist you?" queries Anaïs, and Joaquin counters playfully: "I will seduce you" (*I* 210). "If Anaïs the diarist is to be believed," remarks Bair, Nin and her father "indulged in a nonstop orgiastic frenzy" after the initiation of their affair at Valescure (174). "Nin's seduction of her father in the summer of 1933," writes Diane Richard-Allerdyce, "was part of the process of facing and taking hold of a past trauma in order to take leave of it" (32).
14. Joanne Rock declares in "Her Father's Daughter" that "the most disturbing element of the incest is Nin's illusory sense of victory" (36). Rock hypothesizes that Nin might have introduced into her journal candid descriptions of Joaquin as her "double" and a consummate Don Juan figure in order to intrigue Dr. Otto Rank and convince him to take her on as a psychoanalytic patient. In preparation for her first meeting with Rank, Nin had apparently familiarized herself with *The Don Juan Legend* and *The Double: A Psychoanalytical Study*. See also Jason, "Doubles/Don Juans."
15. "Hope has created a miracle," observes Noel Riley Fitch. "She has won him back" (151). During the nine-day "novena" in Valescure, Anaïs "is disassociated from herself, observing her actions from a distance. . . . She may have finally won her father's approval, but at a cost" (156). Deirdre Bair tends to minimize that cost by speculating that Anaïs "ended the two weeks in a state of euphoria and a belief in the rightness of all she had done and departed feeling free of any lasting repercussion" (176). As Judith Herman tells us, the survivor of childhood sexual abuse "has great difficulty protecting herself in the context of intimate relationships," and the "idea of saying no to the emotional demands

of a parent, spouse, lover, or authority figure may be practically inconceivable" (*Trauma* 111-12). Richard-Allerdyce notes: "Incest, the failure of human family 'law' and of the father-protector function, perpetuates the wounded daughter's inability to incorporate appropriate boundaries" (*Anaïs Nin* 39).

16. Deirdre Bair makes it clear that the father-daughter love affair continued for some time after Anaïs returned to Louveciennes—until she grew exasperated with Joaquin's narcissism, recognized his weakness, and determined to end the affair. This scenario is played out fictionally in "Winter of Artifice." "The split with the father," observes Suzanne Nalbantian, "coincides with the inception of her art" (*Aesthetic Autobiography* 180).

17. Bair tells us that Anaïs was following Rank's instructions when she determined to "jilt" her besotted father, but skeptically points out that "Nin's diary is the only written record of Rank's alleged advice" (190). Later, Anaïs would report that Dr. Inge Bogner considered Joaquin schizophrenic (*D* 5:234). She describes "the shock of realizing with Bogner that he died a schizophrenic" (*D* 6:20) and that he had lived almost entirely without affect, "utterly disconnected" from emotional intimacy (*D* 6:231). For Rank's assessment of Nin's relationship with her father, see his "Preface" to her *Early Diary*.

18. For a discussion of *House of Incest* as surrealistic prose-poem, see Anna Balakian, "Anaïs Nin, the Poet" and Sharon Spencer, "The Music of the Womb." For a superb analysis of the novel in terms of narrative recovery, see Richard-Allerdyce, *Anaïs Nin*, 30-43. According to Richard-Allerdyce, *House of Incest* delineates Nin's "narrative entrance to the psychoanalytic moment in which one can begin to mourn" (30). "Nin's narrator tells the story of embodied trauma and its relation to psychological structure. In the telling, we can hear Nin's own story—that of patriarchy's wounded daughter striving for relief from the hysterical suffering born of that position" (31).

19. "I have had a great yearning for absolution," Nin confesses in *Incest* (279), and all her journals reflect similar sentiments. More than three decades later, Anaïs would beg her therapist, Dr. Inge Bogner, to grant her absolution for daring to enact those fantasies that "other human beings only dream of" (*D* 6:25). Acknowledging a reversion to the Catholic practice of confession, she pleads: "Help me, Dr. Bogner. . . . Give me absolution." (*D* 6:380). According to Deirdre Bair, "Nin credited analysis with helping her to see that she had committed no crime and therefore should feel no Catholic guilt" (478). "Absolution," however, "became an important concept in her life's last decade" (Bair 609). See also Nin's conversation with Krishna Baldev Vaid in *ANAÏS* 5 (1987) and Joaquin Nin-Culmell's letter to Hugh Guiler in "Anaïs Nin, My Sister."

20. "The gap between the two versions," says Richard-Allerdyce, "tells an important story of its own" ("Narrative and Authenticity" 86). Erica Jong reads the

Incest account of Nin's aborted pregnancy sympathetically: "It was a sacrifice she was making and she was well aware of the cost" (23). Miranda Seymour, in a *New York Times* review of Noel Riley Fitch's biography *Anaïs*, accuses Nin of being thoroughly disingenuous with her audience and concludes that her "diaries were a fraud," (18).

21. Deirdre Bair describes the account of Nin's pregnancy and abortion in the posthumously published *Incest* as "heavily edited and substantially rewritten" (562 n.6). Anaïs, she tells us, "insisted that the child was Henry's and not Hugo's, even though she had been intimate with both men during the period of conception. That she had also been intimate with her father did not bear thinking, let alone writing about, and Joaquin Nin was never included in her list of possible fathers" (197). In discussing "Anaïs Nin and Otto Rank," Sharon Spencer mentions that Rank's surviving relatives believe that he was the progenitor (109).

22. Bair is uncertain at what point Miller was informed of Nin's condition and speculates that she did not share the news of her pregnancy for quite some time. Nonetheless, Anaïs implies in her journal that she told Henry about the pregnancy at an early stage, since she refrains from sexual intercourse because of her "condition" and chooses, instead, to engage in fellatio, both with Miller and with Rank. Anaïs was probably correct in her emotional assessment of Miller, though his tribute to her diary in "*Un Être Étoilique*" suggests that he was fully aware of the traumatic impact of paternal desertion on her life and consciousness.

23. For further discussion of Anaïs Nin and D. H. Lawrence, see articles by Gilbert, Karsten, Keller, Hamalian, Markert, and Henke ("Androgynous Creation"), as well as Richard-Allerdyce, *Anaïs Nin*, 15-29.

24. In future discussions and diary entries, Nin would always insist that pregnancy would have been life-threatening because of her small pelvis and because of medical complications due to childhood surgery for appendicitis. On August 5, 1935, she remarks about abortion: "How I regret each time its end, the medicine which makes the uncreative blood flow again. No use. No child possible without cesarean operation and cesarean dangerous to my heart and general condition" (*F* 127). When asked in the 1970s whether she had ever borne a child, Nin responded: "I had surgery when I was nine years old which made it impossible. And we didn't find out until the first child I conceived was still-born—was strangled by adhesions. . . . So nature denied me that. It wasn't by choice" (*WS* 258). At the age of seventy, Anaïs was still parrying with maternal reproaches over her childlessness. "It was nature which decided I could not have children, not me," she protested to her therapist, Dr. Stone, who diagnosed in Nin a powerful residue of Catholic guilt for "evading the duties of woman" so deeply inculcated by Rosa's early training (*D* 7:307).

25. On February 2, 1937, Anaïs notes in *Fire*: "I finally wrote the childbirth story which had been preying on me—fifteen pages of naked, savage truth to be inserted in the diary, as part of the diary" (394). Through the alchemy of her journal, she realizes a glorious transmutation: "instead of wailing, sobbing at the stillbirth experience, I find a moment of ecstasy, even in that" (*D* 6:215). Nin re-creates the experience fictionally in the powerful story "Birth," first published "in the inaugural issue of Dorothy Norman's . . . *Twice a Year* (fall-winter 1938)" (*NM* 22n) and later included in *Under a Glass Bell*. Praised by Lawrence Durrell for this "Dionysiac little birth scene," Anaïs sardonically observes that her readers "warm up, explode over the childbirth story" because it exposes her writing "as a woman" (*NM* 22) In "Ladders to Fire," the first volume of *Cities of the Interior*, Lillian Beye suffers a miscarriage that spares her progeny repudiation by its artist/father, Jay. Nin also introduces a cryptic reference to pregnancy and stillbirth at the end of the novella "Winter of Artifice"—to the bewilderment of her original readers, who speculated about the possibility that the father in this story might have engendered a child with his own infatuated daughter. These various revised and fictional renditions of the trauma narrative are all derivative of, but different from, the fuller account in Nin's *Incest* journal, the prose of which has been culled from the original 150-volume diary manuscripts.
26. Deirdre Bair reports that Nin had at least two subsequent abortions. "On August 22 [1940] Anaïs discovered that she was three months pregnant and Dr. Jacobson arranged an abortion. . . . Hugo knew about the abortion and had accompanied her to the doctor's office, but . . . her problem was to keep it secret from her lover Gonzalo" (259). In the spring of 1947, Anaïs found herself pregnant by Rupert Pole and facetiously remarked: "I didn't tell the Welshman or he would have married me" (Bair 328). Neither of these experiences seems to have had the profound impact of Nin's 1934 abortion, perhaps because they were performed at a much earlier stage of gestation. Later in life, Anaïs adopted a publicly pro-choice stance and, as signatory to an historical testimony published in the first volume of *Ms.* magazine, "lent her name to the list of famous women openly admitting to having had an abortion" (*Conversations* 118). See also her prolific references to the inequities suffered by lower-class women historically denied reproductive choice in France—a dilemma poignantly exemplified by the servant Albertine's self-induced abortion in *Diary* 2:297-98. The event became the basis for Nin's story "Mouse" in *Under a Glass Bell*.
27. See Linde Salber, "Two Lives—One Experiment," for a discussion of Anaïs Nin and Lou Andreas-Salomé. Nin often expressed admiration for this unusual role model and wrote a preface to the paperback edition of *My Sister, My Spouse: A Biography of Lou Andreas-Salomé*, by H. F. Peters—an essay reprinted in the

collection *In Favor of the Sensitive Man*. When I first met Anaïs Nin in February, 1972, she identified Lou Andreas-Salomé as a powerful source of inspiration. See also her references to Andreas-Salomé in *A Woman Speaks*, 44-45, 72, and 89; and *Diary* 7:308.

28. To the counterculture of the 1960s, Nin became something of a literary guru. Some feminist readers have dismissed her writing as narcissistic, essentialist, male-identified and, most recently, politically incorrect. See, for instance, Estelle C. Jelinek's "Critical Evaluation" and Philippa Christmass's "A Mother to Us All?" Throughout her lectures and interviews in the early 1970s, Nin struggled to defend herself against charges of self-absorption (*Conversations* 17, 176). Horrified by Leon Edel's dismissal of the *Diary* as a "narcissus pool," Anaïs objected: "I have never seen a narcissus pool in which a thousand characters appeared at the same time" (*WS* 156). "There was no ego in the Diary, there was only a voice which spoke for thousands, made links, bonds, friendships" (*D* 7:200).

29. Diane Richard-Allerdyce proposes that the "trajectory of Nin's movement from fear and neurosis to creativity . . . provides a literary model for other survivors of early trauma and attests to a process of 'narrative recovery' by which the rendering of oneself in/or as art can be reconstitutive of the damaged self" ("Narrative and Authenticity" 80). Richard-Allerdyce's recent book, *Anaïs Nin and the Remaking of Self*, offers an excellent analysis of "the way Nin's fiction, criticism, and diaries thematize her nearly lifelong struggle to resist the tendency toward despair and to use psychoanalysis in conjunction with writing in a process of 'narrative recovery.'" Nin's diaries, she tells us, "speak especially to the therapeutic potential of writing and the possibility that even someone seriously traumatized early in life can engage in a process of self-making and work through early issues to remake a life into art" (4, 164). Richard-Allerdyce attributes the term "narrative recovery" to a 1993 article by Daniel Morris, though the phrase has since become an integral part of contemporary discourse in narratology. For a history of my own interest in the topic, see the introduction to this volume.

CHAPTER FOUR

1. Lottie Frame, Janet's mother, was talented and poetically minded. She "began publishing her poems each week in the *Wyndham Farmer* and soon became known . . . as the 'local poet'" (*A* 20) who peddled her poetry from door to door during the Depression. Patrick Evans notes that although the "Depression never ended" for the Frames, Janet's school prize of a year's library

membership was so cherished that "its annual renewal became the only luxury the family allowed itself" (20, 22).

2. Patrick Evans reports that Myrtle Frame "was drowned in the Oamaru Public Baths on the afternoon of March 5. It was late summer and the baths were crowded: Myrtle was a strong swimmer and may have suffered some kind of seizure" (23). "The effects of this tragedy upon a closely knit family were obviously marked and lifelong; their influence upon the mind of a child just entering adolescence is beyond conjecture" (24). Janet was in the middle of her thirteenth year when the accident occurred. The psychologist John Bowlby explains that "when loss is sustained during childhood, responses to it frequently take a pathological course" (*Loss* 18). The period of greatest emotional vulnerability "extends over a number of years of childhood (as Freud always held) and into adolescence as well" (36-37).
3. For a relevant discussion of the elegy tradition and its evolution, see Melissa Zeiger, *Beyond Consolation*. Janet did not feel capable of writing elegiac verse until she mourned her mother's passing in 1955 with poetry that echoed the modernist verse of Wallace Stevens and Dylan Thomas (*A* 263-64).
4. Jeanne Delbaere and Mark Williams observe similarities between James Joyce's lexical experimentation and Janet Frame's love of linguistic play. Delbaere feels that Frame's "extraordinary gift for words relates her to James Joyce," since in much of her fiction, she "dislocates the language and rearranges it anew, making words into anagrams, breaking the syntax, placing things in new contexts" (19-20). "Like Joyce," notes Williams, "Frame displays a curiously double attitude towards language. . . . Words . . . become self-enclosed and self-referring structures, and in this loose sense, 'schizophrenic'" (36). For my own analysis of Joyce's *Portrait*, see *James Joyce and the Politics of Desire*, chapter 3.
5. Frame exhibits a similar preoccupation with bodily emissions in *Faces in the Water*. Her protagonist confesses: "My room stank with sanitary napkins. . . . I hid them in the drawer of the landlady's walnut dressing table; . . . everywhere was the stench of dried blood, of stale food thrown from the shelves of an internal house that was without tenants or furniture or hope of future lease" (*FW* 12). As a mental patient, the character Istina Mavet suffers the punitive humiliation of being denied underpants and sanitary napkins: "I went without pants and sometimes without stockings, and I dreaded every month when I would have to ask for sanitary napkins which were supplied by the hospital, for once or twice I was refused them, and told by the overworked besieged staff, 'Use your arse hole.' In the end I did not seem to care; and if I wanted to go to the lavatory . . . and I was refused permission, I would slide from my seat under the table and wet on the floor" (*FW* 95).

6. For an account of the ever-present threat in mental institutions of removal to the dreaded "back wards" for incurables, see Mary Wood, who explains in *The Writing on the Wall*: "Asylums were divided into wards differentiated by the 'severity' of the patient's illness. The 'better' wards were more accessible to public visitors, while the 'worse' wards tended to be in more remote sections of the asylum" (9).
7. In *Anti-Oedipus*, Deleuze and Guattari observe: "*Oedipus is the first idea of an adult paranoiac, before it is the childhood feeling of a neurotic*" (274). "It seems that Freud himself was acutely aware of Oedipus's inseparability from a double impasse into which he was precipitating the unconscious" (80).
8. According to Deleuze and Guattari, schizophrenia "is desiring-production, but it is this production as it functions at the end, as the limit of social production determined by the conditions of capitalism. It is our very own 'malady,' modern man's sickness" (130).
9. Bowlby goes on to postulate: "Clinical experience and a reading of the evidence leaves little doubt . . . that much psychiatric illness is an expression of pathological mourning" (*Loss* 23). He cites the work of Helene Deutsch, who, in a paper on the "Absence of Grief," recognizes "the central place of childhood loss in the production of symptoms and character deviations, and also of a defence mechanism that, following loss, may lead to an absence of affect" (34).
10. Still another interpretation of Frame's behavior might point to symptoms of hysteria. As Claire Kahane reminds us, "Freud also links hysteria and melancholia in his early writings; he writes to Fliess that 'there really is such a thing as hysterical melancholia' and notes such features common to both pathologies as sexual anesthesia and anorexia nervosa" (158n). For further discussion of the construction of the "insane" subject, see Mary Wood.
11. The chronology of events recounted in Frame's *Autobiography* cannot always be correlated directly with the historical record. Patrick Evans explains that Frame, during her years in hospital, "continued to write, encouraged by John Money, her former lecturer in psychology and now a close friend. In 1950 he collected twenty-four of her stories and sketches and persuaded the Caxton Press in Christchurch to publish them" (39). It is not clear when the Hubert Church Memorial Award was first bestowed on this volume. Frame appears to have won the award for *Faces in the Water* in 1961, for *The Lagoon* in 1951 and 1963, and for *Daughter Buffalo* in 1973. Simon Petch suggests that in Frame's autobiographical text, "past and present enter collaborative dialogue with each other, and the argument of autobiography is strengthened while the flow of its 'sequential time' is disrupted" (65). "For her own sense of self, in her autobiography, is fluid, vital, splendidly open to renegotiation, ever reflecting

on its own possibilities, and refreshingly conscious of autobiographical existence as a written and writing fiction" (Petch 70).

12. Petch believes that Frame's "autobiography is always moving towards myth" and that her "writing appeals strongly to myths of nature, fertility, innocence, and initiation" (60). "Experience is enriched by the archetypal tropes of myth and fiction, and reflections multiply with the similes, which reach back to Plato's cave as they mirror the depths of the languages of the imagination" (64). For further discussion of the impact of Platonic ideas on Frame's writing, see Mark Williams's chapter on "Janet Frame's Suburban Gothic" in *Leaving the Highway*.
13. Williams attributes Frame's attitude toward corporality to the influence of her mother's Christadelphian faith, "registered chiefly in her essentially religious sense of the commonplace and in her sense of the body as the only realm of the real" (32). The Christadelphian religion, he explains, follows "a tradition uncontaminated by puritanism, springing . . . from the Blakean sense that Christianity is at heart a message about transforming, not repudiating, physical existence" (33).
14. For an analysis of the difficulty of establishing a credible location from which to speak after incarceration in a mental asylum, see Mary Wood's *The Writing on the Wall*. "After all, how could an insane woman write her own story?" Wood asks, explaining that "these writers take on the task of describing asylum conditions . . . in the face of massive denial that such stories could be true" (1, 5). For a reading of *Faces* as a work amalgamating confessional discourse and fabulation, see Donald Hannah. "Art as therapy?" he asks. "Yes, indeed, and why not?—for *Faces in the Water* demonstrates that therapy can also, on occasions, result in a remarkably successful work of art" (81). Simon Petch notes that "Istina Mavet is born of a creative alliance between autobiography and fiction," and that Frame originally intended for her protagonist to commit suicide after writing these memoirs "to sever any autobiographical connection" (66). Frame told Elizabeth Alley that *Faces in the Water* "was autobiographical in the sense that everything happened, but the central character was invented" (39).
15. Judith Dell Panny identifies in *Faces* a classical trope of *catabasis*, or descent into an infernal underworld from which the hero/protagonist eventually returns a wiser and more knowledgeable individual. Istina's three incarcerations, Panny tells us, simulate three phases of the heroic descent into hell. "[C]atabasis structures the entire novel" (36). For further discussion of *testimonio*, see John Beverley's "The Margin at the Center." "Each individual *testimonio*," he notes, "evokes an absent polyphony of voices, other possible lives and experiences. . . . Rather than a 'decentered' subjectivity, *testimonio* constitutes an affirmation of the individual self in a collective mode" (96-97). The narrator

"speaks for, or in the name of, a community or group, approximating in this way the symbolic function of the epic hero" (95).

16. The worst source of anxiety for Istina Mavet in *Faces in the Water* is the ever-present threat of lobotomy, as it was for Janet Frame. Frame's historical alter ego, Nola, submits to the operation and is left a helpless and degraded zombie who eventually dies. The "legacy of her dehumanising change" remains for Janet a perpetual reminder of the terrible fate she herself escaped so fortuitously. These Gothic memories of souls extinguished in mental institutions "become a living companion, a reminder" (*A* 223). In *Owls Do Cry*, the fictional character Daphne undergoes the lobotomy that Frame herself was spared. In her doctoral dissertation entitled *Un-Naming: The Subject of Madness in Women's Autobiographical Fiction*, Susan Schwartz also places Frame's *Faces in the Water* in the genre of *testimonio*. As Deleuze and Guattari postulate, "Every . . . fantasy is a group fantasy and in this sense a position of reality" (280). Mary Wood observes that as "each writer tells a story of diagnosis, incarceration, and transformation, she discovers and engages the ways that definitions of 'woman' and the 'feminine' intersect with notions of madness. She comes to question the boundary . . . between normality and abnormality, . . . the inside of the asylum and the outside" (21).
17. Brodzki and Schenck observe in *Life/Lines* that the "archetypal female prop of the mirror . . . has historically served to imprison femininity" and propose a bold "feminist reappropriation of the mirror, a framing actively understood, anticipated by the French psychoanalyst Luce Irigaray" (7).
18. Mark Williams explains that, for Frame, the artistic imagination "is not an idealistic vagary but a function of those insistences on reading, seeing, and resisting that informed her family life" (55-56). "The artist must lift up the quotidian, invest the mundane world with religious significance without resorting to the transcendent. It is the world itself that is the occasion of wonder and the mind's best fate is to know itself mortal with a religious intensity. The absence at the basis of being is both terrifying and the source of vision" (54).
19. In *Discerning the Subject*, Paul Smith hypothesizes a paranoid dimension to the process of narrative construction, whereby the "subject" of autobiographical "metadiscourse" functions "like the paranoiac's ego—controls the intention and interpretation of the world it has created in such a way as . . . to protect its own coherence and autonomy" (98). Paranoid delusions, which Smith interprets as "an unhappy parody of imaginative fiction," might be considered "delusions of interpretation and fictionalization, formed to protect the ego from any alteration which might make it unwholesome, unlovable" (97-98).

CHAPTER FIVE

1. In a conversation with Claudia Tate, Lorde describes *Zami* as a "biomythography, which is really fiction. It has the elements of biography and history of myth. In other words, it's fiction built from many sources" (115). Erin Carlston notes that by "maintaining a tension between the roles of the author, the narrator, and the protagonist of *Zami*, intercalating a variety of stylistic devices into the text, and pointedly calling the work a bio*myth*ography, Lorde emphasizes that life is a *story*, produced as dialogue between a subject and society and, most importantly, open to rewriting" (229). Lorde's *Zami*, says Bonnie Zimmerman, "expands the notion of 'real life' beyond fact and 'what really happened,'" since "real life includes myth, legend, fantasy, storytelling, and poetry" (23). Lorde writes in the tradition of earlier African-American authors who, "in their manipulation of received literary conventions . . . engage with and challenge the dominant ideology" (V. Smith, *Self-Discovery* 2). Black women, says Joanne Braxton, "created vital and sometimes hybrid forms, . . . as they grappled with the challenges of freedom and the problem of attaining a public voice" (10). "Unlike the 'solitary . . . male hero,' . . . the black woman autobiographer uses language—sass, invective, impertinence, and ritual invocation—to defend herself physically and psychologically" (205-6).
2. Claudine Raynaud explains that the plural word *zami* is "*patois* for lesbians throughout the Caribbean, based on the French expression *'les amies'*" (236). In Carriacou, Chinosole tells us, "where the male population is small because they must leave this spice-growing island to find work, lesbianism is a known social phenomenon. . . . By tracing her lesbian identity to her family origin and history, Lorde has cleared an important path in Afraamerican literature: freeing the idea of lesbianism from the closet of 'white decadence'" (385-86). In a 1980 interview with Karla Hammond, Lorde postulates that "all Black women are lesbians because we were raised in the remnants of a basically matriarchal society. . . . We're all dykes, including our mommas" (21).
3. Echoing Dianne Sadoff's work on Black matrilineage, Valerie Smith speculates in her article "Black Feminist Theory and the Representation of the 'Other'" about the practice on the part of African-American women writers of grounding their work in both oral and written literary traditions, as well as inherited ritual practices. She observes that "the peril of uniqueness compels an intense need on the part of black women writers to identify a literary matrilineage even as their historical circumstances occasion their ambivalence about the fact and process of mothering" (50). I have, throughout this chapter, followed Audre Lorde in using the uppercase *B* when referring to Black writers. I do so, as well, in memory of my late colleague Eric Hill, whose philosophical defense

of this convention was articulated in a presentation to the University of Louisville Critical Theory Forum, March 1991.

4. "My mother had a strange way with words," Lorde tells Adrienne Rich. "[I]f one didn't serve her or wasn't strong enough, she'd just make up another word, and then that would enter our family language forever. . . . But I think I got another message from her . . . that there was a whole powerful world of nonverbal communication and . . . that was what you had to learn to decipher and use" (*SO* 83).
5. Raynaud similarly notes that "Lorde's conception of the poetic reflects her attachment to the semiotic, to that 'homosexual-maternal-facet,' which Kristeva defines as 'a whirl of words'" (226). In her article on "Speaking in Tongues," Mae Henderson writes: "If glossolalia suggests private, nonmediated, nondifferentiated univocality, heteroglossia connotes public, differentiated, social, mediated, dialogic discourse. Returning from the trope to the act of reading, perhaps we can say that speaking in tongues connotes both the semiotic, presymbolic babble (baby talk), as between mother and child—which Julia Kristeva postulates as the 'mother tongue'—and the diversity of voices, discourses, and languages described by Mikhail Bakhtin" (22).
6. In *The Practice of Love*, Teresa de Lauretis observes that the "fantasmatic relation to the mother and the maternal/female body is central to lesbian subjectivity and desire" (171). She postulates a feminist psychoanalytic project that would undertake "not only a rewriting of the mother as symbolic agent, a theory of her agency and role in the symbolic, but especially an account of her role in symbolic seduction, in the transmission of specifically maternal or female fantasies" (163). "What the Oedipal mother accounts for, finally, is the feminist anti-patriarchal fantasy of a woman-identified community based on the imaginary projection of a mother both narcissistically and symbolically empowering" (183).
7. In *Women Reading Women Writing*, AnaLouise Keating analyzes the confusion precipitated by Linda Lorde's defensive denial of widespread racist practices in U.S. culture. By choosing "to ignore or misname the racism and discrimination she was unable to change," Linda condemns her daughter to suffer protracted "ethnic anxiety" for want of a clearly racialized discourse. Domestic "silence and alienation play important roles in Lorde's construction of a racialized 'blackness'" and evince a "paradoxical process of ethnic identity formation" that "synthesizes invention with discovery" (148-50). In much of her poetry, as well as in *Zami*, Lorde draws on West African myth to reconstruct a beneficent mother-goddess "whose darkness enables her simultaneously to discover and invent her own 'black' ethnic identity" (152).
8. In her introduction to *Black Women Writing Autobiography*, Joanne Braxton analyzes the complex matrifocal heritage of Black women's life-writing: "It was

in the Afra-American autobiography that I first met the outraged mother on the conscious plane. . . . She sacrifices and improvises for the survival of flesh and spirit, and as mother of the race, she is muse to black poets, male and female alike. . . . Implied in all her actions and fueling her heroic ones is outrage at the abuse of her people and her person" (1-2). This maternal figure, says Braxton, "must be the core of our black and female experience, this American Amazon of African descent" (2). The danger for independent Black daughters, however, is the threat of an obsessive "matraphobia"—"the fear of becoming what their mothers had been" (3). For an analysis of "The Literature of Matrilineage," see Nan Bauer Maglin. For further discussion of Lorde's ambivalent relationship with her mother, see Fabian Clements Worsham, "The Poetics of Matrilineage"; Barbara Smith, "The Truth That Never Hurts"; and Barbara Christian, *Black Feminist Criticism*, chapter 15, "No More Buried Lives." *Zami*, says Christian, seems "to be a book about Lorde's reconciliation with her mother, . . . even as she admits . . . the differences between them" (199). Barbara Smith notes: "Lorde connects her lesbianism to the model her mother, Linda, provided—her pervasive, often intimidating, strength; her fleeting sensuality . . . and also to her place of origin" (122).

9. The menarche chapter, notes Carlston, "marks the moment when Audre, the novel's protagonist, begins to converge with Audre the narrator. . . . It recounts her discovery of the relation between West Indian culture (symbolized by the spice mortar), her own female sexuality and sexual power, and her relationship with her mother, now overtly eroticized" (230). "The most erotic scenes in *Zami*, perhaps the most convincingly erotic," says Bonnie Zimmerman, "involve food" (104). "Food is a major motif throughout," adds Chinosole, "and here is a perfect symbol for survival and gratification. . . . West African legends make the mortar and pestle a symbol of the male/female principle as well" (387-88). According to Julia Watson, Lorde "figurally rewrites her mother's destiny in a homely, sensuous story of kitchen erotics" ("Unspeakable Differences" 155).

10. "The first time I ever made love to a woman was crucial to my poetry," Lorde tells Karla Hammond in 1980. "I was able to recognize the connections that existed between myself and my lover. It was crucial to my poetry in terms of power, strength, risking things that I knew but didn't understand" (21). Lorde also reveals her predilection for aesthetic models of ripe, dark female beauty, noting that "Venus of Willendorf's hair is corn rowed, which is an African hair style" (20). In "Audre Lorde's (Nonessentialist) Lesbian Eros," Ruth Ginzberg suggests that the "brilliance of Lorde's lesbian notion of the erotic" lies in its "epistemic and ontological capacity, not a mystical or hedonistic commitment, nor a set of genital activities. Most important, it is a nonessentialist conception of the erotic" (95). According to Teresa de Lauretis in *The Practice of Love*, "the

public presence of a lesbian discourse and self-representation—in various textual and performance modalities, verbal, visual, gestural, etc., including the representation of lesbian sexual practices—may serve as an authorizing social force" (76).

11. After her own mastectomy, Lorde reflects back in *The Cancer Journals* and describes her relationship with Eudora Garrett, the "first woman who totally engaged me in our loving. . . . I was 19 and she was 47. Now I am 44 and she is dead" (*CJ* 35). Lorde recalls in a 1981 interview with Karla Hammond that her sojourn in Mexico offered her a new sense of personal affirmation: "I felt that I could make . . . a real connection between the things that I felt most deeply and those gorgeous words that I needed to spin in order to live" (24).
12. In "An Open Letter to Mary Daly," Lorde challenges Daly's Eurocentric perspective in *Gyn/Ecology*: "Why are her goddess images only white, western european, judeo-christian? Where was Afrekete, Yemanje, Oyo, and Mawulisa? Where were the warrior goddesses of the Vodun, the Dahomeian Amazons and the warrior-women of Dan?" (*SO* 67). In *The Cancer Journals*, Lorde invokes "Seboulisa ma" (*CJ* 11). In *A Burst of Light*, she again feels empowered by prayers to "Black mother goddess, salt dragon of chaos, Seboulisa, Mawu" (*BL* 110).
13. In *Zami*'s epilogue, Lorde celebrates "*MawuLisa, thunder, sky, sun, the great mother of us all; and Afrekete, her youngest daughter, the mischievous linguist, trickster, best-beloved, whom we must all become*" (*Z* 255). In a glossary at the end of *The Black Unicorn*, Lorde explains that in the *Vodu* pantheon, "Mawulisa is the Dahomean female-male, sky-goddess-god principle. Sometimes called the first inseparable twins of the Creator of the Universe, Mawulisa (Mawu-Lisa) is also represented as west-east, night-day, moon-sun. More frequently, Mawu is regarded as the Creator of the Universe, and Lisa is either called her first son, or her twin brother. She is called the mother of all the other *Vodu*, and as such, is connected to the *Orisha* Yemanjá," as well as to Seboulisa, "The Mother of us all" (120-21). Claudine Raynaud talks about MawuLisa as "the great androgynous goddess" and Afrekete as "the black woman of the future" (237). For a fascinating discussion of Lorde's reconfiguration of Dahomean and Fon myth for her own aesthetic purposes, see Keating, 164-179. Lorde apparently appropriates the Fon Eshu/Legba, a "divine linguist and trickster," in her representation of the feminized Afrekete, to emphasize "the transformational power of language, as well as her own linguistic authority" (164-65). By "replacing the Judeo-Christian religio-mythic system with the Yoruban/Fon, she simultaneously discovers and invents the cultural dimensions of her identity" (166). See also DeShazer, 184-88.
14. One might contrast the eucharistic imagery in *Zami* with images of figurative cannibalism in some of Lorde's poetry, such as the mother who cooks up her

daughters in "From the House of Yemanjá" and the erotic image of a voracious MawuLisa in "Letter for Jan" (*The Black Unicorn* 6, 88).

15. The legend of "The Almond Tree" recounted in *Grimms' Fairy Tales* is a tale in which a wicked stepmother slays her stepson, then cooks the boy's corpse in a stew unwittingly ingested by his unsuspecting father. The victim's bones are gathered by his compassionate stepsister Marjory and transmogrified into a magical singing bird that avenges the murder by dropping a millstone on the head of the malicious stepmother. Echoes of the Greek tale of Procne and Itylus notwithstanding, Ella's cynical version of the ballad appears to reverse the gender of victimization. In this contemporary revision of the story, a magically conceived daughter apparently falls victim to her stepmother's malice, and her envious stepbrother connives in his mother's crime by sucking, rather than rescuing, the victim's bones. This particular incarnation of the Bohemian tale may serve as a sly commentary on female vulnerability and male voracity. The song indicts maternal egotism at the same time that it laments infantile helplessness. In the Grimm version, the magical bird sings the following ballad of recrimination:

> It was my mother who murdered me;
> It was my father who ate of me;
> It was my sister Marjory
> Who all my bones in pieces found;
> Them in a handkerchief bound;
> And laid them under the almond tree. (189)

16. According to Mae Henderson, the "complex situatedness of the black woman as not only the 'Other' of the Same, but also the 'other' of the other(s) implies . . . a relationship of difference and identification with the 'other(s)'" (18). "What distinguishes black women's writing, then, is the privileging (rather than repressing) of 'the other in ourselves'" (19). "Lorde's auto-biography," notes Bonnie Zimmerman, "is equally an other-biography. It answers the question—'who is the other woman?'—by showing that she is almost imperceptibly part of one's self" (202). "*Zami*'s final episode," writes Keating, "could be read as Lorde's construction of a multiethnic, gender-specific collective identity, a universalized woman" (173). "By editing out maternity and the signs of her own mortality," remarks Jill Ker Conway, "Lorde could build a triumphalist narrative about the strength derived from women's love for women." Conway suggests that although *Zami* reiterates traditional "romantic quest" plots, as well as a feminist "search for the ultimate earth mother," the book's innovation lies in its "primary focus on erotic experiences and the assumption that erotic experience . . . is *the* experience which gives meaning to life" (137).

17. Claudine Raynaud remarks that in Lorde's "lesbian utopia, a plurality of identities (black, female, lesbian), a line of women (her ancestors, her mothers, her lovers) coalesce into one name. The autobiographical 'I' becomes a collective 'we.' Fragmentation is resolved into wholeness" (223). Erin Carlston interprets Lorde's nostalgic vision of a far-off "home" in Carriacou as "an illusion recognized and utilized as such" (235). According to Julia Watson, "Lorde's myth of destiny as origin remade is less a nostalgic desire for originary unity than a self-conscious strategy for creating a context in which her painful consciousness of the price of her difference can be transformed into celebration" ("Unspeakable Differences" 154).
18. In *Reconstructing Illness*, Anne Hunsaker Hawkins defines the term *pathography* as "a form of autobiography or biography that describes personal experiences of illness, treatment, and sometimes death" (1). Pathographies, she observes, are characterized by an urgent need "to communicate a painful, disorienting, and isolating experience" (10). This subgenre of autobiography has arisen, in part, "as a reaction to our contemporary medical model" (11). The "pathographical act," Hawkins tells us, "constructs meaning by subjecting raw experience to the powerful impulse to make sense of it all" (18). "Indeed, it almost seems as though pathography has replaced the conversion autobiograpy of earlier, more religious cultures" (31). In *Recovering Bodies*, G. Thomas Couser uses the term *autopathography* to designate the "autobiographical narrative of illness or disability" (5). He identifies "illness narrative as a significant and relatively new form of life writing" that tends "to foreground somatic experience in a new way by treating the body's form and function . . . as fundamental constituents of identity" (14, 12).
19. Couser devotes a major chapter of *Recovering Bodies* to breast cancer narratives and points out that, by virtue of their "public mission, an agenda that is in some sense political," these stories "have some affinity with slave narratives, which were also written in the hope of abolishing a threatening condition that their narrators were fortunate enough to escape" (37).
20. Hawkins points out that figurative tropes "of battle and journey are ubiquitous in pathography" (61). Some authors, however, find such military analogies offensive and misleading. See Susan Sontag's *Illness as Metaphor* and Terry Tempest Williams's *Refuge*.
21. Jeanne Perrault situates *The Cancer Journals* in the category of "autography" as a text that "makes up the self it articulates." Lorde's writing "lives close to the vulnerable and uncertain flesh, and yet enjoys rhetorical authority, sureness, and even righteousness. *The Cancer Journals* is the transformation of all that into a powerful text of feminist subjectivity" (30).
22. "Pathographies of death and dying," writes Hawkins, "are a part of the efflorescence in the past two decades of books about this subject" that arise

from "a desperate cultural search for helpful models of 'how' to die" (91-92). Contemporary pathographies about death and dying engage in a struggle "to create a meaningful death out of the fragments of myth available to them" and tend to amalgamate models from stoic, Christian, heroic, and philosophical traditions (97). "The limits of medical discourse are most evident with terminally ill patients," writes Couser (30). Understandably, "few people want to read (and no one wants to write) an autopathography with a tragic plot" (39-40). In the subgenre of breast cancer narratives, he believes, both author and reader must settle for the achievement of "composure" rather than a "facile, premature, and misleading closure" (66).

23. Perrault observes: "If death is silence then life must be (in part at least) language, and giving the self in language, or to language, is a death-defying act" (25). "Lorde connects silence with suppressed differences and language with transformation" (27). In a 1980 interview, Lorde explains to Karla Hammond: "Silence for me is a very negative quality because it's the nameless. As Adrienne [Rich] has said, what remains nameless eventually becomes unspeakable" (18).

24. Couser describes Lorde's *Cancer Journals* as the "most aggressively deconstructive account of breast cancer" he knows, and his remarks about this "series of essays derived from and illustrated by journal entries" apply equally to *A Burst of Light*: "The strength of the book is in its inclusion of both her private responses—cries of pain and outrage—and her political analysis—seasoned, reasoned discourse. Her explicit politics makes her book powerful counter-discourse" (50-51). "In implying that hegemonic culture may be responsible for her illness, she characterizes herself as a martyr to causes long espoused. She imagines, and hopes by her example to recruit, an army of Amazons to take on cancer and patriarchy" (52).

CHAPTER SIX

1. It is beyond the scope of this study to discuss at length the current debate over "recovered memory" and "false memory syndrome." As Charles Whitfield makes clear, the term "false memory syndrome" has never been recognized by mental health professionals and, in fact, "has no scientific credibility" (5). Thorough and convincing discussions of the phenomenon of recovered memory can be found in Whitfield's *Memory and Abuse* and in Jennifer Freyd's *Betrayal Trauma*. Sidestepping what she calls the "Great Recovered Memory Debate," Freyd approaches traumatic amnesia and repression from the standpoint of a psychological investigation of betrayal trauma and its consequences. She offers overwhelming evidence of "information blockage as a natural and inevitable reaction

to childhood sexual abuse" (4-5). For an account of the neurobiology of memory repression, see Bessel A. van der Kolk, "The Body Keeps Score."

2. Like Elly Danica's autofiction *Don't: A Woman's Word*, Fraser's narrative "interpolates the reader as one who will not misread." In each of these autobiographical texts, the author requires the reader "to not only believe her story but to vicariously participate" (Williamson 140). According to Janice Williamson, this kind of autobiographical text "provides a safe place for verbal re-enactment and repetition within an analytic scene that refuses the traditional therapeutic authorization of the analyst over the analysand" (141). "Writing reconstitutes the writer's body and world, making survival possible in a sensorium of particulars," and "announces a new subject whose recuperation depends upon a shared collective rereading of her body in pain" (145). Although Williamson's remarks refer specifically to Danica's work, similar narratological strategies appear to be operative in Fraser's memoir.
3. "Father-daughter incest," writes Judith Herman, "represents a paradigm of female sexual victimization. . . . The actual sexual encounter may be brutal or tender, painful or pleasurable; but it is always, inevitably, destructive to the child. The father, in effect, forces the daughter to pay with her body for affection and care which should be freely given" (*Incest* 4).
4. "On one level of imagination," Hortense Spillers declares, "incest simply cannot occur and never does. Under the auspices of denial, incest becomes the measure of an absolute negativity, the paradigm of the outright assertion *against*—the resounding no! But on the level of the symbolic, at which point the 'metaevent' is sovereign, incest translates into the unsayable which is all the more sayable by very virtue of one's muteness before it" (128). For an informative history of therapeutic responses to the "common occurrence" of incest trauma, see chapter 1 of Judith Herman's *Father-Daughter Incest*. According to Herman, a "vastly elaborated intellectual tradition which served the purpose of suppressing the truth about incest . . . originates in the works of Freud" (9). For an excellent history of the role of psychoanalysis in "society's betrayal of the child," see Alice Miller's *Thou Shalt Not Be Aware*. See also Florence Rush, chapter 9, "A Freudian Cover-up"; Christine Froula, "The Daughter's Seduction"; and Ulman and Brothers, *The Shattered Self*, chapters 1 and 2.
5. Herman reports that in the incestuous families that she and Lisa Hirschman studied, "[p]uritanical and negative sexual attitudes were common. . . . Sex was a taboo subject. . . . Bodies, particularly women's bodies, were considered dirty" (Herman *Incest* 110). Karin Meiselman presents similar findings in chapters 4 and 5 of *Incest*. Some of the survivors interviewed by Louise Armstrong sardonically reported that their Catholic fathers chose incest over the sin of adultery (237).

6. Herman, Freyd, Armstrong, Meiselman, and Rush stress emphatically the child's powerlessness in the face of adult incestuous demands. Children, Herman reminds us, "are essentially a captive population, totally dependent upon their parents or other adults for their basic needs" (*Incest* 27). "In certain kinds of abusive betrayals of children, . . . escape is not an option" (Freyd 10). See also Alice Miller's *The Drama of the Gifted Child* and *Thou Shalt Not Be Aware*. In the latter, Miller explains that a "child in his or her helplessness awakens a feeling of power in insecure adults" (6).
7. It is common, says Meiselman, for young children to interpret the perpetrator's ejaculate as urine and to feel humiliated, but to have "no clear idea of the sexual significance of ejaculation" (151). The erect penis might, for instance, be described by the bewildered infant as a "finger part" (Freyd 127). Herman reports that in the study which she and Lisa Hirschman conducted, the sexual abuse survivors who had been "too young to have a clear idea of the significance of the father's behavior" nonetheless realized from his "furtive attitude . . . that there was something wrong with what they were doing. . . . Most of the daughters . . . 'froze up' or pretended that 'it wasn't really happening'" (*Incest* 86).
8. Ironically, many perpetrators try to cope with their own emotional insecurities and weak ego structures through a hypermasculine stance of authoritarian bullying. Meiselman reports that although the incestuous father wants to be acknowledged as the family patriarch, he generally lacks "a secure sense of his masculine identity" and seeks "to compensate for his feelings of inadequacy" (91-92). The abusive father is generally "a prudish man . . . heavily involved in his church" (103). The paradoxes of such hypocritical behavior are clearly evident in Fraser's portrait of her father, as well as in the novel *Pandora*.
9. "Incest isn't the taboo," says one of Louise Armstrong's witnesses. "Talking about it is" (239). Secrecy is the litmus test that Judith Herman proposes to distinguish abusive fathers from those whose behavior is tacitly seductive. She and her research partner, Lisa Hirschman, "defined a sexual relationship to mean any physical contact that had to be kept a secret" (*Incest* 70). Jennifer Freyd cites Eric Lister's hypothesis that secrecy itself comprises a "secondary trauma" for the victimized child (77-78). The abusive father, notes Meiselman, "soon realizes that he must rely on a child to keep a secret the disclosure of which might subject him to divorce, humiliation in the eyes of the community, or even a prison term" (168).
10. Threats of abandonment are apparently common in cases of abuse and, according to Freyd, prove a powerful source of inhibition to the terrified child. Fear of abandonment by a parent or caregiver is at the very heart of betrayal trauma, where the victim's "dissociative response is adaptive" (88). In *Father-Daughter Incest*, Herman reports that abusive fathers often threaten their daugh-

ters "with the most dreadful consequences" if they break silence and warn that these little squealers will be punished and "sent away from home." Thus, "guarding the incest secret" becomes "part of their obligation to keep the family together" (88). "Patients who have been . . . sexually abused," writes Alice Miller, "also have a stake in keeping secret or covering up what has happened to them or in blaming themselves for it" (*Thou Shalt Not Be Aware* 7).

11. Janice Haaken explains, "The theory that the experience of extreme childhood trauma leads to a dual consciousness or splits in consciousness was initially advanced by Pierre Janet in the late nineteenth century. . . . In order to survive emotionally overwhelming experiences, the individual splits off the memory of the traumatic experience from consciousness. The dissociated memories are preserved in an alter ego state, or alter personality, through an amnesic barrier protecting one part of the personality from knowledge of the abuse" (1075). Fish-Murray, Koby, and van der Kolk observe in "The Effect of Abuse on Children's Thought" that chronically abused subjects often engage in self-hypnosis, whereby they "learn to leave their bodies to the abuser, to become invisible and let a part of themselves float free, . . . thus laying the groundwork for dissociative disorders, including multiple personalities" (103). For an illuminating discussion of traumatic amnesia, see Freyd's *Betrayal Trauma*, chapter 5. Freyd cites extensive psychological studies relating "incest and other forms of childhood sexual abuse to psychogenic amnesia and other dissociative symptoms" (38). In fact, "for victims of childhood sexual abuse, *forgetting the abuse is not unusual*," and "partial amnesia for abuse events accompanied by a mixture of delayed recall and delayed understanding is the most common pattern observed clinically" (43). Citing Bessel van der Kolk's research linking "traumatic memories to neuroanatomical dissociations between the hippocampus and amygdala," Freyd defends the hypothesis that traumatic memories "are not reconstructed narratives as are most memories, but the reactivation of undistorted sensory and affective traces" (99-101). See also van der Kolk and Kadish, "Amnesia, Dissociation, and the Return of the Repressed."

12. Both repression and knowledge isolation, Freyd tells us, can be motivated by the "avoidance of information that threatens a necessary attachment" (22). "The more the victim is dependent on the perpetrator . . . the more the crime is one of betrayal. This betrayal by a trusted caregiver is the core factor in determining amnesia for a trauma" (63). "For the child to withdraw from a caregiver he or she is dependent on could be life-threatening. Thus the trauma of childhood sexual abuse . . . requires that information about the abuse be blocked from the mental mechanisms that control attachment" (75). "Forgetting occurs . . . to stay alive" (165).

13. Problematizing analogies made between sexual abuse and the Holocaust in recovery literature, Janice Haaken points out that whereas "the Holocaust is often invoked to dramatize the private, unacknowledged pain of survivors, it also trivializes the vast distinctions in the magnitude and nature of trauma suffered by various oppressed groups" and "collapses the range of experiences currently carried under the sexual abuse banner" (1079n).

14. "Psychosomatic complaints characteristic of depression" are common in incest survivors, says Meiselman. "In various ways, they acted as if they wished to be punished for the incest and earn their mothers' forgiveness." Some exhibited a "compulsive masochistic reaction" manifested in "sexual acting out . . . and attempts at suicide" (188-89). Numerous incest survivors interviewed in Louise Armstrong's book *Kiss Daddy Goodnight* testify to self-destructive practices, as well as to the maintenance of a double life throughout childhood and adolescence. "I couldn't take my anger out on the people that really hurt me the most," explains one woman. "So instead I did bodily harm to myself. I've got scars all over my body . . . from burning myself with an iron when I was mad. From just taking a knife when I was angry and slicing my finger or my hand" (221).

15. Herman reports that clinical studies of incest victims reveal "various kinds of sexual dysfunction. . . . They had more difficulty in interpersonal relationships, more marital conflicts, more physical problems, and more complaints in general" (*Incest* 32). "For many of the daughters, marriage appeared to be the passport to freedom" (94), but the "isolation these women felt was compounded by their own difficulty in forming trusting relationships" (99). Freyd confirms that incest survivors "commonly suffer damage to their ability to enjoy their sexuality. Their sexual behavior may be either excessively restricted or excessively promiscuous" (172-173).

16. As Adrienne Rich notes in *Of Woman Born*, the "twentieth-century, educated young woman, looking perhaps at her mother's life, or trying to create an autonomous self in a society which insists that she is destined primarily for reproduction, has with good reason felt that the choice was an inescapable either/or: motherhood or individuation, motherhood or creativity, motherhood or freedom" (154). "The depths of this conflict, between self-preservation and maternal feelings, can be experienced . . . as a primal agony" (155). Incest victims, explains Herman, lack "any internal representation of an adequate, satisfactory mother" (*Incest* 107).

17. According to Judith Herman, the "theme of maternal absence . . . is always found in the background of the incest romance" (*Incest* 44). The mother in an incestuous family "is unusually oppressed" and "extremely dependent upon and subservient to her husband" (49). The mothers of incest victims generally "conveyed to their daughters the belief that a woman is defenseless against a

man, that marriage must be preserved at all costs, and that a wife's duty is to serve and endure" (78). The testimonies in *Kiss Daddy Goodnight* strongly confirm these observations. Meiselman notes that the most common profile of an incestuous family shows a father/husband who "is over-controlling, emotionally cold, and even physically abusive." Obsequious to this tyrannical personality, the mother/wife suffers from low self-esteem and exhibits characteristics of "passivity, dependency, and masochism" (119). For obvious reasons, the wife is likely to suffer sexual aversion to the authoritarian bully who dominates her life; so it is not surprising that a "constant finding in studies of father-daughter incest has been that the father has lost sexual access to the mother" (123).

18. The incestuous family, notes Herman, represents "a pathological extreme of male dominance" (*Incest* 124). Almost without exception, incest occurs in father-dominant families where the tyrannical head of household attempts to control every aspect of family life. "Implicitly the incestuous father assumes that it is his prerogative to be waited upon at home, and that if his wife fails to provide satisfaction, he is entitled to use his daughter as a substitute" (49).

19. Meiselman cites studies that associate neurotic symptoms linked to incest with "attempts to 'relive' the traumatic experience" (190). "Another hypothesis . . . states that the incestuous daughter unconsciously seeks 'father figures' in her adult heterosexual relationships, either to regain the positive aspects of the incest affair or to work through the conflicts created by it" (211). "There is a real possibility," says Janice Haaken, "for the trauma story to become a kind of gothic fairytale or a Cinderella story with the prince as the perpetrator. The reversals are important, but the narrative elements are the same: the fantasy of discovering the missing object . . . that will make women whole" (1090).

20. Judith Herman tells us that, in the study she conducted with Lisa Hirschman, the majority of incest victims "tended to overvalue and idealize men. . . . Many had affairs with much older or married men, in which they relived the secrecy and excitement of the incestuous relationship. As the 'other woman,' however, they had little power to define the terms of the relationship, and they had to content themselves with lovers who were capricious and often unavailable" (*Incest* 103). According to Meiselman, the devastating legacy of incest trauma includes persistent "sexual dysfunction," as well as an enduring "masochistic orientation" that inhibits the selection of a "nonabusive sexual partner" (244-45).

21. Unfortunately, Sylvia's childhood friend "Joker" Nash is not an anomaly. Karin Meiselman cites the 1975 edition of the *Comprehensive Textbook of Psychiatry*, which instructs mental health professionals that in cases of father-daughter incest, "the father is aided and abetted in his liaison by conscious or

unconscious seduction by his daughter and by his wife's collusion" (quoted in Meiselman 162). Jennifer Freyd mentions the 1953 Kinsey report, which, in a naive gesture of sexual liberalism, insists: "It is difficult to understand why a child, except for its cultural conditioning, should be disturbed at . . . specific sex contacts" (quoted in Freyd 37). For commentary on this tendency to blame the incest victim, see Rush, chapter 9, "The Demon Nymphette." For a critique of the Kinsey report, see Diana E. H. Russell, *The Secret Trauma*, pp. 5-9. In *Incest: The Last Taboo*, Rubin and Byerly describe a *Time* magazine article of April 14, 1980, entitled "Attacking the Last Taboo": "The pro-incest position argues that some incestuous relationships between consenting family members may be beneficial or neutral" (121). The piece includes comments by Wardell Pomeroy, one of Kinsey's colleagues, and by John Money, the sex researcher who was responsible for Janet Frame's first hospitalization. Rubin and Byerly also summarize a *New York Times* article of December 3, 1979, which reports a "controversial speech given by Professor LeRoy G. Schultz" suggesting "that some incest 'may be either a positive, healthy experience or at worst, neutral and dull'" (128). Florence Rush cites Dr. Suzanne M. Sgroi's response: "'I have never knowingly talked to a happy, well-adjusted, unconcerned incest victim'" (1). See also Armstrong, passim, and Russell's *The Secret Trauma*, especially chapters 10, 11, and 12. Contemporary magnetic resonance imaging of the brain offers startling evidence of neurobiological damage resulting from the physiological effects of post-traumatic stress disorder. In "The Body Keeps Score," Bessel van der Kolk cites studies "showing major neuroendocrine disturbances in sexually abused girls" and at least a "7 percent reduction in hippocampus volume" (in comparison with an 8 percent reduction in the case of Vietnam veterans suffering from post-traumatic stress disorder) (228, 232). At a recent conference on "Trauma and Cognitive Science," J. Douglas Bremner reported a 12 percent reduction in hippocampal volume in the case of abuse survivors, as well as memory deficits for immediate and delayed recall and a severe, long-term loss of declarative memory. It is indeed shocking that chronic sexual abuse can, quite literally, cause hormonal brain damage and produce neurobiological disturbances almost identical to the effects of combat neurosis.

22. Janice Williamson criticizes Fraser's "version of the 'happy ending,' an epiphanic scene of forgiveness where the child imagines the father as victim also." In contrast, for incest survivor Elly Danica, "any forgiveness is out of the question" (Williamson 138). As Sonia Apgar points out, narratives of incest trauma "offer a safe space in which to make sense of, and subsequently diminish, the psychological damage. By (re)inscribing a positive sense of self-identity and (re)constructing her subject position through writing, a survivor empowers herself" (57).

23. Interpreting *My Father's House* in the genre of *testimonio*, Jill Johnston feels that Fraser's autobiography reveals to an apathetic audience "what could be done to change society through the affecting, self-observing literary enterprises of victims" (50).

List of Works Cited and Consulted

Abraham, Nicolas and Maria Torok. *The Wolf Man's Magic Word: A Cryptonymy*. Trans. Nicholas Rand. Foreword by Jacques Derrida. Minneapolis: University of Minnesota Press, 1986.

Adams, Timothy Dow. *Telling Lies in Modern American Autobiography*. Chapel Hill: University of North Carolina Press, 1990.

Adell, Sandra. *Double-Consciousness/Double Bind: Theoretical Issues in Twentieth-Century Black Literature*. Urbana: University of Illinois Press, 1994.

Alcoff, Linda and Laura Gray. "Survivor Discourse: Transgression or Recuperation?" *Signs: Journal of Women in Culture and Society* 18.2 (1993): 260-90.

Allen, Jeffner and Iris Marion Young, eds. *The Thinking Muse: Feminism and Modern French Philosophy*. Bloomington: Indiana University Press, 1989.

Alley, Elizabeth and Mark Williams, eds. *In the Same Room: Conversations with New Zealand Writers*. Auckland: Auckland University Press, 1992.

American Psychiatric Association. *Diagnostic and Statistical Manual of Mental Health Disorders*. 4th ed., rev. Washington, D.C.: American Psychiatric Association, 1994.

Anderson, Charles M. and Marian MacCurdy. *Writing and Healing: The Techne of Wholeness*. Urbana: NCTE Press, forthcoming.

Andrews, William L. *To Tell a Free Story: The First Century of Afro-American Autobiography, 1760-1865*. Urbana: University of Illinois Press, 1986.

Apgar, Sonia C. "Fighting Back on Paper and in Real Life: Sexual Abuse Narratives and the Creation of Safe Space." In Kuribayashi and Tharp, 47-58.

Armstrong, Louise. *Kiss Daddy Goodnight: A Speak-Out on Incest*. 1978; rpt. New York: Pocket Books, 1979.

Ashley, Kathleen, Leigh Gilmore, and Gerald Peters, eds. *Autobiography and Postmodernism*. Amherst: University of Massachusetts Press, 1994.

Augustine, Jane. "H. D. and the Moravian 'Sifting Time.'" Modern Language Association Convention, December 27, 1993.

Bair, Deirdre. *Anaïs Nin: A Biography*. New York: G. P. Putnam's Sons, 1995.

Balakian, Anna. "Anaïs Nin, the Poet." In Nalbantian, *Anaïs Nin*, 63-78.

———. "The Poetic Reality of Anaïs Nin." In Zaller, 113-31.

Barthes, Roland. *Roland Barthes by Roland Barthes*. 1975. Trans. Richard Howard. New York: Hill & Wang, 1977.

Bass, Ellen, and Laura Davis. *The Courage to Heal: A Guide for Women Survivors of Child Sexual Abuse*. New York: Harper, 1994.

Begos, Jane Dupree. "Art and Therapy." *ANAÏS* 3 (1985): 21-26.

Bell, Susan Groag and Marilyn Yalom, eds. *Revealing Lives: Autobiography, Biography, and Gender*. Albany: SUNY Press, 1990.

Benet, Mary Kathleen. *Writers in Love: Katherine Mansfield, George Eliot, Colette and the Men They Lived With*. Boston: G. K. Hall, 1984.

Benjamin, Jessica. *The Bonds of Love: Psychoanalysis, Feminism, and the Problem of Domination*. New York: Pantheon, 1988.

Benstock, Shari. "Authorizing the Autobiographical." In Benstock, *The Private Self*, 10-33.

———. *Women of the Left Bank, Paris, 1900-1940*. Austin: University of Texas Press, 1986.

———. ed. *The Private Self*. Chapel Hill: University of North Carolina Press, 1988.

Bergland, Betty. "Postmodernism and the Autobiographical Subject: Reconstructing the 'Other.'" In Ashley, Gilmore, and Peters, 130-66.

Beverley, John. "The Margin at the Center: On *Testimonio* (Testimonial Narrative)." In Smith and Watson, *De/Colonizing the Subject*, 91-114.

Bloom, Lynn Z. "Heritages: Dimensions of Mother-Daughter Relationships in Women's Autobiographies." In Davidson and Broner, 291-303.

Bloom, Lynn Z. and Orlee Holder. "Anaïs Nin's *Diary* in Context." In Hinz, *World*, 191-202.

Boose, Lynda E. and Betty S. Flowers, eds., *Daughters and Fathers*. Baltimore: Johns Hopkins University Press, 1989.

Bowlby, John. *Attachment and Loss*, 3 vols. Vol. 3, *Loss: Sadness and Depression*. 1980; rpt. Harmondsworth: Penguin Books, 1986.

Braham, Jeanne. *Crucial Conversations: Interpreting Contemporary American Literary Biographies by Women*. New York: Teachers College Press, 1995.

Braxton, Joanne M. *Black Women Writing Autogiography: A Tradition Within a Tradition*. Philadelphia: Temple University Press, 1989.

Braxton, Joanne M. and Andrée Nicola McLaughlin, eds. *Wild Women in the Whirlwind: Afra-American Culture and the Contemporary Literary Renaissance*. New Brunswick: Rutgers University Press, 1990.

Breé, Germaine. "Autogynography." In Olney, *Studies*, 171-79.

Bremner, J. Douglas. "Lasting Effects of Childhood Abuse on Memory and the Hippocampus." Trauma and Cognitive Science Conference, University of Oregon, Eugene, OR, July 18, 1998.

Brodzki, Bella and Celeste Schenck, eds. *Life/Lines: Theorizing Women's Autobiography*. Ithaca: Cornell University Press, 1988.

Brooks, Peter. *Reading for the Plot: Design and Intention in Narrative*. New York: Alfred A. Knopf, 1984.

Brown, Cheryl L. and Karen Olson, eds. *Feminist Criticism: Essays on Theory, Poetry and Prose*. Metuchen, NJ: Scarecrow Press, 1978.

Brown-Guillory, Elizabeth, ed. *Women of Color: Mother-Daughter Relationships in 20th-Century Literature*. Austin: University of Texas Press, 1996.

Brumberg, Joan Jacobs. *Fasting Girls: The History of Anorexia Nervosa*. Cambridge: Harvard University Press, 1988.

Bruner, Jerome. "The Autobiographical Process." In Folkenflik, 38-56.

Bruss, Elizabeth. *Autobiographical Acts: The Changing Situation of a Literary Genre*. Baltimore: Johns Hopkins University Press, 1976.

Bruzzi, Zara. "'The Fiery Moment': H. D. and the Eleusinian Landscape of English Modernism." *Agenda* 25 (Autumn/Winter 1987-88): 97-112.

Buck, Claire. *H. D. and Freud: Bisexuality and a Feminine Discourse*. New York: St. Martin's Press, 1991.

Burgin, Victor, James Donald, and Cora Kaplan, eds. *Formations of Fantasy*. London: Methuen, 1986.

Burnett, Gary. *H. D. Between Image and Epic: The Mysteries of Her Poetics*. Ann Arbor: UMI Research Press, 1990.

Butler, Judith. *Bodies That Matter*. New York: Routledge, 1993.

———. *Gender Trouble*. New York: Routledge, 1990.

Butterfield, Stephen. *Black Autobiography in America*. Amherst: University of Massachusetts Press, 1974.

Calder, Alex. "The Closure of Sense: Janet Frame, Language, and the Body." *Antic* 3 (1987) 93-104.

Camden, Vera, ed. *Compromise Formations: Current Directions in Psychoanalytic Criticism*. Kent, OH: Kent State University Press, 1989.

Card, Claudia, ed. *Adventures in Lesbian Philosophy*. Bloomington: Indiana University Press, 1994.

Carlston, Erin. "*Zami* and the Politics of Plural Identity." In Wolfe and Penelope, 237-50.

Caruth, Cathy, ed. *Trauma: Explorations in Memory*. Baltimore: Johns Hopkins University Press, 1995.

———. *Unclaimed Experience: Trauma, Narrative, and History*. Baltimore: Johns Hopkins University Press, 1996.

Caruth, Cathy, and Deborah Esch, eds. *Critical Encounters: Reference and Responsibility in Deconstructive Writing*. New Brunswick: Rutgers University Press, 1995.

Centing, Richard R. "Emotional Algebra: The Symbolic Level of *The Diary of Anaïs Nin, 1944-1947*." In Zaller, 169-76.

Chinosole. "Audre Lorde and Matrilineal Diaspora: 'moving history beyond nightmare into structures for the future.'" In Braxton and McLaughlin, 379-94.

Chisholm, Dianne. *H. D.'s Freudian Poetics: Psychoanalysis in Translation*. Ithaca: Cornell University Press, 1992.

Chodorow, Nancy. *The Reproduction of Mothering: Psychoanalysis and the Sociology of Gender*. Berkeley: University of California Press, 1978.

Christian, Barbara. *Black Feminist Criticism: Perspectives on Black Women Writers*. New York: Pergamon Press, 1985.

Christmass, Philippa. "A Mother to Us All?: Feminism and 'The Diary of Anaïs Nin.'" *ANAÏS* 14 (1996): 35-41.

Cixous, Hélène. "Castration or Decapitation?" Trans. Annette Kuhn. *Signs* 7 (1981): 41-55.

———. *The Hélène Cixous Reader*. Ed. Susan Sellers. New York: Routledge, 1994. Abbreviated *HCR*.

———. and Catherine Clément. *The Newly Born Woman*. Trans. Betsy Wing. Minneapolis: University of Minnesota Press, 1986.

Coe, Richard. *When the Grass Was Taller: Autobiography and the Experience of Childhood*. New Haven: Yale University Press, 1984.

Colette. *Break of Day*. 1928. Trans. Enid McLeod. New York: Farrar, Straus and Giroux, 1961. (Abbreviated *BD*.)

———. *Earthly Paradise*. Ed. Robert Phelps. Trans. Helen Beauclerk, Briffault, et. al. Harmondsworth, Middlesex: Penguin Books Ltd., 1966. (Abbreviated *EP*.)
———. *Letters from Colette*. Trans. Robert Phelps. New York: Ballantine Books, 1983.
———. *My Apprenticeships*. 1936. Trans. Helen Beauclerk. 1957; rpt. New York: Farrar, Straus and Giroux, 1978. (Abbreviated *MA*.)
———. *My Mother's House and Sido*. 1922, 1929. Trans. Una Vicenzo Troubridge and Enid McLeod. New York: Farrar, Straus and Giroux, 1953. (Abbreviated *MMH* and *S*.)
———. *The Pure and the Impure*. 1932. Trans. Herma Briffault. New York: Farrar, Straus and Giroux, 1966. (Abbreviated *PI*.)
———. *Recollections: Journey for Myself and The Evening Star*. 1946. Trans. David Le Vay. New York: Macmillan, 1972.(Abbreviated *R*.)
———. *The Shackle*. 1913. Trans. Antonia White. New York: Farrar, Straus and Giroux, 1976. (Abbreviated *TS*.)
———. *The Vagabond*. 1911. Trans. Enid McLeod. New York: Farrar, Straus and Giroux, 1955. (Abbreviated *V*.)
Collecott, Diana. "A Double Matrix: Re-reading H. D." *Iowa Review* 16.3 (1986): 93-122.
Collins, Patricia Hill. *Black Feminist Thought*. Boston: Unwin Hyman, 1990.
Contemporary Literature: H. D. Centennial Issue. 27.4 (1986).
Conway, Jill Ker. *When Memory Speaks: Reflections on Autobiography*. New York: Alfred A. Knopf, 1998.
Couser, G. Thomas. *Recovering Bodies: Illness, Disability, and Life Writing*. Madison: University of Wisconsin Press, 1997.
Cox, James M. *Recovering Literature's Lost Ground: Essays in American Autobiography*. Baton Rouge: Louisiana State University Press, 1989.
Crews, Frederick, et al. *The Memory Wars: Freud's Legacy in Dispute*. New York: *The New York Review of Books* Press, 1995.
Crosland, Margaret. *Colette: The Difficulty of Loving*. New York: Dell Publishing Company, 1973.
Culley, Margo. *American Women's Autobiography: Fea(s)ts of Memory*. Madison: University of Wisconsin Press, 1992.
Cummings, Katherine. *Telling Tales: The Hysteric's Seduction in Fiction and Theory*. Stanford: Stanford University Press, 1991.
Cutler, Carolyn. "Words and Images in H. D.'s *Tribute to Freud*." *Psychoanalytic Review* 76 (Spring 1989): 107-13.
Daly, Mary. *Gyn/Ecology: Metaethics of Radical Feminism*. Boston: Beacon Press, 1983.
———. *Pure Lust: Elemental Feminist Philosophy*. Boston: Beacon Press, 1984.
Danica, Elly. *Don't: A Woman's Word*. San Francisco: Cleis Press, 1988.
Davidson, Cathy N., and E. M. Broner, eds. *The Lost Tradition: Mothers and Daughters in Literature*. New York: Frederick Ungar, 1980.
Davis, Robert Con, ed. *Lacan and Narration: The Psychoanalytic Difference in Narrative Theory*. Baltimore: Johns Hopkins University Press, 1983.
De Lauretis, Teresa. *The Practice of Love: Lesbian Sexuality and Perverse Desire*. Bloomington: Indiana University Press, 1994.
———. *Technologies of Gender: Essays on Theory, Film and Fiction*. Bloomington: Indiana University Press, 1987.

Delbaere, Jeanne, ed. *The Ring of Fire: Essays on Janet Frame*. Aarhus, Denmark: Dangaroo Press, 1992.

Deleuze, Gilles, and Felix Guattari. *Anti-Oedipus: Capitalism and Schizophrenia*. Trans. Robert Hurley, Mark Seem, and Helen R. Lane. Minneapolis: University of Minnesota Press, 1983.

De Man, Paul. "Autobiography as De-facement." *Modern Language Notes* 94 (1979): 919-30.

Dembo, L. S. "H. D. *Imagiste* and Her Octopus Intelligence." In King, 209-26.

Demetrakopoulos, Stephanie A. "Archetypal Constellations of Feminine Consciousness in Nin's First *Diary*." In Hinz, *World*, 121-37.

Derrida, Jacques. *The Ear of the Other*. Ed. Christie McDonald. Trans. Peggy Kamuf. New York: Schocken, 1985.

———. *Writing and Difference*. Trans. Alan Bass. London: Routledge, 1978.

DeSalvo, Louise. *Conceived with Malice: Literature as Revenge in the Lives and Works of Virginia and Leonard Woolf, D. H. Lawrence, Djuna Barnes, and Henry Miller*. New York: Plume, 1994.

———. *Virginia Woolf: The Impact of Childhood Sexual Abuse on Her Life and Work*. Boston: Beacon Press, 1989.

DeShazer, Mary K. *Inspiring Women: Reimagining the Muse*. New York: Pergamon Press, 1986.

DiBernard, Barbara. "*Zami*: A Portrait of an Artist as a Black Lesbian." *Kenyon Review* 13.4 (1991): 195-213.

Doolittle, Hilda [H. D.]. *Advent*. In *Tribute to Freud*, 115-87.

———. *Asphodel*. Ed. Robert Spoo. Durham: Duke University Press, 1992. (Abbreviated *A*.)

———. *Bid Me To Live [Madrigal]*. 1960; rpt. London: Virago Press, 1984. (Abbreviated *B*.)

———. *The Collected Poems, 1912–1944*. Ed. Louis L. Martz. New York: New Directions, 1983.

———. *The Gift* [1941–43]; Abridged by Griselda Ohannessian. New York: New Directions, 1982 (abbreviated *G*.) Unabridged: Chapter 1 ("The Dark Room"), *Montemora* 8 (Aug. 1981): 57-76 (abbreviated *G1*); Chapter 2 ("The Fortune Teller"), *Iowa Review* 16.3 (1986): 18-41 (abbreviated *G2*); Chapter 3 ("The Dream"), *Contemporary Literature* 10.4 (1969): 605-26 (abbreviated *G3*).

———. *The Gift* [Typescript]. H. D. Papers. The Collection of American Literature, Beinecke Rare Book Room and Manuscript Library. Yale University. New Haven, Connecticut. (Abbreviated *GTs*.)

———. "H. D. by *Delia Alton*." [1948]. *Iowa Review* 16.3 (1986): 180-221. (Abbreviated *DA*.)

———. *HERmione* [*HER*]. 1981; rpt. London: Virago Press, 1984.

———. *Notes on Thought and Vision & The Wise Sappho*. Ed. Albert Gelpi. San Francisco: City Lights Books, 1982.

———. *Paint It Today*. Ed. Cassandra Laity. New York: New York University Press, 1992.

———. *Tribute to Freud*. 1956; rpt. New York: New Directions, 1974. (Abbreviated *TF*.)

———. *Tribute to the Angels*. London: Oxford University Press, 1945.

———. *Trilogy [The Walls Do Not Fall; Tribute to the Angels; The Flowering of the Rod]*. New York: New Directions, 1973.

DuBow, Wendy M. "The Elusive Text: Reading 'The Diary of Anaïs Nin, Volume I, 1931–1934.'" *ANAÏS* 11 (1993): 22-36.

DuPlessis, Rachel Blau. *H. D.: The Career of That Struggle*. Brighton: Harvester Press, 1986.

———. "Language Acquisition." *Iowa Review* 16.3 (1986): 252-83.

———. "A Note on the State of H. D.'s *The Gift*." *Sulfer* 9 (1984): 178-82.

———. *The Pink Guitar: Writing as Feminist Practice*. New York: Routledge, 1990.

———. "Romantic Thralldom in H. D." In Friedman and DuPlessis, *Signets*, 406-29.

———. *Writing beyond the Ending: Narrative Strategies of Twentieth-Century Women Writers*. Bloomington: Indiana University Press, 1985.

DuPlessis, Rachel Blau and Susan Stanford Friedman. "'Woman is Perfect': H. D.'s Debate with Freud." *Feminist Studies* 7 (1981): 417-30.

Eakin, Paul John. *Fictions in Autobiography: Studies in the Art of Self-Invention*. Princeton: Princeton University Press, 1985.

———. *Touching the World: Reference in Autobiography*. Princeton: Princeton University Press, 1992.

———. ed. *American Autobiography*. Madison: University of Wisconsin Press, 1991.

Edmunds, Susan. *Out of Line: History, Psychoanalysis and Montage in H. D.'s Long Poems*. Stanford: Stanford University Press, 1994.

Eisinger, Erica M. and Mari McCarty, eds. *Colette: The Woman, The Writer*. University Park: The Pennsylvania State University Press, 1981.

Ender, Evelyne. *Sexing the Mind: Nineteenth-Century Fictions of Hysteria*. Ithaca: Cornell University Press, 1995.

Evans, Mari, ed. *Black Women Writers (1950–1980)*. London: Pluto Press, 1985.

Evans, Oliver. *Anaïs Nin*. Carbondale: Southern Illinois University Press, 1968.

Evans, P. D. *Janet Frame*. Boston: Twayne, 1977.

Farwell, Marilyn R. *Heterosexual Plots and Lesbian Narratives*. New York: New York University Press, 1996.

Feldstein, Richard and Marleen S. Barr, eds. *Discontented Discourses: Feminism/Textual Intervention/Psychoanalysis*. Urbana: University of Illinois Press, 1989.

Felman, Shoshana. "Education and Crisis, or the Vicissitudes of Teaching." In Caruth, *Trauma*, 13-60.

———. *Writing and Madness: Literature, Philosophy, Psychoanalysis*. Trans. Evans, Felman, and Massumi. 1978; rpt. Ithaca: Cornell University Press, 1985.

Felman, Shoshana, and Dori Laub. *Testimony: Crises of Witnessing in Literature, Psychoanalysis, and History*. New York: Routledge, 1992.

Felski, Rita. *Beyond Feminist Aesthetics: Feminist Literature and Social Change*. London: Hutchinson Radius, 1989.

Finlayson, Judith. "Connecting with the Universe: Ira Progoff and the Intensive Journal." *ANAÏS* 3 (1985): 31-34.

Firchow, Peter E. "Rico and Julia: The Hilda Doolittle–D. H. Lawrence Affair Reconsidered." *Journal of Modern Literature* 8 (1980): 51-76.

Fish-Murray, Caroline C., Elizabeth V. Koby, and Bessel A. van der Kolk. "Evolving Ideas: The Effect of Abuse on Children's Thought." In Van der Kolk, *Psychological Trauma*, 89-110.

Fitch, Noel Riley. *Anaïs: The Erotic Life of Anaïs Nin*. Boston: Little, Brown and Co., 1993.

Flanner, Raymond B., Jr. *Post-Traumatic Stress Disorder*. New York: Crossroad, 1995.

Flieger, Jerry Aline. *Colette and the Fantom Subject of Autobiography*. Ithaca: Cornell University Press, 1992.

Folkenflik, Robert. "Introduction: The Institution of Autobiography." In Folkenflik, 1-20.

———. ed. *The Culture of Autobiography: Constructions of Self-Representation*. Stanford: Stanford University Press, 1993.

Foucault, Michel. *The Archeology of Knowledge and the Discourse On Language*. Trans. A. M. Sheridan Smith. 1971; rpt. New York: Pantheon Books, 1972.

———. *The Care of the Self*. Vol. 3 of *The History of Sexuality*. Trans. Robert Hurley. 1984; rpt. New York: Random House, 1986.

———. *Discipline and Punish: The Birth of the Prison*. Trans. Alan Sheridan. London: Allen Lane, 1978.

———. *The History of Sexuality*. Vol. 1, *An Introduction*. Trans. Robert Hurley. London: Allen Lane, 1978.

———. *Madness and Civilization: A History of Insanity in the Age of Reason*. Trans. Richard Howard. 1961; rpt. New York: Random House, 1965.

———. *The Use of Pleasure*. Vol. 2 of *The History of Sexuality*. Trans. Robert Hurley. 1984; rpt. New York: Random House, 1985.

Franklin, Benjamin V., ed. *Recollections of Anaïs Nin*. Athens, OH: Ohio University Press, 1996.

Franklin, Benjamin V., and Duane Schneider. *Anaïs Nin: An Introduction*. Athens, OH: Ohio University Press, 1979.

Frame, Janet. *An Angel at My Table*. Autobiography 2. 1984; rpt. London: Collins Publishing Group, 1987.

———. *An Autobiography*. Vol. 1: *To the Is-land*. Vol. 2: *An Angel at My Table*. Vol. 3: *The Envoy from Mirror City*. New York: George Braziller, 1991. (Abbreviated *A*.)

———. "Beginnings." *Landfall* 19.1 (1965): 40-47.

———. *The Envoy from Mirror City*. Autobiography 3. 1985; rpt. London: Collins Publishing Group, 1987.

———. "Interview. By Elizabeth Alley." In Alley and Williams, 39-54.

———. *Faces in the Water*. 1961; rpt. London: Women's Press, 1980. (Abbreviated *FW*.)

———. *Owls Do Cry*. 1957; rpt. London: Women's Press, 1987.

———. *To the Is-land*. Autobiography 1. 1982; rpt. London: Collins Publishing Group, 1987.

Fraser, Sylvia. *My Father's House: A Memoir of Incest and Healing*. 1987; rpt. New York: Harper and Row, 1989. (Abbreviated *MFH*.)

———. *Pandora*. Toronto: McClelland and Stewart, 1972. (Abbreviated *P*.)

Freedman, Diane P., Olivia Frey, and Frances Murphy Zauhar, eds. *The Intimate Critique: Autobiographical Literary Criticism*. Durham: Duke University Press, 1993.

Freibert, Lucy. "Conflict and Creativity in the World of H. D." *Journal of Women's Studies in Literature* 1 (1979): 258-71.

Freud, Sigmund. *The Standard Edition of the Complete Psychological Works of Sigmund Freud.* 24 vols. Ed. and trans. James Strachey. London: Hogarth, 1953-74. (Abbreviated *SE* and volume no.)

Freyd, Jennifer. *Betrayal Trauma: The Logic of Forgetting Childhood Abuse.* Cambridge, MA: Harvard University Press, 1996.

Friedman, Ellen G. "Escaping from the House of Incest: On Anaïs Nin's Efforts to Overcome Patriarchal Constraints." *ANAÏS* 10 (1992): 39-45.

Friedman, Ellen G. and Miriam Fuchs, eds. *Breaking the Sequence: Women's Experimental Fiction.* Princeton: Princeton University Press, 1989.

Friedman, Susan Stanford. "Against Discipleship: Intimacy and Collaboration in H. D.'s Analysis with Freud." *Literature and Psychology* 33 (1987): 89-108.

———. "Creativity and the Childbirth Metaphor: Gender Difference in Literary Discourse." *Feminist Studies* 13 (1986): 49-82.

———. "Emergences and Convergences." *Iowa Review* 16.3 (1986): 42-56.

———. *Penelope's Web: Gender, Modernity, H. D.'s Fiction.* New York: Cambridge University Press, 1990. (Abbreviated *PW*.)

———. "Portrait of the Artist as a Young Woman: H. D.'s Rescriptions of Joyce, Lawrence, and Pound." In Jones, 23-41.

———. *Psyche Reborn: The Emergence of H. D.* Bloomington: Indiana University Press, 1981.

———. "Return of the Repressed in H. D.'s Madrigal Cycle." In Friedman and DuPlessis, *Signets*, 233-52.

———. "Women's Autobiographical Selves: Theory and Practice." In Benstock, 34-62.

———. "The Writing Cure: Transference and Resistance in a Dialogic Analysis." *H. D. Newsletter* 2 (Winter 1988): 25-35.

Friedman, Susan Stanford, and Rachel Blau DuPlessis, eds. *Signets: Reading H. D.* Madison: University of Wisconsin Press, 1990.

Froula, Christine. "The Daughter's Seduction: Sexual Violence and Literary History." In Boose and Flowers, 111-35.

Fuchs, Miriam. "H. D.'s *The Gift*: 'Hide and Seek' with the 'Skeleton-Hand of Death.'" In Morgan and Hall, 85-102.

Gallop, Jane. *Feminism and Psychoanalysis: The Daughter's Seduction.* Ithaca: Cornell University Press, 1982.

———. *Reading Lacan.* Ithaca: Cornell University Press, 1985.

———. *Thinking Through the Body.* New York: Columbia University Press, 1988.

Garner, Shirley Nelson, Claire Kahane, and Madelon Sprengnether, eds. *The (M)other Tongue: Essays in Feminist Psychoanalytic Interpretation.* Ithaca: Cornell University Press, 1985.

Gates, Henry Louis, Jr., ed. *Black Literature and Literary Theory.* New York: Methuen, 1984.

———. *Reading Black, Reading Feminist.* New York: Meridian, 1990.

Gauper, Stephanie A. Demetrakopoulos. "Anaïs Nin and the Feminine Quest for Consciousness: The Quelling of the Devouring Mother and the Ascension of the Sophia." In Jason, 29-44.

Gelpi, Albert. "The Thistle and the Serpent." Introduction to Doolittle [H. D.]. *Notes on Thought and Vision & The Wise Sappho*. San Francisco: City Lights Books, 1982.

Genova, Judith, ed. *Power, Gender, Values*. Edmonton: Academic Printers and Publishers, 1987.

Gersie, Alida. *Storytelling in Bereavement: Dragons Fight in the Meadow*. London: Jessica Kingsley Publishers, 1991.

Gilbert, Sandra M. "Feminism and D. H. Lawrence." *ANAÏS* 9 (1991): 92-100.

Gilbert, Sandra M., and Susan Gubar. *No Man's Land: The Place of the Woman Writer in the Twentieth Century, Vol. 1, The War of the Words*. New Haven: Yale University Press, 1988.

Gilligan, Carol. *In a Different Voice*. Cambridge: Harvard University Press, 1982.

Gilman, Sander L., et al., eds. *Hysteria Beyond Freud*. Berkeley: University of California Press, 1993.

Gilmore, Leigh. *Autobiographics: A Feminist Theory of Women's Self-Representation*. Ithaca: Cornell University Press, 1994.

———. "The Mark of Autobiography: Postmodernism, Autobiography, and Genre." In Ashley, Gilmore, and Peters, 3-18.

———. "Policing Truth: Confession, Gender, and Autobiographical Authority." In Ashley, Gilmore, and Peters, 54-78.

Ginzberg, Ruth. "Audre Lorde's (Nonessentialist) Lesbian Eros." In Card, 81-97.

Goudeket, Maurice. *Close to Colette: An Intimate Portrait of a Woman of Genius*. New York: Farrar, Straus and Cudahy, 1957.

Greene, Gayle, and Coppelia Kahn, eds. *Making a Difference: Feminist Literary Criticism*. London: Methuen, 1985.

Grimm, J. L. C. and W. C. *Grimms' Fairy Tales*. Hertfordshire: Wordsworth Editions Ltd., 1993.

Grosz, Elizabeth. *Sexual Subversions*. London: Allen and Unwin, 1989.

———. *Volatile Bodies: Toward a Corporeal Feminism*. Bloomington: Indiana University Press, 1994.

Guest, Barbara. *Herself Defined: The Poet H. D. and Her World*. Garden City, NY: Doubleday, 1984.

Gunn, Janet Varner. *Autobiography: Toward a Poetics of Experience*. Philadelphia: University of Pennsylvania Press, 1982.

Gusdorf, Georges. "Conditions and Limits of Autobiography." 1956. Trans. James Olney. Rpt. in Olney, *Autobiography*, 28-48.

Haaken, Janice. "The Recovery of Memory, Fantasy, and Desire: Feminist Approaches to Sexual Abuse and Psychic Trauma. *Signs* 21.4 (1996): 1069-94.

Hacking, Ian. "The Making and Molding of Child Abuse." *Critical Inquiry* (1990-91): 253-88.

Hamalian, Leo. "A Spy in the House of Lawrence: Tracing the Signposts of Anaïs Nin's Development As a Writer." *ANAÏS* 13 (1995): 14-26.

Hammond, Karla M. "Audre Lorde: Interview." *Denver Quarterly* 16.1 (1981): 10-27.

———. "An Interview with Audre Lorde." *The American Poetry Review* (March/April 1980): 18-21.

Hannah, Donald. "*Faces in the Water*: Case-History or Work of Fiction?" In Delbaere, 74-81.
Harms, Valerie. "Anaïs and Her Analysts, Rank and Allendy: The Creative and Destructive Aspects." In Nalbantian, 112-19.
———. ed. *Celebration of Anaïs Nin*. Riverside, CT: Magic Circle Press, 1973.
Hawkins, Anne Hunsaker. *Reconstructing Illness: Studies in Pathography*. West Lafayette, IN: Purdue University Press, 1993.
Heilbrun, Carolyn G. *Writing a Woman's Life*. New York: Ballantine, 1988.
Henderson, Mae Gwendolyn. "Speaking in Tongues: Dialogics, Dialectics, and the Black Woman Writer's Literary Tradition." In Wall, 16-37.
Henke, Suzette A. "Androgynous Creation: From D. H. Lawrence to Djuna Barnes: Anaïs Nin's Aesthetic Evolution," *ANAÏS* 15 (1997): 85-94.
———. "Anaïs Nin: A Freudian Perspective." *Under the Sign of Pisces* 11.1 (1980): 6-14.
———. "Anaïs Nin's *Journal of Love*: Father Loss and Incestuous Desire." In Nalbantian, 112-35.
———. "A Confessional Narrative: Maternal Anxiety and Daughter Loss in Anaïs Nin's *Incest*." *ANAÏS* 14 (1996): 71-77.
———. "Frances Farmer: *Will There Really Be a Morning?*" In Rhodes, 112-13.
———. *James Joyce and the Politics of Desire*. New York: Routledge, 1990.
———. "Life-Writing: Art as Diary, Fiction, Therapy." *ANAÏS* 16 (1998): 79-87.
———. "Lillian Beye's Labyrinth: A Freudian Exploration of *Cities of the Interior*." *ANAÏS* 2 (1984): 113-26.
———. "A Portrait of the Artist as a Young Woman: Janet Frame's Autobiography." *SPAN: Journal of the South Pacific Association for Commonwealth Literature* 31 (1991): 85-94.
———. "Recalling Anaïs Nin." In Franklin, 119-25.
———. "Sexuality and Silence in Women's Literature." In Genova, 45-62.
———. "Toward a Feminist Semiotics of Revulsion: Literary Abjection in the Age of Atrocity." *Mattoid* 48 (1994): 96-108.
Herman, Judith Lewis. *Trauma and Recovery*. New York: Harper Collins, 1992.
Herman, Judith Lewis, with Lisa Hirschman. *Father-Daughter Incest*. Cambridge: Harvard University Press, 1981.
Herman, Judith Lewis and Bessel A. van der Kolk. "Traumatic Antecedents of Borderline Personality Disorder." In van der Kolk, *Psychological Trauma*, 111-26.
Heywood, Leslie. *Dedication to Hunger*. Berkeley: University of California Press, 1996.
Hinz, Evelyn J. *The Mirror and the Garden: Realism and Reality in the Writings of Anaïs Nin*. 1971; rpt. New York: Harcourt Brace Jovanovich, 1973.
———. "A Speculative Introduction: Life-Writing as Drama." In Hinz, v-xii.
Hinz, Evelyn J., ed. *Data and Acta: Aspects of Life-Writing*. Winnipeg, Canada: University of Manitoba, 1987.
———. ed. *The World of Anaïs Nin: Critical and Cultural Perspectives*. (*Mosaic* 11.2) Winnipeg: University of Manitoba Press, 1978.
Hirsch, Elizabeth A. "Imaginary Images: 'H. D.,' Modernism, and the Psychoanalysis of Seeing." In Feldstein and Barr, 141-59.
Hirsch, Marianne. *The Mother/Daughter Plot: Narrative, Psychoanalysis, Feminism*. Bloomington: Indiana University Press, 1989.

Hogan, Rebecca. "Engendered Autobiographies: The Diary as a Feminine Form." In Neuman, *Autobiography*, 95-107.

Hollenberg, Donna. *H. D.: The Poetics of Childbirth and Creativity*. Boston: Northeastern University Press, 1991.

hooks, bell. *Feminist Theory: From Margin to Center*. Boston: South End Press, 1984.

Hoy, Nancy Jo. "The Poetry of Experience: How to Be a Woman and an Artist." *ANAÏS* 4 (1986): 52-66.

Hull, Gloria T. "Living on the Line: Audre Lorde and *Our Dead Behind Us*." In Wall, 150-72.

Hull, Gloria T., Patricia Bell Scott, and Barbara Smith, eds. *All the Women Are White/ All the Blacks Are Men/ But Some of Us Are Brave: Black Women's Studies*. Old Westbury, NY: Feminist Press, 1982.

Humm, Maggie. *Feminist Criticism: Women as Contemporary Critics*. Brighton, Sussex: Harvester, 1986.

Iowa Review. *H. D. Centennial Issue*, ed. Adalaide Morris. 16.3 (1986).

Irigaray, Luce. *The Irigaray Reader*. Ed. Margaret Whitford. Oxford: Blackwell, 1991 (Abbreviated *IR*.)

———. *Speculum of the Other Woman*. Trans. Gillian C. Gill. Ithaca: Cornell University Press, 1985.

———. *This Sex Which Is Not One*. Trans. Catherine Porter and Carolyn Burke. Ithaca: Cornell University Press, 1985.

Jacobs, Janet Liebman. *Victimized Daughters: Incest and the Development of the Female Self*. New York: Routledge, 1994.

Jardine, Alice A. *Gynesis: Configurations of Woman and Modernity*. Ithaca: Cornell University Press, 1985.

Jason, Philip K. *Anaïs Nin and Her Critics*. Columbia, SC: Camden House, 1993.

———. "Doubles/Don Juans: Anaïs Nin and Otto Rank." In Hinz, *World*, 81-94.

———. "Dropping Another Veil." *ANAÏS* 6 (1988): 27-32.

———. ed. *The Critical Response to Anaïs Nin*. Westport, CT: Greenwood Press, 1996.

Jay, Karla and Joanne Glasgow. *Lesbian Texts and Contexts: Radical Revisions*. New York: New York University Press, 1990.

Jay, Paul. *Being in the Text*. Ithaca, NY: Cornell University Press, 1984.

Jelinek, Estelle C. "Anaïs Nin: A Critical Evaluation." In Brown and Olson, 312-23.

———. *The Tradition of Women's Autobiography: From Antiquity to the Present*. Boston: Twayne, 1986.

Jelinek, Estelle C., ed. *Women's Autobiography: Essays in Criticism*. Bloomington: Indiana University Press, 1980.

Johnston, Jill. "Divided against Her Father." *New York Times Book Review* 94 (21 May 1989): 50.

Jones, Suzanne, ed. *Writing the Woman Artist: Essays on Poetics, Politics, and Portraiture*. Philadelphia: University of Pennsylvania Press, 1991.

Jong, Erica. "A Story Never Told Before: Reading the New, Unexpurgated *Diary* of Anaïs Nin." *ANAÏS* 12 (1994): 15-25.

Joseph, Gloria I., and Jill Lewis. *Common Differences: Conflicts in Black and White Feminist Perspectives*. New York: Anchor, 1981.

Joyce, James. *A Portrait of the Artist as a Young Man*. 1916; rpt. ed. Chester G. Anderson. New York: Viking Press, 1968.

Kacandes, Irene. "Narrative Strategies in Contemporary Prose Fiction of/as Trauma." Society for the Study of Narrative Literature Conference, April 21, 1995.

Kadar, Marlene. "Whose Life Is It Anyway?: Out of the Bathtub and into the Narrative." In Kadar, 152-61.

———. ed. *Essays on Life Writing: From Genre to Critical Practice.* Toronto: University of Toronto Press, 1992.

Kahane, Claire. *Passions of the Voice: Hysteria, Narrative, and the Figure of the Speaking Woman, 1850–1915.* Baltimore: Johns Hopkins University Press, 1995.

Kamboureli, Smaro. "Discourse and Intercourse, Design and Desire in the Erotica of Anaïs Nin." In Jason, 89-103.

Kamuf, Peggy. *Fictions of Feminine Desire.* Lincoln: University of Nebraska Press, 1982.

Kaplan, Caren. "Resisting Autobiography: Out-Law Genres and Transnational Feminist Subjects." In Smith and Watson, *De/Colonizing the Subject*, 115-38.

Kaplan, Louise J. *Female Perversions: The Temptations of Emma Bovary.* New York: Bantam Doubleday Dell, 1991.

Karsten, Julie A. "Self-Realization and Intimacy: The Influence of D. H. Lawrence on Anaïs Nin." *ANAÏS* 4 (1986): 36-42.

Keating, AnaLouise. *Women Reading Women Writing: Self-Invention in Paula Gunn Allen, Gloria Anzaldua, and Audre Lorde.* Temple University Press, 1996.

Keller, Jane Eblen. "Living à la Lawrence: Anaïs Nin's Revelations of Passional Experience." *ANAÏS* 15 (1977): 12-25.

Kerenyi, C. *Eleusis: Archetypal Image of Mother and Daughter.* Trans. Ralph Manheim. New York: Schocken, 1977.

Ketchum, Anne Duhamel. "Colette and the Enterprise of Writing: A Reappraisal." In Eisinger and McCarty, 22-31.

King, Michael, ed. *H. D.: Woman and Poet.* Orono, ME: National Poetry Foundation, 1986.

Klein, Melanie. *Love, Guilt and Reparation and Other Works, 1921–1945.* New York: Delacorte Press, 1975.

———. *The Selected Melanie Klein.* Ed. Juliet Mitchell. Harmondsworth, England: Penguin Books, 1986.

Klein, Yvonne. "Myth and Community in Recent Lesbian Autobiographical Fiction." In Jay and Glasgow, 330-38.

Kloepfer, Deborah Kelly. *The Unspeakable Mother: Forbidden Discourse in Jean Rhys and H. D.* Ithaca: Cornell University Press, 1989.

Knapp, Bettina. *Anaïs Nin.* New York: Frederick Ungar, 1978.

Kohut, Heinz. *The Restoration of the Self.* 1977; rpt. Madison, CT: International Universities Press, 1977.

Kristeva, Julia. *Desire in Language: A Semiotic Approach to Literature and Art.* Ed. Leon S. Roudiez. Trans. Thomas Gora, Alice Jardine, and Leon S. Roudiez. New York: Columbia University Press, 1980. (Abbreviated *DL.*)

———. *The Kristeva Reader.* Ed. Toril Moi. New York: Columbia University Press, 1986. (Abbreviated *KR.*)

———. *Powers of Horror: An Essay on Abjection.* Trans. Leon S. Roudiez. New York: Columbia University Press, 1982.

———. *Revolution in Poetic Language.* Trans. Margaret Waller. New York: Columbia University Press, 1984.

Krizan, Kim. "Illusion and the Art of Survival." *ANAÏS* 10 (1992): 18-28.
Kuribayashi, Tomoko and Julie Tharp, eds. *Creating Safe Space: Violence and Women's Writing*. Albany: SUNY Press, 1998.
La Belle, Jenijoy. *Herself Beheld: The Literature of the Looking Glass*. Ithaca: Cornell University Press, 1988.
Lacan, Jacques. *Écrits: A Selection*. Trans. Alan Sheridan. New York: Norton, 1977.
———. *The Four Fundamental Concepts of Psycho-Analysis*. Trans. Alan Sheridan. New York: Norton, 1981.
———. *Speech and Language in Psychoanalysis*. Trans. Anthony Wilden. Baltimore: Johns Hopkins University Press, 1968.
LaCapra, Dominick. *Representing the Holocaust: History, Theory, Trauma*. Ithaca: Cornell University Press, 1994.
Laing, R. D. *The Politics of Experience*. 1967; rpt. New York: Ballantine Books, 1971.
Lanser, Susan Snaider. *The Narrative Act: Point of View in Prose Fiction*. Princeton: Princeton University Press, 1981.
Laplanche, Jean. *Life and Death in Psychoanalysis*. Trans. Jeffrey Mehlman. Baltimore: Johns Hopkins University Press, 1976.
Lawlor, Patricia. "Beyond Gender and Genre: Writing the Labyrinth of the Selves." *ANAÏS* 7 (1989): 23-31.
Lejeune, Philippe. *On Autobiography*. Ed. Paul John Eakin. Trans. Katherine Leary. Minneapolis: University of Minnesota Press, 1989.
Lilienfeld, Jane. "The Magic Spinning Wheel: Straw to Gold—Colette, Willy, and Sido." In Perry and Brownley, 165-79.
Lionnet, Françoise. *Autobiographical Voices: Race, Gender, Self-Portraiture*. Ithaca: Cornell University Press, 1989.
———. *Postcolonial Representations: Women, Literature, Identity*. Ithaca: Cornell University Press, 1995.
Loesberg, Jonathan. "Autobiography as Genre, Act of Consciousness, Text." *Prose Studies* 4 (1981): 169-85.
Lorde, Audre. *The Black Unicorn*. New York: Norton, 1978.
———. *A Burst of Light*. Ithaca: Firebrand Books, 1988. (Abbreviated *BL*.)
———. *The Cancer Journals*. San Francisco: Aunt Lute Books, 1980. (Abbreviated *CJ*.)
———. *Sister Outsider: Essays and Speeches by Audre Lorde*. Freedom, CA: The Crossing Press, 1984. (Abbreviated *SO*.)
———. *Undersong: Chosen Poems Old and New*. New York: Norton, 1992.
———. *Zami: A New Spelling of My Name*. Freedom, CA: The Crossing Press, 1982. (Abbreviated *Z*.)
McConnell-Ginet, Sally, Ruth Borker, and Nelly Furman, eds. *Women and Language in Literature and Society*. New York: Praeger, 1980.
McDowell, Deborah E. "Reading Family Matters." In Wall, 75-97.
McFarlane, Alexander C. and Bessel A. Van der Kolk. "Trauma and Its Challenge to Society." In van der Kolk et al., 24-46.
———. "Conclusions and Future Directions." In Van der Kolk et al., 559-75.
McFarlane, Alexander C. and Rachel Yehuda. "Resilience, Vulnerability, and the Course of Posttraumatic Reactions." In Van der Kolk et al., 155-81.
McLaughlin, Joan Bobbitt. "Truth and Artistry in the *Diary of Anaïs Nin*." In Jason, 190-98.

Maglin, Nan Bauer. "'Don't never forget the bridge that you crossed over on': The Literature of Matrilineage." In Davidson and Broner, 257-67.

Makward, Christiane. "Colette and Signs: A Partial Reading of a Writer 'Born *Not* to Write.'" In Eisinger and McCarty, 185-92.

Mandel, Barrett J. "Full of Life Now." In Olney, 49-72.

Marcus, Jane. "Invincible Mediocrity: The Private Selves of Public Women." In Benstock, 114-46.

Markert, Lawrence Wayne. "Speaking with Your Skeleton: D. H. Lawrence's Influence on Anaïs Nin." In Nalbantian, 223-35.

Marks, Elaine. *Colette*. New Brunswick, NJ: Rutgers University Press, 1960.

Marks, Elaine, and Isabelle de Courtivron, eds. *New French Feminisms: An Anthology*. Amherst: University of Massachusetts Press, 1980.

Martin, Joan. "The Unicorn is Black: Audre Lorde in Retrospect." In M. Evans, 277-91.

Meese, Elizabeth A. *Crossing the Double-Cross: The Practice of Feminist Criticism*. Chapel Hill: University of North Carolina Press, 1986.

———. *(Ex)tensions: Re-Figuring Feminist Criticism*. Urbana: University of Illinois, 1990.

Meiselman, Karin C. *Incest: A Psychological Study of Causes and Effects with Treatment Recommendations*. London: Jossey-Bass Ltd., 1978.

Merchant, Hoshang. "Out of and into the Labyrinth: Approaching the Aesthetics of Anaïs Nin." *ANAÏS* 8 (1990): 59.

Metzger, Deena. "The *Diary*: The Ceremony of Knowing." In Zaller, 133-43.

Meyers, Diana Tietjens. *Subjection and Subjectivity: Psychoanalytic Feminism and Moral Philosophy*. New York: Routledge, 1994.

Milicia, Joseph. "*Bid Me To Live*: Within the Storm." In King, 279-300.

Miller, Alice. *Breaking Down the Wall of Silence: The Liberating Experience of Facing Painful Truth*. Trans. Simon Worrall. 1990; rpt. New York: Dutton, 1991.

———. *The Drama of the Gifted Child*. Trans. Ruth Ward. 1979; rpt. New York: Harper Basic Books, 1990.

———. *For Your Own Good: Hidden Cruelty in Child-Rearing and the Roots of Violence*. Trans. Hildegarde and Hunter Hannum. 1980; rpt. New York: Farrar Straus Giroux, 1984.

———. *Thou Shalt Not Be Aware: Society's Betrayal of the Child*. Trans. Hildegarde and Hunter Hannum. 1981; rpt. New York: New American Library, 1986.

Miller, Edmund. "Erato Throws a Curve: Anaïs Nin and the Elusive Feminine Voice in Erotica." In Nalbantian, 164-84.

Miller, Henry. *Letters to Anaïs Nin*. Ed. Gunther Stuhlmann. New York: G. P. Putnam's Sons, 1965.

———. "*Un Être Étoilique*." In Zaller, 5-23.

Miller, Margaret. "Diary-Keeping and the Young Wife." *ANAÏS* 3 (1985): 39-44.

Miller, Nancy K. "The Anamnesis of a Female 'I': In the Margins of Self-Portrayal." In Eisinger and McCarty, 164-75.

———. *Getting Personal: Feminist Occasions and Other Autobiographical Acts*. New York: Routledge, 1991.

———. ed. *The Poetics of Gender*. New York: Columbia University Press, 1986.

———. *Subject to Change: Reading Feminist Writing*. New York: Columbia University Press, 1988.

Millett, Kate. "Anaïs—A Mother to Us All: The Birth of the Artist as Woman." *ANAÏS* 9 (1991): 3-8.

Mitchell, Juliet, and Jacqueline Rose, eds. *Feminine Sexuality: Jacques Lacan and the 'école freudienne'*. Trans. Jacqueline Rose. New York: Norton, 1982.

Moffat, Mary Jane. "Does the Diary Have a Future?" *ANAÏS* 3 (1985): 35-38.

Mohanty, Chandra Talpade, Ann Russo, and Lourdes Torres, eds. *Third World Women and the Politics of Feminism*. Bloomington: Indiana University Press, 1991.

Moi, Toril. *Sexual/Textual Politics: Feminist Literary Theory*. London: Methuen, 1985.

Moorjani, Angela. *The Aesthetics of Loss and Lessness*. New York: St. Martin's Press, 1992.

———. "Fetishism, Gender Masquerade, and the Mother-Father Fantasy." In Smith and Mahfouz, 22-41.

Morgan, Janice. "Subject to Subject/Voice to Voice: Twentieth-Century Autobiographical Fiction by Women Writers." In Morgan and Hall, 3-19.

Morgan, Janice and Colette T. Hall, eds. *Redefining Autobiography in Twentieth-Century Women's Fiction*. New York: Garland, 1991.

Moraga, Cherrie, and Gloria Anzaldua. *This Bridge Called My Back: Writings by Radical Women of Color*. New York: Kitchen Table Press, 1981 and 1983.

Morris, Adalaide. "Autobiography and Prophecy: H. D.'s *The Gift*." In King, 227-36.

———. "The Concept of Projection: H. D.'s Visionary Powers." *Contemporary Literature* 25.4 (1984): 411-36.

———. "A Relay of Power and of Peace: H. D. and the Spirit of the Gift." *Contemporary Literature* 27 (1986): 493-524.

Morris, Daniel. "My Shoes: Charles Simic's Self-Portrait." *a/b: Autobiography Studies* 11.11 (1996): 109-27.

Munt, Sally, ed. *Lesbian Criticism: Literary and Cultural Readings*. New York: Columbia University Press, 1992.

Nalbantian, Suzanne. *Aesthetic Autobiography*. New York: St. Martin's Press, 1994.

———. "Aesthetic Lies." In Nalbantian, 3-22.

———. ed. *Anaïs Nin: Literary Perspectives*. London: Macmillan, 1997.

Neuman, Shirley. "Autobiography: From Different Poetics to a Poetics of Difference." In Kadar, 213-230.

———. ed. *Autobiography and Questions of Gender*. London: Frank Cass & Co. Ltd., 1991.

———, and Smaro Kamboureli, eds. *A/Mazing Space: Writing Canadian Women Writing*. Edmonton: Longspoon/NeWest, 1986.

Newton, Judith, and Deborah Rosenfelt, eds. *Feminist Criticism and Social Change: Sex, Class, and Race in Literature and Culture*. New York: Methuen, 1985.

Nicholson, Linda, ed. *Feminism/Postmodernism*. New York: Routledge, 1990.

Niemeyer, Doris. "How to Be a Woman and/or an Artist: The Diary as an Instrument of Self-Therapy." Trans. Gunther Stuhlmann. *ANAÏS* 6 (1988): 67-74.

Nin, Anaïs. *Cities of the Interior*. 1959; rpt. Chicago: Swallow Press, 1974. (Abbreviated *CI*.)

———. *Conversations with Anaïs Nin*. Ed. Wendy M. DuBow. Jackson: University Press of Mississippi, 1994.

———. *Delta of Venus: Erotica*. New York: Harcourt Brace, 1977. (Abbreviated *DV*.)

———. *The Diary of Anaïs Nin*. 7 Vols. Ed. Gunther Stuhlmann. New York: Swallow and Harcourt Brace, 1966-80. (Abbreviated *D* and volume no.)

———. *D. H. Lawrence: An Unprofessional Study*. Paris: Edward W. Titus, 1932; rpt. Denver: Swallow Press, 1964.

———. *The Early Diary of Anaïs Nin. Volume 1, Linotte—1914–1920; Volume 2, 1920–1923; Volume 3, 1923–1927;* and *Volume 4, 1927–1931*. All volumes with prefaces by Joaquin Nin-Culmell. New York and London: Harcourt Brace, 1978, 1982, 1983, 1985. (Abbreviated *ED* and volume no.)

———. *Fire: From "A Journal of Love," The Unexpurgated Diary of Anaïs Nin, 1934–1937*. New York: Harcourt Brace, 1986. (Abbreviated *F*.)

———. *Henry and June: From "A Journal of Love," The Unexpurgated Diary of Anaïs Nin, 1931–1932*. New York: Harcourt Brace, 1986. (Abbreviated *HJ*.)

———. *House of Incest*. Chicago: Swallow Press, 1958. (Abbreviated *HI*.)

———. *Incest: From "A Journal of Love," The Unexpurgated Diary of Anaïs Nin 1932–1934*. New York: Harcourt Brace, 1992. (Abbreviated *I*.)

———. *In Favor of the Sensitive Man and Other Essays*. New York: Harcourt Brace, 1976. (Abbreviated *SM*.)

———. *Little Birds: Erotica*. London: W. H. Allen, 1979; rpt. Star, 1980. (Abbreviated *LB*.)

———. *Nearer the Moon: From "A Journal of Love," The Unexpurgated Diary of Anaïs Nin, 1937–1939*. New York: Harcourt Brace, 1996. (Abbreviated *NM*.)

———. *The Novel of the Future*. New York: Macmillan, 1968.

———. *Under a Glass Bell*. Denver: Swallow Press, 1961.

———. *Winter of Artifice: Three Novelettes ["Stella," "Winter of Artifice," and "The Voice"]*. 1948; rpt. Athens: Ohio University Press, 1997. (Abbreviated *WA*.)

———. *A Woman Speaks: The Lectures, Seminars and Interviews of Anaïs Nin*. Ed. Evelyn J. Hinz. Chicago: Swallow Press, 1975. (Abbreviated *WS*.)

Nin-Culmell, Joaquin. "Anaïs Nin, My Sister." In Nalbantian, 23-26.

Nussbaum, Felicity A. *The Autobiographical Subject: Gender and Ideology in Eighteenth-Century England*. Baltimore: Johns Hopkins University Press, 1989.

Ofshe, Richard, and Ethan Watters. *Making Monsters: False Memories, Psychotherapy, and Sexual Hysteria*. New York: Scribner, 1994.

Olney, James. "Autobiography and the Cultural Moment: A Thematic, Historical, and Bibliographical Introduction." In Olney, *Autobiography*, 3-27.

———. *Metaphors of Self: The Meaning of Autobiography*. Princeton: Princeton University Press, 1972.

———. "Some Versions of Memory/Some Versions of *Bios*: The Ontology of Autobiography." In Olney, *Autobiography*, 236-67.

———. ed. *Autobiography: Essays Theoretical and Critical*. Princeton: Princeton University Press, 1980.

———. ed. *Studies in Autobiography*. New York: Oxford University Press, 1988.

Ostriker, Alicia Suskin. *Stealing the Language: The Emergence of Women's Poetry in America*. Boston: Beacon, 1986.

Panny, Judith Dell. *I Have What I Gave: The Fiction of Janet Frame*. 1992; rpt. New York: George Braziller, 1993.

Papachristou, Sophia. "The Body in the Diary: On Anaïs Nin's First Erotic Writings." *ANAÏS* 9 (1991): 58-66.

Pascal, Roy. *Design and Truth in Autobiography*. Cambridge: Harvard University Press, 1960.

Pennebaker, James. *Opening Up: The Healing Power of Confiding in Others*. New York: Avon, 1992.

Perrault, Jeanne. *Writing Selves: Contemporary Feminist Autography*. Minneapolis: University of Minnesota Press, 1995.

Perry, Ruth, and Martine Watson Brownley, eds. *Mothering the Mind: Twelve Studies of Writers and Their Silent Partners*. New York: Holmes and Meier, 1984.

Personal Narratives Group, ed. *Interpreting Women's Lives: Feminist Theory and Personal Narratives*. Bloomington: Indiana University Press, 1989.

Petch, Simon. "Janet Frame and the Languages of Autobiography." *Australian and New Zealand Studies in Canada* 5 (1991): 58-71.

Plaza, Monique. "The Mother/The Same: Hatred of the Mother in Psychoanalysis." *Feminist Issues* 2.1 (1982): 75-100.

Poston, Carol. "Childbirth in Literature." *Feminist Studies* 4.1 (1978): 18-31.

Probyn, Elspeth. *Sexing the Self: Gendered Positions in Cultural Studies*. New York: Routledge, 1993.

Progoff, Ira. *At a Journal Workshop*. New York: Dialogue House Library, 1975.

Pryse, Marjorie, and Hortense Spillers, eds. *Conjuring: Black Women and Literary Tradition*. Bloomington: Indiana University Press, 1985.

Pynoos, Robert S., Alan M. Steinberg, Armen Goenjian. "Traumatic Stress in Childhood and Adolescence: Recent Developments and Current Controversies." In Van der Kolk et al., 331-358.

Rainer, Tristine. "Anaïs Nin's *Diary I*: The Birth of the Young Woman as an Artist." In Zaller, 161-68.

———. *The New Diary*. Los Angeles: J. P. Tarcher, 1978.

———. "The Uses of Ambivalence." *ANAÏS* 3 (1985): 27-30.

Rank, Otto. *Art and Artist: Creative Urge and Personality Development*. Trans. Charles Francis Atkinson. New York: Knopf, 1932; rpt. Agathon Press, 1975.

———. *The Incest Theme in Literature and Legend: Fundamentals of a Psychology of Literary Creation*. Trans. Gregory C. Richter. 1912; rpt. Baltimore: Johns Hopkins University Press, 1992.

———. "On the *Early Diary*: A Preface." *ANAÏS* 2 (1984): 20-23.

Raynaud, Claudine. "'A Nutmeg Nestled Inside Its Covering of Mace': Audre Lorde's *Zami*." In Brodzki and Schenck, 221-42.

Relyea, Suzanne. "Polymorphic Perversity: Colette's Illusory 'Real.'" In Eisinger and McCarty, 150-63.

Renza, Louis A. "The Veto of the Imagination: A Theory of Autobiography." In Olney, *Autobiography*, 268-95.

Rhodes, Carolyn, ed. *First Person Female, American*. Troy, NY: Whitson Press, 1980.

Rich, Adrienne. *Of Woman Born: Motherhood as Experience and Institution*. New York: Norton, 1976; rpt. Bantam, 1977.

Richard-Allerdyce, Diane. *Anaïs Nin and the Remaking of Self: Gender, Modernism, and Narrative Identity*. DeKalb: Northern Illinois University Press, 1998.

———. "Anaïs Nin's Mothering Metaphor: Toward a Lacanian Theory of Feminine Creativity." In Camden, 86-98.

———. "Narrative and Authenticity: The *Diary* Now and Then." *ANAÏS* 13 (1995): 79-94.

Richardson, Joanna. *Colette*. New York: Dell, 1983.

Ricoeur, Paul. "Life: A Story in Search of a Narrator." In *A Ricoeur Reader: Reflection and Imagination*. Ed. Mario J. Valdés. Toronto: University of Toronto Press, 1991. 425-37.

———. *Time and Narrative*. 3 vols. Trans. Kathleen McLaughlin and David Pellauer. Chicago: University of Chicago Press, 1984-1988.

Riddel, Joseph. "H. D. and the Poetics of Spiritual Realism." *Contemporary Literature* 10: 435-46.

———. "H. D.'s Scene of Writing." *Studies in the Literary Imagination*. 12: 41-59.

Riley, Denise. *"Am I That Name?" Feminism and the Category of "Women" in History*. Minneapolis: University of Minnesota Press, 1988.

Rimmon-Kenan, Sholomith. *Discourse in Psychoanalysis and Literature*. London: Methuen, 1987.

Rivière, Joan. "Womanliness as Masquerade" (1929). In Burgin et. al., 33-44.

Robertson, Robert T. "Bird, Hawk, Bogie: Janet Frame, 1952–62." In Delbaere, 31-40.

Robinson, Janice S. *H. D.: The Life and Work of an American Poet*. Houghton Mifflin, 1982.

———. "What's in a Box? Psychoanalytic Concept and Literary Technique in H. D." In King, 237-58.

Rock, Joanne. "Her Father's Daughter: A Re-evaluation" *ANAÏS* 13 (1995): 29-38.

Rose, Jacqueline. *Sexuality in the Field of Vision*. London: Verso, 1986.

Rowell, Charles H. "Above the Wind: An Interview with Audre Lorde." *Callaloo* 14.1 (1991): 83-95.

Rubenstein, Roberta. *Boundaries of the Self: Gender, Culture, Fiction*. Urbana: University of Illinois Press, 1987.

Rubin, Rick and Greg Byerly. *Incest: The Last Taboo. An Annotated Bibliography*. New York: Garland, 1983.

Rush, Florence. *The Best Kept Secret: Sexual Abuse of Children*. New York: McGraw-Hill, 1980.

Russell, Diana E. H. *The Secret Trauma: Incest in the Lives of Girls and Women*. New York: Basic Books, 1986.

Rutherford, Anna. "Janet Frame's Divided and Distinguished Worlds." In Delbaere, 41-52.

Salber, Linde. "Two Lives—One Experiment: Lou Andreas-Salomé and Anaïs Nin." Trans. Gunther Stuhlmann. *ANAÏS* 9 (1991): 78-91.

Sarde, Michèle. *Colette: Free and Fettered*. Trans. Richard Miller. 1978; rpt. New York: William Morrow, 1980.

Sartre, Jean-Paul. *Being and Nothingness*. Trans. Hazel E. Barnes. New York: Philosophical Library, 1956.

Sayers, Janet. *Sexual Contradictions: Psychology, Psychoanalysis, and Feminism*. London: Tavistock, 1986.

Schacter, Daniel L. *Searching for Memory: The Brain, the Mind, and the Past*. New York: Basic Books, 1996.

Scheman, Naomi. *Engenderings: Constructions of Knowledge, Authority, and Privilege*. New York: Routledge, 1993.

Schneider, Duane. "Anaïs Nin in the *Diary*: The Creation and Development of a Persona." In Hinz, *World*, 9-19.

Scholar, Nancy. *Anaïs Nin*. Boston: Twayne, 1984.

Schor, Naomi. *Breaking the Chain: Women, Theory, and French Realist Fiction*. New York: Columbia University Press, 1985.
———. *Reading in Detail: Aesthetics and the Feminine*. London: Methuen, 1987.
Schor, Naomi and Elizabeth Weed, eds. *The Essential Difference*. Bloomington: Indiana University Press, 1994.
Schwartz, Susan. *Un-Naming: The Subject of Madness in Women's Autobiographical Fiction*. PH. D. Diss., University of Melbourne, 1996.
Scott, Bonnie Kime, ed. *The Gender of Modernism*. Bloomington: Indiana University Press, 1990.
Seymour, Miranda. "Truth Wasn't Sexy Enough." Review of *Anaïs: The Erotic Life of Anaïs Nin* by Noel Riley Fitch. *New York Times Book Review*. (17 October, 1993): 18.
Showalter, Elaine. *The Female Malady: Women, Madness, and English Culture, 1830–1980*. New York: Pantheon, 1985.
———. "Hysteria, Feminism, and Gender." In Gilman, et al., 286-344.
———. *Hystories: Hysterical Epidemics and The Modern Media*. New York: Columbia University Press, 1997.
———. *Sexual Anarchy*. New York: Viking, 1990.
———. ed. *The New Feminist Criticism: Essays on Women, Literature, and Theory*. New York: Pantheon Books, 1985.
Silverman, Kaja. *Male Subjectivity at the Margins*. New York: Routledge, 1992.
Slater, Philip E. *The Glory of Hera: Greek Mythology and the Greek Family*. 1968; rpt. Boston: Beacon Press, 1971.
Slavney, Phillip R. *Perspectives on "Hysteria."* Baltimore: Johns Hopkins University Press, 1990.
Slawy-Sutton, Catherine. "Lies, Half-truths, Considerable Secrets: Colette and Re-Writing the Self." In Morgan and Hall, 23-44.
Smith, Barbara. "The Truth That Never Hurts: Black Lesbians in Fiction in the 1980s." 1989; rpt. in Mohanty et al., 101-29.
Smith, Joseph H. and Afaf M. Mahfouz, eds. *Psychoanalysis, Feminism, and the Future of Gender*. Baltimore: Johns Hopkins University Press, 1994.
Smith, Paul. *Discerning the Subject*. Minneapolis: University of Minnesota Press, 1988.
Smith, Sidonie. *A Poetics of Women's Autobiography: Marginality and the Fictions of Self-Representation*. Bloomington: Indiana University Press, 1987.
———. *Subjectivity, Identity, and the Body*. Bloomington: Indiana University Press, 1993.
Smith, Sidonie, and Julia Watson, eds. *De/Colonizing the Subject: The Politics of Gender in Women's Autobiography*. Minneapolis: University of Minnesota Press, 1992.
———. *Getting a Life: Everyday Uses of Autobiography*. Minneapolis: University of Minnesota Press, 1996.
Smith, Valerie. "Black Feminist Theory and the Representation of the 'Other.'" In Wall, 38-57.
———. *Self-Discovery and Authority in African-American Narratives*. Cambridge: Harvard University Press, 1987.
Snyder, Robert, ed. *Anaïs Nin Observed: From a Film Portrait of a Woman as an Artist*. Chicago: Swallow Press, 1976.
Sojourner, Sabrina. "From the House of Yemanjá: The Goddess Heritage of Black Women." In Spretnak, 57-63.

Sommer, Doris. "Not Just a Personal Story": Women's *Testimonios* and the Plural Self." In Brodzki and Schenck, 107-30.

Sontag, Susan. *Illness as Metaphor*. New York: Farrar, Straus and Giroux, 1978.

Spencer, Sharon. "Beyond Therapy: The Enduring Love of Anaïs Nin for Otto Rank." In Nalbantian, 97-111.

———. *Collage of Dreams: The Writings of Anaïs Nin*. 1977; rpt. New York: Harcourt Brace, 1981.

———. "The Music of the Womb: Anaïs Nin's 'Feminine' Writing." In Friedman and Fuchs, 161-73.

Spencer, Sharon, ed. *Anaïs, Art and Artists, A Collection of Essays*. Greenwood, FL: Penkeville, 1986.

Spengemann, William. *The Forms of Autobiography: Episodes in the History of a Literary Genre*. New Haven, CT: Yale University Press, 1980.

Spillers, Hortense. "'The Permanent Obliquity of an In(pha)llibly Straight': In the Time of the Daughters and the Fathers." In Wall, 127-49.

Spoo, Robert. "H. D.'s Dating of *Asphodel*: A Reassessment." *H. D. Newsletter*. 4.2 (1991): 31-40.

Spretnak, Charlene, ed. *The Politics of Women's Spirituality: Essays on the Rise of Spiritual Power Within the Feminist Movement*. Garden City, NY: Doubleday, 1982.

Sprinker, Michael. "Fictions of the Self: The End of Autobiography." In Olney, *Autobiography*, 321-42.

Stanton, Domna. *The Female Autograph: Theory and Practice in Autobiography from the Tenth to the Twentieth Century*. Chicago: University of Chicago Press, 1984.

Stern, Daniel. "The Novel of Her Life: *The Diary of Anaïs Nin*, Volume IV (1944–47)." In Zaller, 153-56.

Stewart, Joan Hinde. *Colette*. Boston: Twayne Publishers, 1983.

Stone, Albert E. *Autobiographical Occasions and Original Acts: Versions of American Identity from Henry Adams to Nate Shaw*. Philadelphia: University of Pennsylvania Press, 1982.

Sturrock, John. "Theory Versus Autobiography." In Folkenflik, 21-37.

Sukenick, Lynn. "Anaïs Nin: The Novel of Vision." In Zaller, 157-60.

Suleiman, Susan R., ed. *The Female Body in Western Culture: Contemporary Perspectives*. Cambridge: Harvard University Press, 1986.

Tate, Claudia, ed. *Black Women Artists at Work*. New York: Continuum, 1983.

Tate, Trudi. *Modernism, History, and the First World War*. Manchester: Manchester University Press, 1998.

Terr, Lenore. *Unchained Memories: True Stories of Traumatic Memories, Lost and Found*. New York: Basic Books, 1994.

Trebilcott, Joyce, ed. *Mothering: Essays in Feminist Theory*. Totawa, NJ: Rowman and Allenheld, 1983.

Ulman, Richard B. and Doris Brothers. *The Shattered Self*. Hillsdale, NJ: Analytic Press, 1988.

Vaid, Krishna Baldev. "Writing and Wandering: A Talk with Anaïs Nin." *ANAÏS* 5 (1987): 49-55.

Van Boheemen, Christine. *The Novel as Family Romance: Language, Gender and Authority from Fielding to Joyce*. Ithaca: Cornell University Press, 1987.

Van der Kolk, Bessel A. "The Body Keeps Score: Approaches to the Psychobiology of Posttraumatic Stress Disorder." In Van der Kolk et al., 214-41.

———. "The Psychological Consequences of Overwhelming Life Experiences." In Van der Kolk, *Psychological Trauma*, 1-30.

———. "Trauma and Memory." In Van der Kolk et al., 279-302.

———. ed. *Psychological Trauma*. Washington, D.C.: American Psychiatric Press, 1987.

Van der Kolk, Bessel A., Alexander C. McFarlane, Lars Weisaeth, eds. *Traumatic Stress: The Effects of Overwhelming Experience on Mind, Body, and Society*. New York: The Guilford Press, 1996.

Van der Kolk, Bessel A. and Mark S. Greenberg. "The Psychobiology of the Trauma Response: Hyperarousal, Constriction, and Addiction to Traumatic Reexposure." In Van der Kolk, *Psychological Trauma*, 63-87.

Van der Kolk, Bessel A. and William Kadish. "Amnesia, Dissociation, and the Return of the Repressed." In Van der Kolk, *Psychological Trauma*, 173-90.

Van der Kolk, Bessel A. and Alexander McFarlane. "The Black Hole of Trauma." In van der Kolk et al., 3-23.

Van der Kolk, Bessel A., Lars Weisaeth, Onno van der hart. "History of Trauma in Psychiatry." In Van der Kolk et al., 47-74.

Veith, Ilza. *Hysteria: The History of a Disease*. Chicago: University of Chicago Press, 1965.

Wagner-Martin, Linda W. "H. D.'s Fiction: Convolutions to Clarity." In Friedman and Fuchs, 148-60.

Wakerman, Elyce. *Father Loss*. 1984; rpt. New York: Henry Holt, 1987.

Wakoski, Diane. "A Tribute to Anaïs Nin." In Zaller, 145-52.

Wall, Cheryl A., ed. *Changing Our Words: Essays on Criticism, Theory, and Writing by Black Women*. New Brunswick, NJ: Rutgers University Press, 1989.

Walker, Alice. *In Search of Our Mother's Gardens*. New York: Harcourt Brace, 1984.

Wasson, R. Gordon, Albert Hofman, and Carl A. P. Ruck, eds. *The Road to Eleusis: Unveiling the Secret of Mysteries*. New York: Harcourt Brace, 1978.

Watson, Julia. "Toward an Anti-Metaphysics of Autobiography." In Folkenflik, 57-79.

———. "Unspeakable Differences: The Politics of Gender in Lesbian and Heterosexual Women's Autobiographies." In Smith and Watson, *De/Colonizing the Subject*, 139-68.

Waugh, Patricia. *Feminine Fictions: Revisiting the Postmodern*. London: Routledge, 1989.

Weedon, Chris. *Feminist Practice and Poststructuralist Theory*. Oxford: Basil Blackwell, 1987.

Weintraub, Karl J. *The Value of the Individual: Self and Circumstance in Autobiography*. Chicago: University of Chicago Press, 1978.

Whitfield, Charles L. *Memory and Abuse: Remembering and Healing the Effects of Trauma*. Deerfield Beach, FL: Heath Communications, Inc., 1995.

Williams, Mark. *Leaving the Highway: Six Contemporary New Zealand Novelists*. Auckland, New Zealand: Auckland University Press, 1990.

Williams, Terry Tempest. *Refuge: An Unnatural History of Family and Place*. New York: Random House, 1992.

Williamson, Janice. "'I Peel Myself out of My Own Skin': Reading *Don't: A Woman's Word*." In Kadar, 133-51.

Willis, Susan. *Specifying: Black Women Writing the American Experience*. Madison: University of Wisconsin Press, 1987.

Wilson, Anna. "Audre Lorde and the African-American Tradition: When Family is Not Enough." In Munt, 75-94.

Wolfe, Susan J. and Julia Penelope, eds. *Sexual Practice Textual Theory: Lesbian Cultural Criticism*. Cambridge, MA: Blackwell, 1993.

Wood, Lori A. "Between Creation and Destruction: Toward a New Concept of the Female Artist." *ANAÏS* 8 (1990): 15-26.

Wood, Mary Elene. *The Writing on the Wall: Women's Autobiography and the Asylum*. Urbana: University of Illinois Press, 1994.

Woolf, Virginia. *Moments of Being: Unpublished Autobiographical Writings*. Ed. Jeanne Schulkind. 2nd. ed. New York: Harcourt Brace, 1957.

Worsham, Fabian Clements. "The Poetics of Matrilineage: Mothers and Daughters in the Poetry of African American Women, 1965–1985." In Brown-Guillory, 117-31.

Wright, Elizabeth. *Psychoanalytic Criticism: Theory in Practice*. London: Methuen, 1984.

Yaeger, Patricia. *Honey-Mad Women: Emancipatory Strategies in Women's Fiction*. New York: Columbia University Press, 1987.

Yalom, Marilyn. *Maternity, Mortality and the Literature of Madness*. University Park: Pennsylvania State University Press, 1985.

Young, Iris Marion. *Throwing Like a Girl and Other Essays in Feminist Philosophy and Social Theory*. Bloomington: Indiana University Press, 1990.

Zaller, Robert, ed. *A Casebook on Anaïs Nin*. New York: New American Library, 1974.

Zeiger, Melissa F. *Beyond Consolation: Death, Sexuality, and the Changing Shapes of Elegy*. Ithaca: Cornell University Press, 1997.

Zilboorg, Caroline, ed. *Richard Aldington & H. D.: The Early Years in Letters*. Bloomington: Indiana University Press, 1992. (Cited as Zilboorg 1.)

———. *Richard Aldington & H. D.: The Later Years in Letters*. Manchester: Manchester University Press, 1995. (Cited as Zilboorg 2.)

Zimmerman, Bonnie. *The Safe Sea of Women: Lesbian Fiction 1969–1989*. Boston: Beacon Press, 1990.

Index

Printed in the United States
134480LV00001B/37/P

9 780312 230982